A WINDOW ON RUSSIA

BOOKS BY EDMUND WILSON

AXEL'S CASTLE

THE TRIPLE THINKERS

TO THE FINLAND STATION

THE WOUND AND THE BOW

THE SHOCK OF RECOGNITION

MEMOIRS OF HECATE COUNTY

CLASSICS AND COMMERCIALS

THE SHORES OF LIGHT

FIVE PLAYS

RED, BLACK, BLOND AND OLIVE

A PIECE OF MY MIND

THE AMERICAN EARTHQUAKE

APOLOGIES TO THE IROQUOIS

WILSON'S NIGHT THOUGHTS

PATRIOTIC GORE

THE COLD WAR AND THE INCOME TAX

O CANADA

THE BIT BETWEEN MY TEETH

EUROPE WITHOUT BAEDEKER

GALAHAD and I THOUGHT OF DAISY

A PRELUDE

THE DUKE OF PALERMO and OTHER PLAYS

THE DEAD SEA SCROLLS: 1947–1969

UPSTATE

A WINDOW ON RUSSIA

EDMUND WILSON

A WINDOW ON RUSSIA

*for the Use
of Foreign Readers*

Peter the Great, in Pushkin's *Bronze
Horseman:* "Here it has been ordained
for us by Nature that we shall break
a window through to Europe."

MACMILLAN

SBN 333 13755 8

First published in the United States of America 1972
First published in Great Britain 1973 by
MACMILLAN LONDON LIMITED
London and Basingstoke
Associated companies in New York Toronto
Dublin Melbourne Johannesburg and Madras

Printed in Great Britain by
A. WHEATON & CO.
Exeter

Most of these pieces have appeared in *The Atlantic
Monthly, The Nation, The New Yorker,* and *The New
York Review of Books.*

CONTENTS

I

Notes from the Forties
    Russian Language   3
    Pushkin   15
    Tyutchev   28
Gogol: The Demon in the Overgrown
   Garden   38
Seeing Chekhov Plain   52
Turgenev and the Life-Giving Drop   68
Sukhovo-Kobylin: "Who Killed the
   French Woman?"   148
Notes on Tolstoy   161
Notes on Pushkin   185
A Little Museum of Russian Language   197

II

The Strange Case of Pushkin and Nabokov   209
Svetlana and Her Sisters   238
Solzhenitsyn   270

Dearest Elena: When Eugène-Melchior de Vogüé had married your great-aunt Alexandra Mikhailovna Annenkova in 1878, he would retire from time to time to her family place in the Ukraine and work on his book *Le Roman Russe*, which was published in 1886. This book turned out to be a landmark in the knowledge and popularity of Russian literature abroad. It introduced to French readers Tolstoy, Dostoevsky and the rest. Vogüé knew Russian and Russia well. He had been secretary to the French Embassy in Russia from 1876 to 1882 and must always have had in his wife a reliable source of information. I, on the other hand, have spent only five months in Russia, in the summer of 1935, and my Russian was so inadequate when you and I first married that when we tried to communicate in a language which other people could not understand, I spoke so very badly and you with such easy fluency that we were unable to understand one another. I owe, however, to you, whose mother was Russian, and to your Russian family and friends, a great debt in connection with this book, which pretends to so little in comparison with Vogüé's. It is a handful of disconnected pieces, written at various times when I happened to be interested in the various authors. It has no logical sequence or coherence, and it is anything but comprehensive. Some of the pieces are probably dated. There has come to be now in the United States much more interest in the study of Russian than there was when I began to write, and the misapprehensions which I mentioned in 1943 are no doubt no longer widely held. This collection (which includes all the pieces on Russian subjects that I have not collected in other volumes) is intended, as I indicate in the subtitle, mainly for English-speaking readers, and I am well aware that its statements will be greeted with protest and even indignation by many literary Russians; but I am also aware that in Russia the social and regional differences in language are more divergent than in most other countries, so that the foreigner can never be sure of being safe; and that, with writers such as Pushkin and Gogol especially, who are likely to have been first read by Russians in childhood, the naïve impressions of childhood are likely to be carried on into later life, when these writings have not been reread with the insight and intelligence of an adult.

In any case, I am grateful for all you have contributed to this book, and for your undiscouraged patience with my effort to understand Russian customs and states of mind. You have never ceased to exemplify the most attractive Russian qualities: sensitivity, humor, human sympathy, capacity (with limitations) for adaptability to different milieux and proficiency in the preparation of such dishes as *kulebyaka, kisel* and *bliny.*

With my love as ever,

Edmund

I

Notes from the Forties

RUSSIAN LANGUAGE

These notes need a word of explanation, if not a word of excuse. They are merely first impressions of the Russian classics by a reader who has learned Russian in his forties; and they may often seem quite wrong to Russians who hear the language as they read, and who see the whole background behind the book as the foreigner with his dictionary cannot do.

Such jottings can find their only justification in the fact that the reports of visitors to little-frequented countries supply for subsequent travellers a kind of information which cannot always be found in the studies of even the most intelligent natives. Those phenomena which most puzzle the visitor, to which he may find it most difficult to adjust himself, are likely to be things which the native takes so completely for granted that he has never thought about them at all.

Now there has been very little written on Russian literature by English-speaking writers who read Russian (though there is one first-rate book in French: *Le Roman Russe* by the Vicomte E.-M. de Vogüé). So far as my experience goes, the only commentaries of any interest are the rather meager writings of Maurice Baring and Oliver Elton. Yet it has certainly become very important for the English-speaking countries to establish cultural relations based on something more than attendance at the Russian ballet, the reading in translation of a few nineteenth-century novels, and a vague notion of the Marxism of Lenin.

The complete neglect in the West, on the part of our education, of Russian language and history has left us badly prepared to communicate with or to understand the Russia of the Revolution, which will certainly emerge from the war as one of the dominant powers of the world. The colleges are doing something to remedy this lack, and it may be that Russian studies will eventually have almost the importance that German studies did in the period that ended with World War I. In the meantime, these notes on reading are intended as a stimulus to learning Russian and acquiring some firsthand knowledge of what is certainly one of the great modern literatures.

The novelists of Russia have come through to us and made us admire their genius solely through the interest of their content, of the stories they have to tell. We should never suspect from our translations, of which the style is often so colorless and so undistinguished, that Russian, as a literary language, has immense and unique resources.

"The Russian language," wrote Lomonosov, the great founder of the literary medium in the middle of the eighteenth century, "the sovereign of so many others, is superior to all the other languages of Europe, not only in the extent of the regions where it reigns, but also in its peculiar comprehensiveness and abundance. Charles V, the [Holy] Roman emperor, used to say that one ought to talk Spanish with God, French with one's friends, German with one's enemies, and Italian with the ladies. But if he had learned Russian, he would certainly have added that one could speak it appropriately to all of them. For he would have found in it the majesty of Spanish, the vivacity of French, the strength of German, the tenderness of Italian, and, besides these, the richness and the concision, so vigorous in its imagery, of the Greek and Latin tongues."

Yet the factors that make of Russian so admirable a medium for literature are in some cases precisely those that make it difficult for the foreigner to master.

In the first place, there are the resources of the vocabulary. The Russian language is compounded of a variety of linguistic elements: Slavonic, Oriental, and Western, which have provided an immense number of synonyms with different shades of meaning. In this it somewhat resembles English, which mixes Teutonic and Latin, and is at the opposite pole from French, with its almost one hundred per cent Latinity.

In the second place, Russian presents itself to a foreigner as a language almost entirely composed of idioms. In this, too, it is the opposite of French, so codified and sensibly ordered, so generalized and formularized. The differences between Russian and French are worth dwelling on in this connection, because they serve better than any other contrast to illuminate the nature of Russian. This contrast, indeed, has created a great cultural issue in Russian literature from Pushkin's and Griboyedov's time through Tolstoy's and Dostoevsky's to the last novel by Mark Aldanov. The French language in tsarist Russia became, in the eighteenth century, the social medium of the upper classes; it was Pushkin's second language.

French played a very important role in influencing the locutions and the word formations in the development of modern Russian; and it was principally in imitating French models that the Russians of Pushkin's generation learned elegance, polish and point. Yet there has always been a latent antagonism between the Russians who have borrowed from the West and the French to whom they owe so much. The invasion of Napoleon may have contributed to this, but it was inherent in the cultural relation. The French cannot help regarding the Russians as barbarians and children: in spite of the best efforts of Mérimée and Vogüé to explain the Russians to the French, the Russian genius remains alien to them. And, on the other hand, to the Russians the French inevitably appear stereotyped and dry, the victims of a standardized language which seems to write their books itself with only a nominal intervention by the author and of a social code which dictates their behavior and leaves little place for spontaneity.

Tolstoy has dramatized this situation in *War and Peace* and *Anna Karenina,* where he often makes the characters speak or write in French, and gets a vivid effect by playing up their natural personalities when they are talking or thinking in Russian, against their artificial French personalities imposed by education. This effect, which has its bearing on the great themes of both these novels, is largely lost in the English translations—especially where, as in Aylmer Maude's and Constance Garnett's, much of the French is translated, too; so that the reader misses the contrast between, say, the conventional letters in French between the Princess Maria and her Moscow friend in their role of well-brought-up *jeunes filles*, and the rapid impulsive gusts, so full of affectionate diminutives, of Natasha talking Russian. The transmutation of

Natasha into a nice little English girl seems to be one of the unavoidable calamities of the importation of Tolstoy into English.

But we can see Tolstoy's point quite plainly in the episode where Rostopchin, after buying his escape from the mob by throwing it a political prisoner, is obliged, as he drives off in his carriage, to justify himself to himself in French: "*J'avais d'autres devoirs. Il fallait apaiser le peuple. Bien d'autres victimes ont péri et périssent pour le bien public*"; or in the scene where the Princess Hélène, in explaining why it is proper and necessary for her to get a divorce from Pierre, resorts to speaking French, because it has always seemed to her that "her case did not seem quite clear" in Russian.

French is a logical and social language, Russian an illogical and intimate one; and when the Russian of the old regime changed from one of the Western languages to Russian, it was likely to be with relief and a burst of expansive geniality, for, with its long Homeric patronymics, its humorous or tender or derogatory versions of people's Christian names, and its special set of words to designate the various kinds of sisters-in-law and brothers-in-law (that still lingers from a time when it was important, in order to prevent inbreeding in the tribe, to have all such relationships clear), it spoke with the accents of the Russian land, the all-night Russian drinking party, the patriarchal-feudal relations, the humor, the enthusiasm, the quick give-and-take between different classes of people. It was a language with few formulas of politeness, clumsy for abstract thought, but more expressive than the Western languages of the feelings and the impressions of the senses in proportion as it was closer to the primitive emotions—a language that had sprouted from the people as the birch woods had grown from the Russian soil.

But all this makes trouble for students. Teachers of Russian report that their classes start out with enthusiasm, but that always the moment arrives when they suddenly melt away. The student is encouraged at first by the discovery that the queer-looking alphabet is easy. This alphabet, in the weeded-out form in use since the Revolution, though it has more characters than the English alphabet, is a much more practical affair. It really fits the sounds of the language as our English letters do not do: there are few anomalies of spelling in Russian compared with either English or French. But when the student has got a little farther, far enough to grasp the difficulties of Russian grammar, he is likely to become appalled and give up the whole thing.

Let us suppose, however, that he perseveres. He may think it is almost too much that a language spoken today like Russian should be the same kind of language as Latin and Greek, a kind that he had supposed obsolete; and that he should have even to learn six cases to the Greek four and the Latin five, and a separate set of adjectival endings that are sometimes quite different from the endings of the nouns. At least, in Latin and Greek you do not have the complication, as you sometimes do in Russian, of special forms in the same case for animate and inanimate objects, with the annoying exception that collective nouns such as народ, *people*, are treated as if the members were inanimate. But let us suppose that the student faces these dreadful declensions—that he tries even not to long for the happy simplicities of Goodwin and Allen and Greenough when he discovers that there is no rule for neuter plurals: you simply have to learn the different ones; and that he may even suppress a rising oath when he discovers that such expressions as *a pound of tea* require a special form of the genitive. He is still not so far from the classical tongues.

But the true horrors of Russian still await him. It is natural for him to assume that in any major language of Europe, especially in the language of a people that undertakes Five-Year Plans, the numerals should be easy to handle, or that, at least, in spite of the fact that everything is encumbered by endings so that every time you mention a date you have to decline almost every digit, they should represent a uniform progression. But the normal expectation of the student is brazenly flouted and mocked by the nation of Peter the Great and Stalin. The writer of the article on Russian language in the *Encyclopaedia Britannica* says correctly of the Russian numerals—with what sounds like a note of irritation—that "a compromise between grammar and logic has produced a kind of maze." The student may well finally lose patience with a system which owes its complications to the survival of such features as a difference in usage, based on counting on the fingers of one hand, between numbers up to five and numbers from five on, and as a primitive dual number which, instead of sticking to two as it does in Greek, has been trailed along through three and four. The student may, however, decide when confronted with these and other peculiarities, which seem so much more quaint than practical, that he will have to content himself with recognizing the meaning when reading and hoping to be understood when, in speaking, he uses the wrong endings, or perhaps the wrong word altogether, since certain nouns are not to be used with the number five or beyond.

Yet, I should say, from my own experience, that it is at this point in studying Russian that the second phase of discouragement sets in. The student is under the impression that he can pretty well make out what he reads; but then gradually and chillingly creeps in the realization that he has really not got it at all: that he is missing a part of the meaning and even making vital mistakes.

This condition of uncertainty may be mainly due to a habit, in connection with the verbs, of falling back upon the rough-and-ready policy that he has adopted in the case of the numerals. It is one of the peculiarities of the Slavic verbs that, besides having several of the usual kind of tenses, they are subject to metamorphoses called *aspects*. If you have started with an old-fashioned grammar, you may have learned that the verbs have five aspects: imperfective— он стучал, *he was knocking;* perfective— он постучал, *he knocked;* semelfactive—он стукивал, *he knocked once;* iterative—он стукивал, *he used to knock;* and inchoative—он застучал, *he began to knock.* This may seem exotic, but logical enough, and you are prepared to master the rules for forming the different aspects; but it then turns out to your dismay that стучать, the grammarian's showpiece, is about the only verb in Russian which exhibits all five of these aspects and forms them in a regular way. Every verb, in respect to its aspects, seems to behave in a different manner, and often the various aspects are represented by quite unpredictable words which have not even the root in common. The situation is further complicated in the case of certain verbs by the imperfective aspect's splitting up into two further aspects called the abstract and the concrete—so that you have to use a different verb when you say, *Birds fly,* from the verb that you use when you say, *The birds are flying.* The student is likely to end, as I understand the Soviet schools have done, by partly disregarding the aspects and trying to fasten these forms in the memory by represent-int them as independent verbs.

II

I have described some of these difficulties thus specifically to warn the prospective student what he is going to encounter in Russian. One must accept from the beginning the true situation: one is up against something quite different from the more orderly languages one is used to; one has to deal with language which—to confess the whole truth—one cannot really get hold of through the grammar.

What, then, is one to do about Russian? Well, the only way to learn to speak it is to pick it up colloquially from Russians, and the only way to learn to read it is to become so much interested in it that the constant anomalies cease to irritate us because they help us to see inside the Russian mind—and to enjoy its combination of vivid perceptions with closeness to half-primitive conditions; and because they are a fundamental factor in the subtlety and richness of the Russian poems and plays and novels.

Thus the student, as I have indicated above, will sooner or later find out that he must grapple with what may seem to him the formidable task of memorizing long lists of verbs; but this task will become attractive from the moment that he understands how very inter-esting these Russian verbs are. The way to approach them is not grimly, with the scarcely repressed hostility of the foreigner who cannot become reconciled to the fact that their meanings do not correspond to the meanings of the verbs in his own language. One must

observe the Russian verbs as the bird-watcher does
birds, collect them as the lepidopterist does butterflies;
one must group them for oneself in families: verbs of
divergent meanings that are based on common roots;
verbs, alike or unlike in form, that the dictionary
may give as synonyms but that have quite distinct
uses and meanings. One will at first be amused, for
example, to discover that there are special Russian
verbs which have no equivalents in English or in any
other language one knows, for special phenomena
that one may already have observed as characteristic of
Russians: пропиваться, *to squander all one's money on
drink;* перепарывать, *to whip everybody all around;*
дожидаться, *to attain by waiting;* запортоваться,
to let one's tongue run away with one; напяливать,
to put on a tight garment with a certain amount of effort.
Then one may become aware of whole classes of words
which particularize among things to which we pay
relatively little attention in English. A curious example
of this is the multiplication of verbs to designate expressions of the eyes. In reading *Anna Karenina,* I collected
some fifteen of these (counting aspects, not primary
verbs), of which it was impossible to find out the real
meanings from the Russian-English dictionary: you
have to get a Russian to illustrate them.

The Russian habit of narrowing or closing the eyes
may indicate various attitudes on the part of the person
who does it; and our only simple English word is
squint, which does not describe Russian expressions
at all. A curious example is зажмурить глаза, which
means a voluntary closing of the eyes. A child who
has been waked up in the morning closes its eyes to
steal a few minutes' sleep; a woman is talking to another
woman about the trials of a third woman whose husband
drinks, and the listener drops her lids in taking dignified

cognizance of the scandal. In either case, зажмурить глаза is in order.

When one has become really familiar with the Russian conception of aspects and has ceased to attempt to force them into the Western conception of tenses, one comes to understand for the first time the Russian perception of time—a sense of things beginning, of things going on, of things to be completed in the future but not at the present moment, of things that have happened in the past all relegated to the same plane of pastness, with no distinction between perfect and pluperfect; a sense, in short, entirely different from our Western sense of clock-time, which sets specific events with exactitude in relation to an established and unvarying chronology. The timing of much Russian literature—of Pushkin or Tolstoy—is perfect; but it is not like the timing of a well-made French play, where the proportions, the relations and the development have something in common with mathematics. It is a timing that plays on our most intimate experience of the way in which things happen, which appeals to the natural rhythms of an alert and unregimented attention.

The great paradox of Russian, then, is that it is at once as highly inflected as Latin, and so lends itself, in Pushkin's poetry, to an Horatian tightness and a Catullian tenseness, and as flexible and fluent as Shakespeare's English. And we must recognize further the anachronism of a widely spoken modern language that deals with the realities of the Western world in terms of an equipment several centuries more primitive than that of Elizabethan English at the time when Ben Jonson wrote his grammar. The new Soviet society, of course, is partly altering this. Just as the clumsy and complicated system of designating family relationships gave way, under the influence of the West, to *cousin* and *beau-frère* and *belle-mère,* so the old terminology of Russian society, with its крестьянство and мещанство and дворянство and all the other ancient distinctions, has given way to the German terminology of the economic categories of Marxism. Fine old feudal words like the one just mentioned which means *to have everybody thoroughly flogged,* have been displaced by the abstract and euphemistic, the sinister and hypocritical ликвидиро-вать, *to liquidate.* But the problems of contemporary Russian need not concern us here. We shall be dealing with the last century's classics; and the point is that the Russian in which Tolstoy, say, depicts the hunting party in *War and Peace* is as colloquial and rank and wild, for all Tolstoy's coolness and clearness, as the English which John Masefield, in *Reynard the Fox,* is able, in our own day, to manage with only a slight effect of semi-archaic incongruity.

November, 1943

PUSHKIN

We have long entertained in the West certain notions about Russian literature—which have been shared by such critics as Virginia Woolf with the ordinary literary journalists. These assumptions may be formulated somewhat as follows:

(1) That the Russians are formless and unkempt;
(2) That they are gloomy;
(3) That they are crudely realistic;
(4) That they are morbid and hysterical;
(5) That they are mystical.

These ideas are all very misleading. They are not susceptible of being applied as generalizations even to the three or four novelists who are usually read by the West. They are obviously not true of Turgenev, but the Westerners get around this by asserting that Turgenev is exceptional: that he acquired a European refinement and became virtually a French writer—though Turgenev's graceful form and not too heavy touch are typical of one Russian tradition. Chekhov also has form, of course, but then he is unquestionably gloomy. Tolstoy is not hysterical till he gets to *The Kreutzer Sonata,* which comes late in his literary career. Dostoevsky, when one looks into the matter, turns out to be the figure who, *par excellence,* represents the Westerner's ideal of what

a Russian writer ought to be; but, even in the case of
Dostoevsky, our preconceived ideas about Russians
partly prevent us from seeing in him the qualities that
are really there.

Now the great fountainhead of Russian literature is
Pushkin. From him all these other Russian writers in
more or less degree derive; and the qualities of Pushkin
are the opposites of the qualities which are usually attrib-
uted to the Russians by French and English readers.

The Russians are in the habit of comparing Pushkin
with Mozart, and this is perhaps the nearest one can
come to a simple comparison. Pushkin does, through
both his career and his qualities, somewhat recall
Mozart: he is able to express through an art that is
felicitous and formal a feeling that is passionate and
exquisite; he has a wide range of moods and emotions,
yet he handles them all with precision; and—what is
hard to make Westerners believe—he achieved in the
poetry of his time a similar preëminence to Mozart's
in music.

Mozart's career itself was in some ways characteristic of the generation that followed his rather than of
the eighteenth century. The poets that overlapped the
century or were born in the early eighteen hundreds,
who lived in the stimulating disturbing time between
the old world and the new, tend, in the very disorder of
their lives, to repeat the same evolution. They are
precocious, they soon make themselves masters of their
art; they do personal and original work, and they are
likely to try their hands at several genres; they die before
their time, of disease or dissipation or the results of
reckless living, leaving productions that make the later
nineteenth century look rather banal and soggy and
that yet constitute a fragmentary lifework. Byron, Keats,
Shelley, Heine, Poe, Musset—here the earliest date

(Byron's birth) is 1788 and the latest (Musset's death) 1857, with all these writers except the tough Heine dying in their twenties or thirties or forties (as Mozart died at thirty-five). If one adds from another department the work of Jane Austen (1775–1817), also consummate and also uncompleted, and of Stendhal (1783–1842), similarly original, non-official and squeezed out, as it were, by the stresses of the age, you get a distinct picture of this brilliant intermediate generation.

Now, though Goethe is of course the figure who dominates the perilous swing out of the past into the modern world, Pushkin, born in 1799, exiled in his youth, censored in his maturity, and shot in a duel in 1837, is the great figure of this short-lived group. Unlikely though it may seem, he had something in common with every one of the writers named above. He is the universal poet of that moment. Pushkin's cultural roots and branches reach out about him in every direction; he studied Latin and Greek, and he made a beginning with Hebrew; he digested the age of Voltaire and derived from it all that he needed; he tried his hand at translating Wordsworth, exploited Barry Cornwall by borrowing the form of the Englishman's *Dramatic Scenes,* and he achieved a perspective on Byron which few of the European romantics had, by a careful reading of Shakespeare, from whom he learned what he required for his chronicle play, *Boris Godunov;* he established with the Polish poet Mickiewicz one of those intimate literary relationships, half-competitive, half-coöperative, that are likely to be so profitable to both parties, and he exchanged, for Prosper Mérimée's pioneer work in learning Russian and translating him and Gogol into French, translations which improved the originals, of Mérimée's forged Slavic folk-songs; and in the field of Russian culture itself, he retold the Russian fairy stories as perhaps the fairy stories of no other nation have ever been retold; he acted as literary godfather to Gogol, giving him the cues to his artistic development and supplying him with the themes of *Dead Souls* and *The Inspector General*; bequeathed to the Russian composers enough subjects for ballets and operas to last all the rest of the century, and sowed the seeds of a Russian realism united with a fine sensibility that has been flourishing ever since. Pushkin had a mastery of language as remarkable certainly as that of any other nineteenth-century poet; and, with this, a kind of genius which none of the other poets had, and few of the novelists to the same degree: the genius for dramatic projection.

In this rare combination of qualities, it seems to me that Pushkin is the only modern poet in the class of Shakespeare and Dante. It may seem unbelievable that Pushkin's achievement in his bare thirty-eight years can be comparable to Shakespeare's or Dante's; yet, after all, Shakespeare at thirty-eight had written *Julius Caesar* and *Hamlet,* and Dante had had his vision and is thought to have composed at least the first seven cantos of the *Divina Commedia*. If Pushkin's latest poems and plays and the final version of *Evgeni Onegin* do not precisely correspond to these, it is only because *Hamlet* and the opening of the *Inferno* are each the beginning of an immense mature work which the poet feels the assurance that he will be able to live to finish. With Pushkin, it is as if his impending death were anticipated by him all along, as if he knew from the first that he must find the way to put into the work of his thirties all his intensity and all his variety. The scale of Pushkin's work is different because his life-span is different. Just as the subject of Shakespeare is the full experience of a man who is young and passes through middle age and finally grows old, and as Dante's whole project depends for its force on a discipline in organizing

experience through self-discipline and an ultimate aloof
contemplation hardly attainable before late middle age
(Dante died at fifty-six, as soon as his poem was finished); so Pushkin, incongruously situated in the Russia
of the Decembrist uprising, where he had felt all his life
at the back of his neck the pressure of a remorseless paw,
found a way to make his fate itself both the measure
and the theme of his work, with a dignity, an objectivity,
a clear and pure vision of human situations which
remove him completely from the category of the self-
dramatizing romantic poets.

II

To write properly of Pushkin is so large a task that
such hints as I here have space for may imply their
excuse by their obvious lameness.

First of all, Pushkin's mastery of form. He is one
of the few writers who never seem to fall—from the
point where he has outgrown his early models—into
formulas of expression. He finds a special shape and a
special style for every successive subject; and, even
without looking for the moment at his dramatic and
narrative poems, one is amazed at the variety of his
range. You have lyrics in regular quatrains that are as
pointed and spare as Greek epigrams or as forceful and
repercussive as the *Concord Hymn,* and you have lyrics
in broken accents: soliloquies that rise out of sleep or
trail off in unspoken longings—where the modulated
meter follows the thought; you have the balladry and
jingling of folk-songs, and you have set-pieces like *To a
Magnate* (К Вельможе)* (in the meter and rhyme

---

* I have included the Russian title in the cases of works of which the
translated title might not always be readily identifiable.

scheme of Boileau's epistles) of a rhetorical solidity and brilliance that equals anything in Pope or the Romans; you have droll little ribaldries like the *Tsar Nikita*, informal discursive poems like *Autumn* that are like going to visit Pushkin for a week-end in the country, and forgings of fierce energetic language, now metallic and unmalleable, now molten and flowing, like *The Upas Tree* and *The Prophet*. You have, finally, dramatic lyrics like *The Fiends* and *Winter Evening*, for which it is hard to find phrases or comparisons because they are as purely and intensely Pushkin as *Furi et Aureli, comites Catulli* is purely and intensely Catullus or *Sweeney among the Nightingales* Eliot.

As for the texture of Pushkin's language and its marvelous adaptation to whatever it describes, one is helpless to give any idea of it without direct quotation from his poetry; but a passage or two may be mentioned in which the patterns and motifs must be obvious even to readers who do not know Russian. *Count Nulin* is a little tale in verse which Pushkin said he wrote to show that the history of Rome might have taken quite a different turn if Lucretia had slapped Tarquin's face instead of submitting to him. The poem is relatively light, yet artistically it is perfect; a genre picture of country life as accurately and vividly sketched as any episode in a Russian novel. Here is the passage in which the slap occurs. The Lucretia is a landowner's lady, and the Tarquin a fashionable traveller returning to Russia from France.

> Но тут опомнилась она,
> И честной гордости полна,
> А впрочем, может быть, и страха,
> Она Тарквинию с размаха
> Даёт пощёчину, да, да!

Пощёчину, да ведь какую!
Сгорел граф Нулин от стыда,
Обиду проглотив такую;
Не знаю, чем бы кончил он,
Досадой страшною пылая,
Но шпиц косматый, вдруг залая,
Прервал Параши крепкий сон.

But here she recovers herself, and, incited by her pride of chastity, and perhaps by fear as well, she gives Tarquin a swinging slap—Yes, yes!—And what a slap!

Count Nulin burned with shame to swallow such an insult; I don't know what he might have done, consumed with dire chagrin, if the woolly Spitz had not begun to bark and waked Parasha from her heavy slumber.

The word for *slap* here is пощёчина, but the actual impact of the slap is conveyed by the first syllable of даёт, and the да, да, *yes, yes!* at the end of the line, and reinforced by да ведь in the next line. Then it goes on stinging in the lines that follow, the да cropping up again in the last syllable of стыда, *shame,* and fading somewhat but still clearly perceptible in обиду and досадой, *insult* and *chagrin,* all these words thus referring by their meaning to Nulin's injured feelings and by their sound to his tingling cheek. In the last two lines the lap dog begins to yap in the alternating *p*'s and *k*'s, which have already been prepared for by the consonants in the description of the earlier shock.

Another charming example is in *The Tale of the Tsar Saltan,* when the brave little prince, adrift with his mother, begins his appeal to the sea:

Ты, волна моя, волна!
Ты гульлива и вольна . . .
"O thou, my sea, my sea!
So indolent and free" . . .

Here the *v*'s alternate with *l*'s, and the soft *l*'s alternate
with hard *l*'s. The rhyme words—*sea* and *free*—are
identical except for this difference in the *l*'s. Pushkin
here uses metonymically the word for *wave* for *sea;*
and the whole effect is smooth and undulating like the
movement of a gentle swell. It is curious to note that
Pushkin has here hit upon the same combination both
of consonants and of vowels that Pope, in *Windsor
Forest,* has used for his line on the eel:

The silver eel, in shining volumes rolled . . .

and that these same combinations occur in the Seventh
Book of the *Aeneid* where Virgil describes the serpent
gliding about on the body of Amata:

Ille, inter vestis et levia pectora lapsus,
Volvitur attactu nullo, fallitque furentem,
Viperream inspirans animam; fit tortile collo
Aurum ingens coluber, fit longae taenia vittae,
Innectitque comas, et membris lubricus errat.

It is characteristic of Pushkin that both these passages
should owe their vividness primarily to the representa-
tion of *movement.* Movement is a specialty of Pushkin's.
He can do sounds, landscapes, personalities, and all
the other things, too; but there is probably no other
poet since Virgil, with his serpents, his limping Cyclops,
his wheel of Ixion, and his armies moving off, who has
this sense so completely developed as Pushkin; and
the control of the consistency and pace of the hexameter
can never give the freedom for such effects that Pushkin
finds in his rapider meters. The flood in *The Bronze
Horseman,* the ballet-girl in *Evgeni Onegin,* the hawk
that drops on the chicken-yard in *Ruslan and Lyudmila,*

the cat in *Count Nulin* creeping up and pouncing on a mouse—Pushkin is full of such pictures of actions that seem as we read to take place before our eyes without the intervention of language.

This natural instinct for movement is shown in another way in the poet's command of the movement of his verse and the movement of his play or his story. I have spoken in an earlier note of the timing of Russian fiction. The timing in Pushkin is perfect. He never for a moment bores you, yet—touching on nothing, however briefly, without some telling descriptive stroke—he covers an immense amount of ground. The one hundred and seventy pages of *Onegin* take us through as much of life as many Victorian novels, and give us the feeling of having lived it more intimately. A Russian lady once told me that when she had looked up *The Gypsies* after not having read it for many years, she was surprised to find how short it was: the impression left in her memory by this succession of ten little scenes had been that of having gone, like the hero, to wander a long time with a caravan. In the case of a writer like Flaubert, for example, we *see* a story take place: it is a panorama reeled off before us, and its pace is the pace of the showman. With Pushkin, we *live* the vicissitudes of Aleko as we live the campaigns of *War and Peace*.

III

But what of Pushkin's larger themes? I should have neither the space nor the confidence to deal with his creations and their meanings. But a foreigner who reads Pushkin for the first time in his forties may derive from his very inexperience one advantage that balances a little the handicaps he suffers from the inadequacy of his Russian. It would be interesting to come upon Shakespeare and to read him all through for his intrinsic interest without ever having studied him at school; and the Russian who has memorized *Poltava* at the same age when English-speaking children are learning *The quality of mercy* . . . may never be able to rid himself of preconceptions about Pushkin as national poet that actually obscure his understanding of Pushkin as critic of life. Having got out of *Evgeni Onegin* what he was capable of getting in his schooldays, he will continue to remember it all his life as a simple and improving story for well-brought-up young men and women. One even finds reactionary Russians writing about *The Bronze Horseman* as if it were simply a glorification of the ruthless authority of Peter the Great, to which the lives of Evgeni and his sweetheart are quite properly sacrificed; yet this is a great deal more obtuse than it would be for an Englishman to see only the patriotism in *Henry V* and not realize that the frustrated Falstaff is more interesting to Shakespeare than Henry. I heard recently at a Russian meeting in celebration of the defense of Leningrad a speaker quote Evgeni's defiance of the statue: "Where dost thou gallop, haughty steed? —And where wilt thou plant thy foot?"—as if it were a battle-cry, and as if it had never occurred to him that the whole point of Pushkin's poem is that the hoof of Peter's charger has crushed the Russians as well as their enemies.

> Куда ты скачешь, гордый конь,
> И где опустишь ты копыта?

That hoof was hanging over Pushkin all through his later work. It was one of the elements of the complex

doom which closed in on him and cut him down—
though this doom, like the doom of Aleko in *The
Gypsies,* depended upon Pushkin's personality, too.
The events that resulted in Pushkin's death make one
of the queerest and most disquieting stories in the whole
of literary history—a story perhaps more dramatic than
anything Pushkin ever invented; and it would provide
one of the most fascinating problems for which literature
affords the opportunity, to try to explain Pushkin's
writing and these happenings in terms of one another.
I am by no means prepared to undertake the explanation, but I am certain that, as Pushkin perfects his art, as
he sharpens the profile of his style and intensifies his
concentration on human personalities and relations, he
is reflecting ever more clearly the internal and external
conflicts in which he finds his spirit involved. Aleko,
who flees to the gypsies from the organized social world,
but finds himself eventually driven to commit among
them the same kind of crime that has originally made
him an outlaw, and so becomes outlawed by the gypsies
themselves; the clerk of *The Bronze Horseman,* who
loses all he has in the flood and yet pays for his rebellion
with madness; the young guardsman in *The Little House in
Kolomna* who dresses as a woman and works as a cook;
the general in *The Nigger of Peter the Great* who can
never make up for his blackness; the young mountaineer
in *Tazit* who refuses to avenge his brother and allows
himself to be made a pariah; the prince in *Rusalka* who
marries a princess only to be alienated from her by the
enchantments of his earlier love, a miller's daughter
turned water-nymph; the merchant's son of *Scenes from
the Age of Chivalry* who is persuaded by the knights to
take service with them and then finds that he has become
their menial—all are the images of Pushkin's false position between the old nobility and the new, between the

B

life of society and the life of art, between the tsardom and the instincts of modern thought, between marriage and the man for himself.

Yet in these dramas the whole situation is usually seen so much in the round, the presentation of opposing forces is so little obscured by animus, that it becomes almost impossible to say that the poet is on either side. In *Onegin* the clever but sterile Evgeni envies the stupid Lensky for his idealism, his poetic aspirations and his capacity for love, and manages to kill him in a duel; in *Mozart and Salieri* the academic composer envies the genius and poisons him. Both themes are plainly the reflections of something that has been deeply experienced by Pushkin and on which he might have brooded with bitterness; yet he handles them in such a way that there is never any melodrama involved: Lensky is extremely sincere, but foolish and perhaps a bad poet; Salieri is a villain, but he states his point of view with so much conviction and dignity that we almost come to respect him. The emotion that we get from reading Pushkin is something outside the picture: it is an emotion, half-comic, half-poignant, at contemplating the nature of things. He gives us the picture created by art— and this is to a considerable extent true even of his personal poetry—and refrains from other comment (his digressions in such stories as *Evgeni Onegin* and *The Little House in Kolomna* always have an artistic value that is different from their ostensible purpose).

We always feel, thus, in reading Pushkin, that there is something behind and beyond, something we can only guess at; and this makes his peculiar fascination— a fascination which has something in common with the inexhaustible interest of Shakespeare, who seems to be giving us his sonnets and *Hamlet* and *Lear* and the rest as the moods and dreams of some drama the actuality of which we never touch.

"Others abide our question. Thou art free.
We ask and ask: Thou smilest and art still . . ."

Pushkin smiles, but he is never free in the sense that Shakespeare in the end is free, and he has always in relation to his art a seriousness and an anxiety of one who knows the night is coming. As his mind grows in clarity and power, the prison of the world grips him tighter; and his final involvement and defiance and defeat are themselves a projection of the drama which is always still behind and beyond.

November, 1943

TYUTCHEV

The literary career and reputation of the poet F. I. Tyutchev have certain points of resemblance to those, respectively and both together, of A. E. Housman and Gerard Manley Hopkins.

Tyutchev was four years older than Pushkin and eleven years older than Lermontov, and he is usually ranked by the Russians as one of the three great poets of his period; but, since he wrote no plays or novels or narrative poems as Pushkin and Lermontov did, he has supplied no opera librettos and no translatable stories, and is therefore quite unknown in the West. He was not a professional writer and did not care to be a literary figure. He was a diplomat who lived out of Russia for the better part of twenty-two years and from time to time sent verses to Pushkin, who published them in the quarterly he was editing. It was not till the early fifties that Nekrasov brought Tyutchev's poetry to the attention of the public and that Turgenev edited a book of his lyrics. The whole work of Tyutchev consists merely of about three hundred short pieces—lyrics and political verses—which, although they are known by Russians as well as we know *A Shropshire Lad,* have no way of getting through to other languages.

The comparisons with Housman and Hopkins may,

however, serve not only to indicate the position of
Tyutchev in Russian poetry, but also to give some idea
of his form and of the kind of poet he is. We must banish
first of all from our minds the idea that Russian literature
is necessarily loose or disorderly. The tendency of
Russian poetry is, if anything, in the opposite direction
of being too uniformly well-turned. Certainly these three
Russian poets of the early nineteenth century are
a good deal more consistently satisfactory from the
point of view of form than any of the English Romantic poets except Keats. There are lyrics of Lermontov's and Pushkin's so classical in achieving their
effects by the mere displacement or change of a word
in the pattern of a line or a quatrain that we can hardly
find anything of the kind in English till we come to A. E.
Housman. And Tyutchev is the great Russian master
of the pregnant and pointed and poignant short poem.

But the landscapes and seasons that Tyutchev prefers
—and he largely lives on landscapes and seasons—
with the feelings that these inspire, are quite different
from the clear autumn bitterness or the sharp summer
irony of Housman. Tyutchev loves the indeterminate
moments between fair and rainy weather, when a
thunderstorm is looming or passing, or between the
night and the dawn or the sunset and the dark, which
reflect indeterminate and variable emotions. There is
a fine little poem of E. A. Robinson's which has something in common with Tyutchev:

> Dark hills at evening in the west,
> Where sunset hovers like a sound
> Of golden horns that sang to rest
> Old bones of warriors under ground,
> Far now from all the bannered ways
> Where flash the legions of the sun,

> You fade—as if the last of days
> Were fading, and all wars were done.

Imagine something halfway between this and certain poems of Léonie Adams's, where the phrases strike out more facets, and the whole thing has a livelier psychological interest. There is piece after piece in *High Falcon* that is amazingly close to Tyutchev (*The Moon and Spectator, The Mysterious Thing, Evening Sky, Sundown, Twilit Revelation, Country Summer* and others).

> How now are we tossed about by a windy heaven,
> The eye that scans it madded to discern
> In a single quarter all the wild ravage of light,
> Amazing light to quiver and suddenly turn
> Before the stormy demon fall of night;
> And yet west spaces saved celestial
> With silver sprinklings of the anointed sun. . . .

For though the stanza of Tyutchev is epigrammatic—he was in conversation a famous wit—his language is delicious and exquisite. He had brought over from an earlier period certain qualities that were alien to the age of Pushkin. The eighteenth century in Russia was distinguished by literary characteristics—a touch of reckless Aeschylean grandiloquence—quite different from anything we mean when we say "eighteenth century" in English, and closer to our seventeenth century. Even the foreign reader is surprised to come upon such a phrase as "a loud crimson exclamation." But in Tyutchev this style has been infinitely refined: there are a liquidity and a shifting suggestiveness that anticipate symbolist poetry. The Russian poets of the end of the century claimed him as a precursor of their school, and were impatient with Turgenev for having ironed out, in editing Tyutchev's poems—rather as Rimsky-Korsakov conventionalized the score of *Boris Godunov*—the metrical innovations of the poet. In this role of rediscovered "ancestor" of an advanced phase of poetry that did not derive from him, Tyutchev occupies a position not unlike that of Hopkins.

The sensibility of Tyutchev lives between light and shadow among the feelings and impressions and reflections of a region so vibrating and rarefied that it makes most English romantic poetry seem relatively sensual and downright. One of the best of his poems is *Italian Villa,* which is certainly all Russian and all Tyutchev in this coincidence of physical with moral awareness. The poet and a woman companion arrive at an Italian villa which has for a long time been uninhabited. You have a charming and lulling description of the old house asleep in the sun, with only the babble of the fountain and the twittering of a swallow rippling the settled silence. But the visitors enter; and in the tranquil darkness where a cypress looks in at the window, they suddenly feel that a change has occurred: the fountain seems to stop; a convulsive shudder runs through the branches of the cypress; there is a queer indistinct whisper like something muttered through sleep. "What was it, friend? Was it that cruel life—the life, alas! then quickening in our veins—that ruthless life, with its rebellious fire, had to no purpose crossed the sacred threshold?"

> Что зто, друг? Иль злая жизнь недаром,
> Та жизнь—увы!—что в нас тогда текла,
> Та злая жизнь, с её мятежным жаром,
> Через порог заветный перешла?

Yet, admirable though Tyutchev is, he is somehow to an Anglo-Saxon a little unsympathetic. He is a little

too weepy for our taste. In his poetry is audible, as it is
not in Pushkin, that incurable minor key of resignation
to grievance and complaint, that may move us when we
hear it in an old Russian song but with which we become
impatient when we find how habitual and incessant it
is in all kinds of connections in Russian life.

In Tyutchev's case, this key is associated with a
humidity of emotional atmosphere that is also rather
alien to us. There are moments when the English-
speaking reader, in his exploration of Russian literature,
seems to come upon something clammy that makes him
instinctively withdraw his hand. He is put off by it
in certain passages of Herzen's fascinating memoirs
where Herzen and his wife and his friends get themselves
into messy mixed-up situations so that everybody
languishes and agonizes and nobody will make a
decision to straighten the thing out. It is a kind of thing
that people objected to in the novels of Dostoevsky when
they were first being read in English, though these
episodes in Dostoevsky are usually brought to an end
by thunderclaps that clear the air; the kind of thing
that used to puzzle and exasperate the first foreign
audiences of Chekhov's plays, though Chekhov exploits
these situations for pathos and humor both. It is something which can perhaps be shortly described as a tendency of Russians in emotional relationships to "stew
in their own juice"—which is a Russian phrase as well
as an English one: masticating and gulping and regur-
gitating their problems, biting upon their suffering and
doting over their guilt, sweating and freezing for years
in the *impasses* of personal involvements as if they were
waiting in Soviet breadlines or the reception rooms of
callous officials.

And something of this complaisance in incurable
heartbreak, this inveterate helpless quaver, one does

find in the poetry of Tyutchev, especially if one reads him in bulk (which perhaps it is unfair to do: Housman, too, is always sounding the same note, and, with him, too, we tend to protest if we read too much at once). Tyutchev is always sighing for Italian suns, and he even thinks nostalgically of the malaria of Rome, by the granite and gray skies of the Neva; he is forever grieving over stricken loves, and he never seems to write when they are flourishing. That lugubrious word роковой, which means *destined, fateful, fatal,* seems to toll on every other page, with its deep recognition of defeat, its certainty that all the affairs of the heart have come out and must always come out badly.

Tyutchev was twice married, both times to German women; and at fifty-one he fell in love with a teacher at a Russian school. Says D. S. Mirsky, "Their love was passionate and profound and an infinite source of torture to both. The young woman's reputation was ruined, and Tyutchev's own gravely tainted, as well as his family happiness. When in 1865 Mlle Denisova died, gloom and despair took possession of Tyutchev. The wonderful tact and forbearance of his wife in the whole affair only increased his suffering by a profound feeling of guilt." Though I am usually interested in the lives of writers, I have not yet been able to bring myself to look this story up. I feel that I have heard enough about it in reading Tyutchev's poems on the subject.

With all this, there are in Tyutchev's pessimism a bitter pride and a noble consistency. But it is as far from A.E. Housman as it is from Alfred de Vigny.

Be still, be still, my soul; it is but for a season:
Let us endure an hour and see injustice done. . . .

says Housman; and,

Gémir, pleurer, prier est également lâche.
Fais énergiquement ta longue et lourde tâche,
Dans la voie où le Sort a voulu t'appeler.
Puis aprés, comme moi, souffre et meurs sans parler.

says Alfred de Vigny's wolf. But Tyutchev, after Mlle
Denisova's death, begs God to dispel his dullness of soul
in order that he may feel his pain more severely, and this
somehow disconcerts the Western reader.

So does Tyutchev's conception of Nature. Nature, for
Housman and Vigny, is indifferent to men, and so they
defy her.

Those are the tears of morning,
That weeps, but not for thee . . .

says Housman; and Vigny:

Vivez, froide Nature, et revivez sans cesse
Sous nos pieds, sur nos fronts, puisque c'est votre loi;
Vivez, et dédaignez, si vous êtes déesse,
L'Homme, humble passager, qui dut vous être un Roi;
Plus que tout votre règne et que ses splendeurs vaines
J'aime la majesté des souffrances humaines:
Vous ne recevrez pas un cri d'amour de moi.

For Wordsworth, the natural world holds a kind of
divine presence that stands always behind what we
see and to feel oneself in touch with which is to be
strengthened, instructed, exalted. But the attitude
of Tyutchev is quite distinct. Nature, in a sense, is
indifferent to man, but man does not need to fight her.
She is neither opponent nor friend: she has a life and
a soul of her own which are larger than the life of man

and which will eventually absorb and obliterate him.
Tyutchev gives final expression to his fundamental
point of view in a poem written not long before his death.
Do the oaks, he asks, that grow on ancient barrows, that
spread their branches and grow grand and speak with
their leaves—do they care into whose dust and memory
they are plunging their long roots? "Nature knows
nothing of the past: our lives to her are alien and phantoms; and, standing in her presence, we dimly apprehend
that we ourselves are but part of her revery. Indiscrimi-
nately, one by one, when they are done with their futile
exploit, she welcomes all her children into her fathomless
depths that swallow and reconcile all."

> Природа знать не знает о былом,
> Ей чужды наши призрачные годы,
> И перед ней мы смутно сознаем
> Себя самих—лишъ грезою природы.
> Поочередно всех своих детей,
> Свершающих свой подвиг безполезный,
> Она равно приветствует своей
> Всепоглощающей и миротворной бездной.

Tyutchev's Nature is Pushkin's Bronze Horseman:
the power that creates and that crushes; and there is a
drama of feeling in relation to it in Tyutchev as there
is in Pushkin. But Tyutchev, who was a reactionary in
politics under Nicholas I and Alexander II and even
held a post in the Censorship, is rather on the masochistic
side, the side that submits to being crushed. And one of
the elements of the Russian character to which it is
most difficult for the Westerner to adjust himself is the
passion for self-immolation.

December, 1944

The Soviet bookstore in New York is now and has always been a rather weird place. I have always felt when I visited it that I was under suspicion of being a spy. On one occasion, in the middle thirties, when I had just come back from the Soviet Union, I went there to get a copy of F. I. Tyutchev's poems. "Ah, Tyutchev, Tyutchev!" said the lady in attendance, "I used to know his poetry by heart!" They are masters of the evasive answer. On a much more recent occasion, when I had asked whether they had any volumes of the jubilee edition of Tolstoy, the answer was, "Perhaps a few." When I asked where they could be found, I was told, "Ah, that would be hard to say." And the lady from whom I was trying to buy a Tyutchev, went on, without offering to sell me one, to point out—what I found to be true—that Tyutchev had written the equivalent of Oscar Wilde's "Each man kills the thing he loves"; though he seems to have been hostile to Wilde himself.

> О, как убийственно мы любим,
> Как в буйной слепоте страстей
> Мы то всего вернее губим,
> Что сердцу нашему милей!

And I found later that just as Oscar Wilde had said that woman was "a sphinx without a secret," Tyutchev had said the same thing of nature:

> Природа—сфинкс. И тем она верней
> Своим искусом губить человека,
> Что, может статься, никакой от века
> Загадки нет и не было у ней.

I wonder, if these are not simple coincidences, whether these similarities may be traced to André Raffalovich,

who wrote on homosexuality and was a lifelong friend
of Wilde's admirer John Gray. I finally succeeded in
buying what I supposed were Tyutchev's collected
poems and conscientiously read them through—only to
discover later that all his religious and political verses
had been excluded by the Soviet publishers in order
to conceal from the public the excessively reactionary
views of this pillar of the old regime. The above essay on
Tyutchev was written in ignorance of the existence of
these. I had to buy another copy of an edition of the
poems printed in Germany for the Russian émigrés in
1921, in order to read Tyutchev the loyalist.

Vladislav Khodasevich has called attention, in an
essay on Tyutchev, to the habitual ineptitude of his
political judgments. He believed, for example, that the
future of Europe would depend on the outcome of a
struggle between revolution and orthodox Russia, and
that the orthodoxy of Russia was destined to save
the day.

1971

GOGOL: THE DEMON

IN THE OVERGROWN GARDEN

The centenary of Gogol's death, February 21, was celebrated by Russians both here and at home and made the subject of a conference at Columbia, but it has not, so far as I know, brought forth any writing in English except a small book by Janko Lavrin, a professor of Slavonic languages at Nottingham University in England: *Nikolai Gogol: A Centenary Survey*. Professor Lavrin is not much of a critic and not much of a master of English, but in his unpretentious way he has been doing useful work in introducing Russian writers to the English-speaking world, and this book has its value for us because it treats certain phases of Gogol's life more satisfactorily than either D. S. Mirsky in his *History of Russian Literature* or Vladimir Nabokov in his own little book on the subject. Both these writers give a rather blurred picture of Gogol's depressing later years, but Professor Lavrin follows, stage by stage, his subject's agonized attempts to find in religion a force that would lift him to the level of the mission—the mission, as he conceived it, of the great Russian writer—of which he had tormenting glimpses but which he never felt confident of being able to fulfil.

The present writer proposes to make use of Professor Lavrin's book as a pretext for adding his own word to the

38

current commemoration of this great and strange writer, the least read and understood in English of the five Russian masters of fiction. It should be noted that an excellent edition of Gogol in six small and cheap volumes has recently been published in the Soviet Union, so that most of his work is now more accessible than it had been for many years, during which the pre-Soviet sets were bringing enormous prices. This new edition is not quite complete, for it omits, along with a number of lesser things, almost the whole of Gogol's last published book, *Selected Passages from Correspondence with Friends,* in which he expressed his reactionary views, but the volumes are well printed and handy, equipped with adequate notes, and full of curious illustrations from the old editions. (Constance Garnett's six-volume translation is unfortunately out of print, but Mr. Nabokov speaks well of B. G. Guerney's more recent translation of *The Overcoat, The Inspector General,* and *Dead Souls.*) The writer has been using this Soviet edition to fill up the gaps in his reading of Gogol and has now been through all his principal works in Russian; so to this extent, at least, he is qualified to write on the subject. It is always rather dangerous for a foreigner who has to work at reading an author to argue about the classics of another country with people who have known them all their lives. (Though Professor Lavrin is a Slovene, he is evidently at home in Russian.) There are sometimes extremely important things about relative rank and quality that the foreigner cannot know, because he has read only scattered works and does not see the whole development of a literature. I have tried to bear in mind, in this connection, a remark that Jean Cocteau once made to me: "Maupassant is a great writer in Russian." Yet the very necessity for the foreigner of paying close attention to every sentence may prevent the story from carrying him along so fast that he fails to notice exactly what is being said and how the author is saying it; and to come fresh to an accepted classic with a mature and unprejudiced mind may make it possible for him to see certain things that have been obscured for readers to whom the language is native, by childhood associations or conventional interpretations. One sometimes has this experience with the works of one's own literature —as when one only discovers in later life the beauty and the meaning of some play of Shakespeare's that bored one when one read it at school.

Apropos of the first of these points and before going on to the second, a word about the impression made by Gogol's style on the reader who attacks him with a dictionary. None of the other Russian classics, so far as my experience goes, presents so many obstacles to the foreigner. The paragraphs confront one like solid walls; the sentences seem to go on for pages. The vocabulary is queer and enormous. In Gogol's Ukrainian stories, the Ukrainian words are a factor that has to be reckoned with, as one has to reckon with Scottish in Scott, and the glossaries provided by Gogol himself fall far short of being complete—though the new editors have done something to supplement them. Then, Gogol was fond of collecting the vocabularies of special occupations and classes as well as the local dialects, and he liked to invent words. You should not be disheartened when you meet, for example, on the threshold of the brilliant fragment *Rome* the rebarbative word *ishcher'*, which is not given in the most comprehensive dictionary, and learn at last from the notes of this new edition that we have only Gogol's assurance that this is an "authentic Russian word" meaning "live coal." If you persist, Gogol's spell will conduct you over all these stumbling blocks; I know of no equally demanding writer who will give you more

for your trouble. Gogol rarely produced a sentence that
was not interesting from the literary point of view—that
is, from the point of view of the special use of language
to create impressions—and any one of his far-stretching
paragraphs will contain so much poetry and humor, apt
phrasing and unexpected imagery, that it makes one's
slow-going delightful. It is as if one were steadily
consuming a big bowl of Ukrainian soup, full of cabbage
and beets and potatoes, chunks of sturgeon and shreds
of beef or duck, with a foundation of sour cream—not
that I know of any such Russian soup (they usually have
fewer ingredients), but then there is no other writer who
seems so to have mixed in everything.

Gogol's style is a variety of that viscous prose which—
for reasons rather difficult to understand—was so
popular in the early nineteenth century. The plum cake
of Charles Lamb is a typical example; so, in a different
field, is the maddeningly impeded narrative style of a
Hawthorne or a Herman Melville. This style allows no
rapid progression. A paragraph seems a mere clot of
words, which might almost as well be read backward as
forward and in which the contrived rhythms have the air
of being ends in themselves, since they are always forcing
the reader to stop and pay attention to them instead
of sweeping him on. This style must have been due
to some very strong pressures, for it is shared to some
extent by a writer who worked on a big scale, like
Balzac; and even by a popular writer, like Scott, who
did want to tell a story. The settings of the stage in
Balzac, the antiquarian preliminaries of Scott, are often
entanglements of this littered non-functional style, which
combines the facetious with the pompous, clumsily handled actualities with jaunty mythological allusions. Now,
Gogol is the master of this prose imbroglio. Though he
may seem to be merely stirring round and round his

thick and nutritious pages, as if they were the strawberry boiled preserve, or the *kasha* to be eaten with currants or honey, or the dough full of hazelnuts and poppy seeds for one of the fancier forms of the rich polymorphous Ukrainian bread that his country people are always eating, this invariably results in a finished dish, which contributes to a well-arranged dinner. The Russian genius for movement, which is one of the great features of Russian literature—I make no apology in this connection for continually changing the metaphor— never allows Gogol's style to get really stuck; there is always a drama on foot that you know will not let you down, and in the meantime the rhapsodies, the inventories, the interpolated anecdotes, and the huge Homeric similes that are whole short stories in themselves are managed with a great sense of rhetoric, so that they do not hold anything up, and they always become in some curious way organic parts of the story. With so much that might be stifling or stagnant, like the life that Gogol depicts, there is always something else that creates suspense—an element of the passionate, the *détraqué,* that may startle us at any moment. In these pages, which in style resemble the tangled forests and the overgrown gardens that are a recurrent motif in Gogol's work, from his earliest goblin tales to Plyushkin's estate in *Dead Souls,* astounding transformations take place: a devil will suddenly appear at the turn of a paragraph, a treasure will be revealed—though the treasures are mirages arranged by the devils—but, as is not always the case with the Gothic novels or the Hoffmannesque tales from which Gogol derived, these visions have a force of emotion, an intense identity and life of their own, that make even Poe seem cerebral and such fancies of Hawthorne's as the Minister's Black Veil and the Black Sabbath of Young Goodman Brown mere phantoms of woven words.

I am still speaking of the early Ukrainian stories—
Evenings on a Farm Near Dikan'ka and its successor, the
Mirgorod series—and this brings me to my second
point: the chance that a foreign reader may be able
to grasp certain things more readily than a native one.
I am going to presume to register dissent from some of
the accounts of these tales that we have had from Lavrin,
Nabokov and Mirsky. This is the department of Gogol's
work that is most taken for granted by Russians. They
first read these stories as fairy tales or farces about comic
villagers. "It was . . . this kind of stuff," says Vladimir
Nabokov, "the juvenilia of the false humorist Gogol,
that teachers in Russian schools crammed down a
fellow's throat. . . . After a lapse of perhaps twenty-five
years I forced myself to reread the *Evenings*—and I
remained as unmoved as I had been in the days when my
teacher could not understand why *The Terrible Vengeance* did not make my flesh creep or *Shponka and
His Aunt* did not make me rock with laughter." *Taras
Bulba,* the longest of the Mirgorod stories, is apparently
prescribed to Russian children somewhat as *Ivanhoe* is,
or was, prescribed to ours—as an exciting historical
romance. It celebrates the exploits of the Cossacks at a
period, rather vaguely indicated, in the sixteenth or
seventeenth century when they were fighting the Poles
and the Tartars. Yet if one comes to these stories after
reading *Dead Souls,* one sees that they are a good deal
closer to Gogol's later work than Mr. Nabokov, for
example, is willing to admit. Taras Bulba himself has a
good deal in common with the boorish and maniacal
landowners encountered by Chichikov in the novel.
In spite of the heroic element, in spite of Gogol's
interpolation of passages that imitate the language of the
folk ballad or the epic, he cannot help making his
Cossack chieftain—who gratuitously starts a war in
order to give his two sons a field for exhibiting their

prowess, then unhesitatingly shoots down one of them
when, infatuated with a Polish princess, the boy has
gone over to the Poles and avenges the death of the
other, who has been captured and executed by the
enemy, by laying waste the whole of Poland—less a hero
than a comic monster. If Pushkin exclaimed over *Dead
Souls,* "God, how sad Russia is!" he might have said
of this earlier epic, "How horrible old Russia was!"
And the arrival of Taras in the Warsaw ghetto in which
he is to hide for a time launches Gogol on a characteristic
but quite non-heroic episode of magnificent comic
squalor.

Nor is the household in *Old-World Landowners,*
the first of the Mirgorod stories, really so different from
the households of *Dead Souls* as one would gather from
the descriptions of this story by Mirsky and Lavrin
(and Mr. Nabokov quotes Mirsky with approval). The
first of these critics says of it that "the vegetable humors
of the old pair, their sloth, their gluttony, their selfish-
ness, are idealized and sentimentalized, and pathetic
sympathy is the main emotion evoked in the reader."
Gogol, says Lavrin, "disgusted by the noise and whirl of
a big town," had turned this old man and his wife "into
an embodiment of his own idea of peace and of that
unruffled pastoral world which he had known in his
childhood." The chronicle of their gluttony, he continues, conveys "no implication of moral censure, since
the whole of it is but an example of man's 'return to
nature,' to the contentment of the vanishing or vanished
patriarchal ways," etc. But is it true that this old-world
couple are much idealized by Gogol? Does he really
approve of their plantlike life? The climax of the story
comes when the old lady's cat is lured away by the outlaw
cats that live in the woods but creep in through a hole
under the barn. The pet comes back to be fed (as the old

man is always being fed); then, when her mistress reaches
out to stroke her, she escapes to freedom again. The old
lady takes this at once as a sign that death has come for
her. She feels, no doubt, that the cat has deserted her,
but an impression is also created that this life of peace,
comfort and overeating, which is not enough for the
cat, is not enough for her either. Yet she cannot slip
away like the cat, she can only escape by dying. Over the
old man's grief at her death Gogol is certainly eloquent
but hardly sentimental; the author makes it plain that
his mourning for his wife is also a vegetable affair, that
he misses her out of "habit," not "passion." The quickly
spent emotions of youth seem childish, the author says,
beside this long and slow habituation to another human
being on the part of a man "who has never been moved
by any strong feeling but whose life has simply consisted
of sitting in a high chair, eating dried pears and mushrooms, and taking part in amiable conversations." But
we do not get the impression that Gogol would be
satisfied with such an existence. No: this household, too,
is a jungle, a condition stuffed with sensual gratifications
that can never be enough for the soul, a way of life in
which, sooner or later, things are bound to take a queer
turn. A wild impulse, an unearthly summons, may
suddenly upset everything. The cats from the forest
have crept in like devils. The widower, walking in the
orchard, by whose fruit trees with their succulent fruit
he, too, has been overgrown, thinks one day that he
hears his wife calling him, and this proves to be an omen
of his death. Gogol tells us here that sometimes in his
childhood he has imagined, on a bright and quiet day,
that he heard a voice calling his name and has fled to find
some other human being who would relieve him of his
sense of desolation. No night of raging storm, he says, in
the heart of a pathless forest could have frightened him

so much as that terrible silence in the midst of a cloudless day. This is a subtle and disturbing story, of which the *Gemütlichkeit* is not the author's but a part of the subject; yet Marc Slonim, in his recent book *The Epic of Russian Literature,* seems to be the only critic in English who has gone even so far as to mention that "under the surface" of it "there lurks Gogol's usual dread of insignificance and triviality."

As for the celebrated *Quarrel of the Two Ivans,* as Lavrin abridges the title, it seems to me a typical example of the classic which everybody knows so well—it is invoked by Russians like the "Alice" books—that no one any longer pays attention to it. It is assumed to be an hilariously funny story—though with a famous sigh and shrug at the end—that exploits a ridiculous quarrel between two queer and crotchety old men, one of whom has called the other a goose. Russians refer to it with the ready-made grin that we have for Tom Sawyer painting the fence or old Weller telling the court to spell his name with a "we." Neither from Lavrin's account of this tale nor from that of any other of these critics would one be able to get an idea of what it is really about, for they all have the quarrel appear meaningless. Lavrin does make it clear that the story is fundamentally bitter but tells us only that the issue between the two old cronies is that "Ivan Ivanovich wanted to buy from his friend an old gun the latter would not part with." Actually, the trouble is that Ivan Ivanovich cannot bear the feeling of inferiority inflicted by the sight of his neighbor's maid hanging out on the line a whole wardrobe of old uniforms, old dress clothes and other signs of his friend's superior rank, and that he begs Ivan Nikophorovich to give him the gun in order to induce the latter to confer on him some sign of equality. The quarrel could never be healed because Ivan Nikophorovich could never refrain, in a crisis, from treating Ivan Ivanovich *de haut en bas,* and Ivan Ivanovich could equally never forgive this. It is a tragedy of provincial snobbery destroying good human relations in a community so dismal and dull that one might think people would try to preserve them—though the point is, of course, that it was certain that Ivan I.'s vulgar insistence would incite Ivan N. to insolence and that, for men with nothing to do, a war of spite that involves a class issue may, by stimulating a certain excitement, prove more satisfactory than a peaceful friendship. In any case, the two Ivans, in their humble way, are monsters that lead up to the more formidable monsters to be later encountered in *Dead Souls.*

From *Dead Souls* all the glory has departed of ancient Ukrainian legend as well as the amusing mythology of Ukrainian peasant lore, and even the gentleness and decency of the comfortable "old-world landowners." We are submerged in the messy and stuffy and smelly and run-to-seed life of landowners who are drunken and quarrelsome, moping and ineffective, brutal and self-assertive or crazily acquisitive or stupidly grasping. After an opening almost Pickwickian, with a man putting up at an inn, this strange book, which never ceases to be humorous, leads us into a domain of horror: another and ranker jungle that is also a stagnant morass. Gogol wallows, like his characters, in the paragraphs of a cluttered, apparently phlegmatic style that has now been brought to perfection; yet this style has a persistent undercurrent of sadness, of disgust, of chagrin; it condemns and it undermines. There is still the same queer suspense that is sometimes disrupted by violence but is never completely relieved. What, we ask ourselves, is meant by this chronicle of Chichikov, the empty soul, who buys up the names of serfs (referred to as "souls" in old Russia) that have died since the last census, in order to pretend he owns them and to borrow money on this credit? Are not the souls of their masters also dead? Are these landowners really devils who appear to Chichikov or is he himself a devil who has come for *them?* Exposed in the district he has been working, he is last seen driving away in his carriage. There is a moment of respite and open horizons—the troika dashing off with its cheerful bells. In this torpid and moldy Russia, something has been set in motion, and Gogol has a moment of exaltation. But where is it going? he asks, and the horizon returns no answer. Nor is he able to escape from this world that is tedious as well as mad; nor has he power to redeem his hero through the Purgatory he plans to succeed this Hell. In the fragments that have come to us of the Second Part, the adventurer Chichikov, though sent to jail, seems to emerge just as much of a scoundrel, and the supposedly virtuous characters are the victims of obsessions like those of the First.

Gogol's life was full of absurdities, and Mr. Nabokov takes advantage of them, rather cruelly, to make his last phase ridiculous. It becomes somewhat more comprehensible in the account of it by Mr. Lavrin. Poor Gogol, who felt it his duty to supply his public with something more positive, to answer himself the question he had sent after the flying troika, now resorted to a sort of sham fanaticism, set up as a preacher and teacher, and published the *Selected Passages from Correspondence with Friends,* in which he glorified the Russian landowner as the agent of God on earth and opposed the education of the peasants, who, he said, should not be allowed even to know of the existence of any book but the Bible. But the indignant retorts of his friends, toward whom he had adopted a didactic tone, seem seriously to have shaken his self-confidence. He came to feel that, for all his pretensions, he had not really yet found God. He visited Palestine in the hope of a new revelation but could not find Him even there, and he finally came under the influence of a strong-minded Russian priest who, bigoted and ignorant of literature, tried to persuade him to give up writing. Ten days before his death—at the insistence, perhaps, of this priest—he burned up the Second Part of *Dead Souls,* on which he had spent years of work, then declared that this had been a mistake, that the Devil had induced him to do it.

The typical situation in Gogol is the sudden falling-out of the bottom of some impressive construction that we have watched being elaborately built. You have, thus, the dissolution of the old-world landowners; the loss of Taras Bulba's sons; the explosion between the two Ivans; the theft of the overcoat in the famous later story; the cataclysmic discoveries, too late, in the plays, of the large-scale imposture of *The Inspector General* and of the confidence game in *The Gamblers;* the abject jumping out the window of the fiancé of *Marriage* at the moment when, with infinite difficulty, his betrothal has been achieved; the breakdown of Chichikov's fraudulent traffic just in his hour of triumph when he is fêted as the toast of the town. So Gogol and his great book, at the moment when Turgenev says that all attention in Russia was centered on him and it, unexpectedly collapsed together.

Gogol presents an unusual case of a frustrating impasse of the spirit, a hopeless neurotic deadlock, combined with a gusto for life, an enormous artistic vitality. So vigorous and so rich is this talent that it must have been difficult for his friends and his readers to foresee that it was doomed to be choked. Lavrin suggests that the trouble may be traced to an Oedipus complex, an explanation of such cases suggested so often that it is coming to seem rather suspect. There is, however, no doubt that Gogol's defeat was bound up with his lifelong failure to arrive at any satisfactory sexual life. Fear of marriage is made the comic theme of the story of *Shponka and His Aunt,* deliberately left unfinished, and of the rather inferior comedy *Marriage,* and Gogol's difficulties in this connection appear in another kind of theme, which he never succeeds in developing: that of the ideal woman, seen briefly and adored from afar—the maidenly *pensionnaire* who makes such an impression on Chichikov; the Italian beauty who gleams in the crowd for the hero of the projected novel on Rome. The magnificent opening of this novel has far more of positive inspiration than anything that has survived from the Second Part of *Dead Souls.* Gogol's longing for a feudal world becomes somewhat more sympathetic when it is dramatized in the person of an Italian prince returning from impoverished exile to discover for the first time his native Rome, but at the moment when it at last becomes necessary, after the long, the monumental buildup, to bring the prince into direct relations with the dazzling Annunziata, the story abruptly breaks off. In *Viy,* of the Mirgorod series, the traveller and the beauty —both Gogol and his heroes are always travelling—do engage, but with a fatal result, and that this fatal result was inevitable to Gogol's vision of life is shown by the turn that he seems to have given to the folk tale from which he derived the story. This is a version of the vampire legend in which a young man must stand watch for three nights by the body of a dead woman, who at midnight comes to life and attacks him. Gogol says that he has followed the folk tale exactly, but in the versions of this story included in the collection of Afanasiev, the Russian Grimm, the young man is always able to defend himself with the Psalter and the sign of the Cross, and finally defeats the witch; and, from these and from the habits of folk tales in general, we may assume that it is Gogol himself—the solid Ukrainian background, more or less realistically presented, is certainly very much Gogol's—who is responsible for making his student succumb at the third vigil and fall dead with fright when the vampire calls in the reinforcements of Hell (just as, in *Taras Bulba,* the young Andrey is destroyed through the irresistible spell that has been cast on him by the Polish princess). It should be noted that the girl is revenging herself. She had fastened herself first on the student in the shape of an old hag, and he had only got rid of her by beating her to death, at which point she had been forced to reveal herself as the typical Gogolian beauty, intimidating and unattainable. In a final ironic scene, the boy's former companions on the walking trip that has had for him this tragic end—back in college now and warming up over their cups—are discussing his fate at their ease. Not having had to share his ordeal, they decide that if he had not been yellow, the witch could have done him no harm: "You've only got to cross yourself and spit on her tail, and nothing can happen to you!" But this rite had never worked for Gogol. It was always the Devil who appeared to him, never the Savior he hoped for, and when the feminine apparition toward whom he aspired comes at all close to any of his heroes, she proves to be a devil, too.

It was only to Dostoevsky, in the next generation, that the Christian revelation came. It is one of the striking features of the continuity of Russian literature that Dostoevsky should not only show strongly the literary influence of Gogol but that he should even give somewhat the impression of being haunted by Gogol's devils and even of saving Gogol's soul.

December 6, 1952

SEEING CHEKHOV PLAIN

To write about Chekhov, for a critic of the English-speaking countries, has usually meant to grope among the incomplete and scrambled translations of Constance Garnett and others. Here is a book on the subject— *Chekhov: A Biographical and Critical Study,* by Ronald Hingley—by an Englishman who knows Russian and who has been able to avail himself of the new material published by the Soviets. It is a curious feature of Soviet life that the pitiless discouragement of talent in the field of contemporary literature has seemed hardly, in the field of scholarship, to have affected the publication of editions of the Russian classics that are sometimes of unprecedented excellence. The *Complete Collected Works and Letters of A. P. Chekhov,* which was brought out in twenty volumes between 1944 and 1951, contains, in chronological sequence, every known piece of writing by Chekhov, published and un-published, with all variants, early drafts, and passages suppressed by the censor. [I have since, however, learned from a paper by Gleb Struve that in the case of Chekhov's letters about the liquidated director Meyerhold, the Soviets have made suppressions of their own. 1971] At the time Mr. Hingley wrote his book, only the first eleven volumes had appeared, but with these, which included an immense amount of stuff that had been printed in magazines but that Chekhov had never collected—reviews and topical skits and captions for humorous drawings, and even a column of Moscow gossip that Chekhov contributed in his youth—Mr. Hingley was in a better position to give an account of Chekhov's work than anyone else, including Russians, who had ever attempted to do so in English. His book is clear, sensible, competent, and it should help to lift the twilight atmosphere that has partly veiled Chekhov in English and that is the result less, as people assume, of his moral and artistic qualities than of the remoteness of Russia from us and of the obstacles between us and his text.

For nothing could be more different from the Western conception of Chekhov than that of the average literate Russian. In England and the United States, Chekhov has been read almost exclusively by a specialized literary public, with whom he has sometimes become a cult and by whom he has been regarded as the master of so exquisite an art, so far from obvious in its themes and technique, that one can only compare the attitude toward him to the attitude toward Henry James at the time when James had not yet come to figure as a pillar of the national pantheon. But Chekhov's first publications were humorous sketches and squibs contributed to magazines of the type of our old *Life* and *Puck,* which he wrote, in his early twenties, in order to scrape together the money to put himself through medical school, and among Russians he has always had a public that, sometimes quite insensitive to his masterpieces, never ceases to be delighted by the fantasy of this early humor. The situation of Chekhov, in fact, from the point when he was encouraged by the novelist Grigorovich, as Mark Twain was

by Howells, to take himself more seriously as a writer
was not unlike that of Mark Twain when, after
publishing *Huckleberry Finn,* he had difficulty in slough-
ing off his original reputation as a popular entertainer.
Some of Chekhov's early comic stories—such as the
one that appears in English under the title *A Horsey
Name*—have had much the same kind of success as
Mark Twain's *Jumping-Frog of Calaveras County.*
They are so funny that Chekhov the artist has had
difficulty in living them down, though the point of
such a joke as *A Horsey Name* is involved with psychological truth in a way that the Frog is not, and
the element of humor in Chekhov—though it certainly
became more refined—has always been a good deal
stronger than non-Russian readers usually grasp.

The transition from the earlier to the later humor is
well shown by David Magarshack, a Russian-born
Britisher who writes in English, in another recent book
on Chekhov, *Chekhov the Dramatist.* This transition
may be clearly traced in the successive revisions that
have now been collected of the humorous dramatic
monologue, *On the Harmfulness of Tobacco,* that
eventually became and still remains a stock piece for
recitation. The first version, of 1886, is a comic vaude-
ville turn full of touches from the barbershop weeklies, in
which a lecturer against tobacco, who has turned up
a little tipsy, loses the thread of his discourse, forgets
himself sufficiently to produce a snuffbox, and confides
in the audience at length on the subject of his shrewish
wife and his many unmarriageable daughters—though
even here it is the human situation that figures as the
basis of the joke, and the lecturer's demoralization has
already a touch of the macabre. The last version of
this piece, written in 1902, at the end of Chekhov's
life, is a horrifying and heartbreaking revelation of

the pathetic personality of the lecturer: "Oh," he cries, in an outburst at the end, "to throw everything over! . . . If only I could run away from this cheap and trashy and common life that's turning me into a pitiful old fool! . . . Oh, to be able to get away somewhere, far far away in the fields, where I could stand like a tree, like a column, like a scarecrow in somebody's vegetable garden, underneath the wide sky, where you could watch the bright quiet moon hanging over you all the night, and forget, forget everything!" Then he catches sight of his slave-driving wife, who is watching him from the wings, and brings his lecture to a proper close. The different stages of this little play show in miniature Chekhov's whole growth.

Yet this humor that runs all through Chekhov is but one of a number of features that the foreigner may miss or misunderstand. If Chekhov has been baffling to Russians, it has been only because they wanted to pin him down to a definite political position, which he always refused to take. His work is not vague but compact and dense, all made up of hard detail and larded with allusions to specific things. Yet his stories as well as his plays, which have fascinated Western readers, have often left them puzzled or blank. To such readers—though, as much as those of Flaubert, as much as the plays of Ibsen or Shaw, these fictions are nailed to their time and place—they have seemed to occur in a realm of dream. "They are not lit [Chekhov's characters]," writes Mr. Somerset Maugham, in the preface to an omnibus of his own stories, "by the hard light of common day but suffused in a mysterious grayness. They move in this as though they were disembodied spirits. It is their souls that you seem to see. The subconscious seems to come to the surface and they communicate with one another directly, without the impediment of speech. Strange, futile creatures, with descriptions of their outward seeming tacked on them like a card on an exhibit in a museum, they move as mysteriously as the tortured souls who crowded about Dante when he walked in Hell. You have the feeling of a vast, gray, lost throng wandering aimless in some dim underworld." We cannot, I think, however, entirely blame pale translations for the misty effect that Chekhov produces on Mr. Maugham. It is true that Constance Garnett made the Russian writers sound all more or less the same, whereas Chekhov's writing, though it sometimes lacks color, is never blurred in Russian; it gives rather the impression of the tight-strung lines of a masterly steel engraving. But, of course, Mr. Maugham is hardly at home in these questions of literary art. It is more interesting that Virginia Woolf should find herself at sea with Chekhov. "Our first impressions of Chekhov," she writes in *The Common Reader,* "are not of simplicity but of bewilderment. What is the point of it, and why does he make a story out of this? we ask as we read story after story. . . . These stories are inconclusive, we say, and proceed to frame a criticism based upon the assumption that stories ought to conclude in a way that we recognize. . . . We have to cast about in order to discover where the emphasis in these strange stories rightly comes. . . . Is it that he is primarily interested not in the soul's relation with other souls but with the soul's relation to health—with the soul's relation to goodness? These stories are always showing us some affectation, pose, insincerity. Some woman has got into a false relation; some man has been perverted by the inhumanity of his circumstances. The soul is ill; the soul is cured; the soul is not cured. Those are the emphatic points in his stories."

It is plain that to both these so different English novelists Chekhov comes as an apparition, rather insubstantial and eerie, abstracted from time and space, telling stories they can only half grasp. "I have little doubt," says Mr. Maugham, with a touch of that patronizing tone that he likes to adopt with his betters, "that Chekhov would have written stories with an ingenious, original, and striking plot if he had been able to think of them. It was not in his temperament. Like all good writers, he made a merit of his limitations." Well, Chekhov did contrive in his early phase—in the novel called in English *A Shooting Party* (Драма на Охоте)—a thriller that is certainly original and that is full of surprise and suspense. (It has recently been used for a Hollywood movie.) This novel, which was written as a job, as a serial for a magazine, is a highly characteristic work of astute social observation and shrewd psychological insight (it is strange to find Mr. Hingley describing this extraordinary story as "not of serious literary merit"); but Chekhov cared so little about plot-fiction that he never brought it out in a book. One cannot expect Mr. Maugham to approve of the precept that Ivan Bunin reports Chekhov's preaching to him: that in writing a short story you should lop off the beginning and the end. But it ought to be obvious to anyone whose notion of storytelling does not stop with the well-oiled plot, with the "wow" in the final paragraph which Chekhov refrained from writing, that the stories and plays of Chekhov are both complex and closely worked out. Mr. Hingley, who sometimes, in retelling Chekhov's stories, suggests that he has not seen their structure, does not bring out Chekhov's sense of form so well as Mr. Magarshack, who analyzes the patterns of the plays and demonstrates the subtlety and terseness of their beautiful workmanship. Yet there is no question that

Western readers have been seriously handicapped with
Chekhov even more than with the other Russian writers
by their unfamiliarity with the cultural and social
background of the world that he is writing about. He
is much more limited and local than Tolstoy or
Dostoevsky, and we do not always catch his allusions
or understand the points he is trying to make. Though
Chekhov is always specific, always quite sure and
sharp, we think him elusive and vague. "These evocative
undertones in the dialogue," Mr. Magarshack correctly
writes of the literary references in Chekhov, "are
completely lost in the translation, with the result
that an English version of a Chekhov play distorts
the emotional reaction it is meant to set up in the
audience, creating the impression that the characters
express themselves so oddly because they are
'Russians.'" Nor are the full social implications of
Chekhov's characters grasped. In the case of Mrs.
Woolf, for example, she has touched upon something
essential in Chekhov, something that can be understood
anywhere, and if Chekhov had no general human
significance, he would not belong to the great Russian
tradition and would never, outside of Russia, have
exerted so strong an influence. Yet it is also in the
Russian tradition to deal critically with Russia's
specific problems, and Chekhov was no exception to
this. He did not have a religious message, as Dostoevsky
and Tolstoy did, and he deliberately kept clear of
politics, but, after all, his story *Ward No. 6* was one
of the contemporary writings that most aroused Lenin
in his youth, and his whole work is a social document
of a powerful if largely negative kind.

A further and unnecessary obstacle to the foreigner's
understanding of Chekhov has been added by the
Garnett translation, which jumbles the stories up,

giving no indication of when they were written and sometimes putting side by side productions divided by decades, in such a way as to destroy completely the sequence of some twenty-five years of work. D. S. Mirsky complained of this in his *Contemporary Russian Literature,* and Mr. Hingley makes the point again. In the Russian editions the stories are usually presented in their proper order, and in the new Soviet edition each has been carefully dated. It is only by reading them thus that it is possible to get any idea of Chekhov's artistic development or his ultimate vision of Russian life.

If we follow this line of development, we see that, beginning with satirical jokes, Chekhov goes on to master the art of the ironic anecdote, so often pathetic or tragic (it would hardly, one would think, be possible to complain of a good many of them that one did not understand the point); these, in turn, begin to expand into something more rounded-out (the dense but concise study of character and situation) and eventually—in what Mr. Hingley calls Chekhov's Tolstoyan period (*A Nervous Breakdown,* for example)—take on a new moral interest or attain, as in his "clinical" one (*The Black Monk*), a new psychological depth. These studies become more comprehensive—*The Steppe, A Dreary Story, Ward No. 6*—in such a way as to cover a whole life *en raccourci* or an experience in fuller detail. Such pieces are not short stories but what Henry James called *nouvelles.* (The earlier *Shooting Party* was Chekhov's only real novel.) Then Chekhov enters his final phase, which extends from 1894 to his death in 1904, and which it seems to me possible to date from the story called *A Woman's Kingdom,* which immediately follows *The Black Monk.* The *Monk* had been a masterpiece of a kind different from any of these later

ones: a story of the supernatural that had something
in common with Hawthorne, though it was also a
"clinical" story of a psychiatric case; and all through
the stories before this, even when they were dealing
with lives that were sordid or uneventful, there had
run a certain vein of the grotesque, of something not
always quite plausible: an element of satiric relief,
of comic exaggeration—even, in certain cases, of
fable and fairy tale. But there is nothing of this in
A Woman's Kingdom, which simply describes a day
in the household of an unmarried woman—a chronicle
of domestic incident, solidly and soberly treated, in
which the rise of the industrial middle class (the theme
of a number of the later stories) is given its first intensive
treatment. The method here changes as well as the scale.
We now rarely get a single situation—as in *Ward
No. 6*—carried through to an ironic climax.

This final series of stories, of which Chekhov managed
to produce only a few a year, become more and more
complex, involving a number of characters and presenting, as his plays of these years do, a whole social
microcosm. These are really compressed novels, and
we soon come to see that Chekhov is composing, in
this latest period, a kind of Comédie Humaine in
miniature. He is covering contemporary Russia in a
sequence of significant studies, each one or each group
of which aims to deal with—and for the purposes of
the author more or less to exhaust—some clearly
defined milieu. He is certainly concentrating here on
an anatomy of Russian society rather than on appraising
the soundness, as Virginia Woolf found him doing,
of this or that individual soul. In *A Woman's Kingdom*
(Бабье Царство), and later on in *A Doctor's Visit*
(Случай из Практики) and *The New Villa*, it is the
recently arrived *bourgeoisie*, who have grown up with

modern factories and modern engineering and now find themselves cut off from the people, from whom they have sprung. In *Three Years,* it is the old Moscow merchant world, almost as self-contained as a ghetto, in which the strength of the older generation, bigoted, harsh, and oppressive, is at last undermined by the defection of its sons, who are marrying into the gentry or attempting, as intelligentsia, to escape to a world of more freedom and more sophistication; but these latter do not pan out, they cannot adapt themselves, and the wife of the brother who has stayed with the business—a woman from a "county" family, who has suffered a good deal from her boorish inlaws—comes to feel in the long run that her husband has chosen the better part. In *The Murder,* it is a family of innkeepers who have learned to read the Bible and are possessed by fanatical religious ideas—a form of illumination that does not save them from benighted savagery. *Peasants* is a study of the peasant world, which Chekhov is far from idealizing, as Tolstoy liked to do, or sentimentalizing, as Turgenev sometimes did. A peasant from the *izba,* who has bettered himself to the extent of becoming a waiter in Moscow, falls ill and returns with a wife and child to his family in the village; here, surrounded by miseries and horrors to which he has become unaccustomed, he is allowed to die of tuberculosis, while his wife and his daughter sink to the sordid and servile level of the older generation. In a companion piece, *In the Ravine,* Chekhov deals with the brutalizing influence of the kulak, prosperous peasant, class. In this somewhat better-off family, the shopkeeper father sells bad meat, one of his sons passes bad money, and an enterprising daughter-in-law, who is building a brickyard on her father-in-law's land and who fears that she may be deprived of it,

eliminates the infant grandson to whom he proposes
to leave it by scalding him to death with boiling water.
Everybody knows about this but the poorer peasants
do not dare protest, and nothing is done about it.
These two stories of peasant life are like cultures of
malignant germs examined through a microscope.
In *The Bishop,* the next-to-last story that Chekhov
lived to complete, he fixes on his slide a specimen of
the not quite diseased yet not very vigorous tissue of the
Greek Orthodox Church: a dying peasant priest, who
has risen above the level of his parents but now finds
he has nobody close to him; who has been turned into
a professional churchman, caught up in the routine
of his duties, without ever having experienced a moment of genuine religious feeling; who should clearly
have been a lay intellectual but has never had the chance
of becoming one. In these, and in the stories that
immediately precede them, are presented a variety
of other types of peasants, ex-peasants, and the lower
middle class that were called in Russia *meshchane,*
together with doctors, professors, petty provincial
officials, and—given the full-scale treatment in *The
Duel* of 1891—the pretentious and inept intelligentsia.

It should be noted that in his stories of this period
Chekhov gives us no comparable picture of the decaying
landowner class that is the subject of three of his later
plays, and that this class, when it does appear—the
story called in English *An Artist's Story* is the only
possible exception—figures usually, as in *My Life,*
in only an incidental role and is shown as degenerate
to the point of squalor. There are here no lakes with
symbolic gulls, no cherry orchards in bloom. Mr.
Magarshack makes a great point of Chekhov's repeated
insistence that *The Cherry Orchard* was meant as a
comedy not far removed from farce, declaring that

the author's intention was betrayed by Stanislavsky when he turned it into something romantic, and it is true that, if one reads the play, one finds that the humor is broader, the glamour laid on less thick, than memories of the Art Theater productions, seen without one's knowing the language, might have led one to expect. Yet the poetry and pathos *are* there—Chekhov put them there. Mr. Magarshack is certainly mistaken when he thinks that it was not Chekhov's purpose to have us think that the old butler Firs is to die in the boarded-up house, abandoned by his irresponsible masters. My own explanation of Chekhov's complaints about Stanislavsky's production of *The Cherry Orchard* is that he felt himself somewhat embarrassed by his tenderness, in these later plays, for the world of the *dvoryane,* the gentry, into which he had not been born and toward which he had otherwise taken a rather disdainful tone. If he seems to protest too much in his letters on the subject of *The Cherry Orchard,* we may guess that he wished to avoid being thought to admire it too much (as Dickens, in *Our Mutual Friend,* disturbed by the threatening power of the parvenu middle class, was moved to a certain nostalgia for the cultivated upper classes he had hitherto ignored or made fun of). Yet Lopakhin, who buys up the cherry orchard—a freed serf, like Chekhov's father—but who cannot, on account of his origins, induce even a poor relation of the original owners to marry him, is hardly more of a hero to Chekhov than the narrator of *A Shooting Party*. This narrator, a clever but common man, a provincial examining magistrate, both despises and envies the local count, proprietor of a run-down estate and a degenerating household not unlike but very much less attractive than those of *The Cherry Orchard,* and murders with impunity, under the nobleman's nose, a girl who has been the mistress of both of them when she shows that she prefers the count, however unappetizing, to the narrator, for whom she feels some physical passion. He completely bluffs the district authorities and succeeds in getting an innocent peasant sent away to Siberia for the crime he himself has committed, and eventually takes the count in to live with him, when the latter has drunk away all his money, still susceptible to the old man's prestige and in consequence enjoying his degradation. This lower-class man who is on the make is the central figure in Chekhov. This is the theme—transposed into terms of a variety of milieux—of every one of the stories mentioned above. And it is much to the point at the present time to inquire how Chekhov judged these characters. For it was people of this kind who came to the top with the success of the Russian Revolution. It is an irony in Chekhov's own manner that, in carefully preserving his work, the Soviet Russians should always assume— when they talk about him in public, at any rate—that his types are all monsters and parasites produced by the corruption of the old regime, when, in their grovelling before authority, their half-baked education and their vulgar ambitions, they have obviously a good deal in common with the people who are running the Soviet Union.

What, then, did Chekhov think of these people, of whom he had been one himself and from whose cowardices, servilities, hypocrisies he prided himself— in a remarkable letter quoted by Mr. Hingley—on having delivered himself, declaring that he had succeeded in finally "squeezing out of myself every drop of servile blood" and becoming "a real human being." He seemed to be well aware that the future belongs to them. Mr. Hingley devotes some space to discussing the unreal problem of whether Chekhov ought to be regarded as an "optimistic" or a "pessimistic" writer. "There is," he says, "general agreement in Russia today that Chekhov was an optimist, both in his writings and in his personal life, and this view has the important support of Chekhov himself." Mr. Magarshack insists that Chekhov's last four plays represent "a drama of courage and hope." Now, it is true that an occasional speech in these plays gives expression to courage or hope, but when any such note is struck—as it is at the end of *The Three Sisters,* when the husbandless, loverless women, unable to make a break with the life of their backwater town, begin to talk of a time when "our sufferings will pass into joy for those who live after us" and "peace and happiness will reign on earth"—such longings and resolutions are always seen in a pathetic perspective. It is true that Chekhov himself was occasionally moved to prophesy in a similar sense. "Do you know," A. A. Kuprin reports him as saying, "in three or four hundred years the whole earth will turn into a blossoming garden." But the immediate prospect for a world administered by Chekhov's characters is not in the least cheerful. One cannot, of course, expect a robust faith from a man who is dying of tuberculosis, though such invalids have their moments of buoyancy, but Chekhov's susceptibility to this disease—from which a number of his later characters, such as Nikolai in *Peasants,* suffer—was itself no doubt partly a product of the hard strain of adaptation, intellectual, social and physical, that so many of his characters undergo. "What the writers who belong to the gentry," he wrote in a letter of 1889, "receive as a gift from nature we

lower-class intelligentsia buy at the cost of our youth,"
and this cost in debilitating effort and the frequent
inadequacy of what it bought were usually in the
foreground with Chekhov. Yet, in one of his best stories,
The Steppe, he makes us feel that the hopes of the
peasants who are sending their boy away to be educated
may be something more than merely touching, that
something new and sound may come of it—though the
bishop of the next-to-last story might well be this boy
grown old, who, cut off from his peasant mother,
has never found his true vocation.

But—what is curious and probably significant, as
it is certainly rather surprising to the reader who has
taken these pieces in their chronological order—the
last story that Chekhov completed, *Betrothed* (Невеста)
(buried by Mrs. Garnett in a volume of pieces of much
earlier date), sounds a note of triumphant self-confidence. A girl from the provinces, an independent
spirit, throws over her provincial fiancé, whose *posh-
lost,* that special combination of commonness,
banality and smugness, she finds that she cannot
stomach. She has been worked on by an artist cousin,
who has told her that she must go to St. Petersburg
and study in the university, that the more people like
her become "dedicated" and trained, "the sooner the
Kingdom of Heaven will descend upon the earth. In
that time, little by little, there will not be left of your
town one stone upon another. Everything will be
turned upside down; everything will be changed, as
if by magic. There will arise large and splendid houses,
marvellous parks, extraordinary fountains, remarkable
people." This cousin, a typical Chekhovian *raté,*
has slipped out of painting into architecture, out of
architecture into working for a lithographer, and has

never been effectual at anything except egging on his women friends to throw over their family life. Unlike the three sisters, the Nadya of this story does succeed in making the break, and she finds, when she returns for vacation, that her home now seems small and ignoble. She is repelled by the ancient tradition, carried on by her mother and grandmother, of crowding all the servants into narrow quarters and making them sleep on the floor. She does not feel very much compunction at discovering that this mother and grandmother have been dropped by their social circle as the result of her improper behavior in jilting her fiancé. She is not even very much moved at receiving a telegram which tells her that the cousin who spurred her on has died of tuberculosis. She shakes off the old house and town—it is as if the old life had burned up and the ashes had blown away—and, alive with excitement and hope, she goes back to her work in the city.

Chekhov, thus, at the end of his life, reminds us of the Watcher by the Way in that fine poem of Edwin Arlington Robinson's, *The Town Down the River*. Robinson was dealing here, within only a few years of Chekhov, with a period in the United States that seemed sometimes, though not for quite the same reasons, as discouraging, as full of frustrations, as the Russia of his time did to Chekhov. Robinson's watcher by the road that leads to a great modern city warns the people who are eagerly journeying there, as the characters of Chekhov do to Moscow and St. Petersburg, of its dangers and disillusions. Yet when his own life is nearly over, and the old and unsuccessful come to him to tell him that they now see he was right and to warn him in turn that his end is near and that they might as well all give up their hopes:

"But your lanterns are unlighted
And the Town is far before you:
Let us hasten, I implore you,"
Said the Watcher by the Way.
"Long have I waited,
Longer have I known
That the Town would have its own,
And the call be for the fated.

"In the name of all created,
Let us hear no more, my brothers;
Are we older than all others?
Are the planets in our way?"—
"Hark," said one; "I hear the River,
Calling always, night and day."—
"Forward, then! The lights are shining,"
Said the Watcher by the Way.

November 22, 1952

TURGENEV

AND THE LIFE-GIVING DROP

The maiden name of Turgenev's mother was Varvara Petrovna Lutovinova. The family knew little of their ancestry before the beginning of the eighteenth century, but they had since then accumulated a fortune by methods which sometimes amounted to plunder. The family history was full of scandals. When Varvara Petrovna was a little girl, her mother married again and took her to live with her stepfather, a drunken country squire, who beat her and humiliated her in ways that she could not bear to talk about. Varvara's mother was hardly gentler: she made favorites of the daughters of her husband and did nothing to defend her own daughter. Turgenev gave the following account of her to one of his German friends: "The quick-tempered old woman was stricken with paralysis, and spent all her time sitting almost motionless in an armchair. One day she got very cross with the little serf boy who was in attendance on her, and in a fierce fit of anger seized a log and hit him over the head with such force that he fell unconscious to the floor. This sight produced a most unpleasant impression on her: she bent down, picked the little boy up, put him beside her on the big armchair, placed a pillow on his bleeding head, and, sitting down on it, suffocated him." The daughter was unattractive but extremely strong-willed, and she knew that she would inherit the family property. When Varvara Petrovna was sixteen, her stepfather tried to rape her, and she ran away, on foot and half-dressed, to the house of an uncle twenty miles away. The uncle took her in, but the atmosphere of the household was not friendly. He kept her under rigorous discipline, and she resented this. By the time she was twenty-six, the relations between them had become so embittered that he threatened to put her out and wanted to disinherit her, but before he had a chance to remake his will, he died of a heart attack.

Varvara Petrovna now found herself mistress of an enormous property—a number of separate estates, tenanted by thousands of serfs (Turgenev's friend Pavel Annenkov says that she possessed five thousand in the Government of Orel alone), whom she ruled with a brutality which rivalled that from which she herself had suffered. She identified herself with the Tsar and referred to her peasants as "subjects." She was not only tyrannical but ogreish. For the slightest deviation from her orders, and sometimes on trumped-up pretexts, she would have her people flogged or send them off to Siberia—though from this latter fate they were sometimes rescued by neighbors, who took them on their own estates, while Varvara Petrovna's household pretended that her sentences had been carried out. She would not allow her maids to have children, because children interfered with their duties, and they threw their babies into a pond. When two of her favorite servants were married to one another, by her orders and without being consulted, she permitted the wife to have children but made her keep them so far away that the mistress could not hear them crying, in a place to which it was rarely possible for the mother to get to see them. On her removal to Moscow for the winter, the mistress forbade this woman to bring her children along, and when she learned that the girl had dared to disobey, she made a terrible scene, which a member of the household has described: "Varvara Petrovna, hoarse with rage, threw herself out of bed, with one hand seized Agatha by the throat, and with the other it seemed as if she tried to tear her mouth to pieces . . . but immediately let go, and almost falling into the nearest armchair, she had an attack of nerves." She gave orders that the children should be sent back to the country, but they were hidden in a servant's room, where they lived locked up all winter, never allowed to go out, for fear the mistress would see them. On one occasion, when the keeper of the linen was having a celebration of her "name day," enlivened, as a matter of course and as Varvara Petrovna well knew, by a liberal consumption of vodka, the mistress played on her servants a morbid and ferocious practical joke. She declared herself to be dying and summoned the fifty members of her household and office staffs to pass before her bedside. Pretending to be only half conscious, she noted which servants did not appear and which had a smell of vodka. Then she quickly recovered, demanded tea and decreed that all these culprits should be punished: "Rascals, drunkards! You were all drunk. You were glad that your mistress was dying! . . . You were drinking and celebrating a name day with your mistress dying!"

There is, of course, in all this the terrible need of a woman who has never been loved to make herself felt by others. She had married a young cavalry officer, of an older and more honorable family, which, however, was going bankrupt. He was handsome and attractive to women, and he had found Miss Lutovinova so

repellent that it had been only by his father's going
down on his knees and begging him to rescue the family
estate, which would otherwise be sold at auction, that
he had been persuaded to marry her. He gave Varvara
three sons—Ivan and his older brother Nikolai and a
younger boy, who died at seventeen—but was continually unfaithful to her. He was allowed by her no
power in the household, and he did nothing to protect
the children, whom their mother sometimes thrashed
every day, for reasons which in some cases were never
explained to them. He died when he was forty-one
and when Ivan was sixteen. Thereafter, Varvara
Petrovna carried on up to the time of her death, when
Ivan was thirty-two, a systematic persecution of her
children. She had nothing but contempt for writers,
and she never forgave Ivan for his interest in literature,
which she considered no career for a Turgenev. But
by refusing to give him an allowance, she forced him
to earn money by his pen and so to become a professional writer, to get published and to prove his
competence, earlier, perhaps, than might otherwise
have happened. By the time he had inherited property,
he had written *A Sportsman's Sketches* and had proved
himself already a master of both storytelling and
Russian prose.

The content of Ivan's early work is mostly in one
way or another a product of his mother's personality.
In the stories Turgenev wrote before 1847, when the
series of *Sketches* was begun, there is an alternation
of two main themes. The salient one is a force of evil
so powerful and so audacious that no resistance to it
is possible—a force that, as long as his mother was
living, appeared in a masculine form. The queer
scoundrels of *The Duellist* (Бретёр) and *Three*

*Portraits**—the latter perhaps an episode from the family history, in which the Lutovinovs appear as Luchinovs—seduce and mishandle women and provoke their more decent rivals to duels in which the latter get killed. In the one-act play *The Indiscretion* (Неосторожность), of 1843, which begins as an amusing comedy, you have the same implacable villain, who bullies and ends by murdering the heroine. This comes as a surprise to the reader, who expects her to extricate herself, and makes the otherwise adroit little piece impossible, one would think, for the stage. Turgenev even added an epigraph, consisting of two lines of dialogue, in which it is shown that this scoundrel was not merely never brought to justice but that he lived to become a respected official.

The complementary theme to this—in *Andrey Kolosov* and *Petushkov*—is the timid or inadequate man who lets the woman down. In *Andrey Kolosov* you have something of both. Andrey wins and drops poor Varya in a selfish cold-blooded way, and the narrator, who worships Andrey—in slavish imitation of his hero—after winning her, drops her, too. Here we find in Turgenev's first story a situation that is to run through all his work and to have its great development in *Fathers and Sons:* two friends, one ruthless, one shy, who become involved with the same woman. In the case of *A Sportsman's Sketches,* the whole impact of the book is a protest against the antiquated

---

* Except for the spelling of proper names, I have usually given Turgenev's titles in the versions of Constance Garnett, unsatisfactory though these sometimes are. I have, however, used *Fathers and Sons* instead of *Fathers and Children* in order to make this title consistent with the translation Mr. Magarshack prefers.

system of serfholding that Varvara Petrovna stood for: without explicit sympathy for the serfs or overt condemnation of the masters, the latter are played off against the former. In this book, Turgenev invented what was really a new genre. He had been able to learn from Pushkin, whom he took for his master, the trick of evading the censorship by telling a story in such a way as to make it convey its moral without any explicit statement, and he was the first Western writer of fiction to perfect the modern art of implying social criticism through a narrative that is presented objectively, organized economically, and beautifully polished in style. The stories of Mérimée—many of them written before Turgenev's—are distinguished by similar qualities, but so were the short stories of Pushkin and those of Lermontov's *A Hero of Our Time*. The following dates will give some idea of the way in which this form was developed: Pushkin's *Tales of Belkin*, 1831; Mérimée's *Mosaïque*, 1833; Lermontov's *A Hero of Our Time*, 1840; *Andrey Kolosov* (Turgenev's first prose short story), 1844; Mérimée's *Carmen*, 1845; the first of *A Sportsman's Sketches*, 1847. But no prose tale before Turgenev attempts, through sheer technical precision, not merely to tell a story but also to hit on the head a social and moral nail. *Madame Bovary* was not begun till 1851 and not published till 1857. *A Sportsman's Sketches* appeared as a book in 1852.

Varvara Petrovna Turgeneva ignored Ivan's stories as they came out in periodicals, and in her last years she worked herself up into paroxysms of hatred against both her sons. Nikolai had outraged his mother by marrying her German *femme de chambre,* and Varvara refused to receive his wife. The most she would do to recognize that a marriage had taken place was to direct

that her little grandchildren be led past the window of
her house in order that she might have a look at them.
She had at last, however, been induced to give her
acceptance of the marriage on condition that Nikolai
should resign from his civil-service job in St. Petersburg
and come to live in Moscow and manage her property
from there. She promised to buy him a house, but
after he had picked one out and signed an agreement
for it, she did not supply the money, and left him with
his furniture on the pavement and his family still in
the capital. It was weeks before she made it possible
for him to complete the sale of the house, and then,
when he had moved to Moscow, she compelled him to
spend every day with her from eleven o'clock in the
morning to three or four in the afternoon, and would
not supply him with further funds, so that, once he
had spent what he had got for the sale of his St.
Petersburg place, he had no way of keeping up his
establishment. Ivan was living in Paris. It had made
him so unhappy to stay at Spasskoye (the estate on
which his mother chose to live), on account of her
crushing cruelty and his powerlessness to do anything
about it—since she received his appeals with indignant
scorn—that he preferred to go away and forget her.
She attempted to make him return by withholding
even the small sums of money she had grudgingly
granted before, and when he would not, she vicariously
revenged herself. Turgenev had had a daughter by a
seamstress who worked for Varvara Petrovna. The
little girl was now seven. Varvara Petrovna, on leaving
Moscow, where she went for the winter months, took
the child away from her mother and sent her to work
in the kitchen. On occasions when she was entertaining
guests, she would sometimes have the little girl cleaned
up and more presentably dressed and brought in to be

exhibited to visitors. She would ask them whom they thought she resembled, and when they at once said Ivan Sergeyevich, she would send her back to the kitchen to become the butt of the servants.

Nikolai and Ivan at last decided to have a showdown with their mother. They appealed to her to give them small incomes, so that at least they could know what to count on. She received this request with calm and proceeded to present them with "deeds of gift," which purported to make over to them two of her other estates but which were actually of no value whatever, since she had not had them legally drawn, and had, in the meantime, as they learned, sent orders that all the corn in both places be sold, and the money forwarded to her, so that there would not be a ruble to be got from them or even a grain left for sowing. She mocked her two sons in a nasty scene, handing them the worthless papers and demanding that they thank her for them. "No one," wrote Pavel Annenkov, "could equal her in the art of insulting a man, of humiliating him and making him unhappy, while preserving decorum and calm and maintaining her own dignity." Nikolai kissed her hand and left the room, but Ivan simply got up and went. The next day his mother challenged him; why had he not thanked her? "Do you mean to say you are still dissatisfied with me?" We have an account of what followed from a member of the household who overheard it:

"Listen, Mamma," began Ivan Sergeyevich at last, "let us drop this conversation. Ah, why do you want to renew it?"

"And why do you not want to speak out?"

"Mamma, once more, I beg you, let us drop it—I know how to be silent, but I cannot lie and pretend.

Do what you will, I cannot. Do not force me to speak—it is too distressing."

"I don't know what you mean by 'distressing,'" continued Varvara Petrovna harshly, "but I am offended. I do everything for you, and then you are dissatisfied with me!"

"Do not do anything for us. We don't ask you for anything now. Please leave the subject alone—we shall continue to live as we have lived."

"Not as you have lived! You have some property now," Varvara Petrovna continued to urge severely.

"Now, why; tell me why do you say such a thing?" At last Ivan Sergeyevich lost patience. "We had nothing yesterday and we have nothing today, and you know it very well!"

"Why nothing!" cried Varvara Petrovna. "Your brother has a house and an estate, and you have an estate."

"A house! And you know that my brother is too honest to look upon that house as his own. He cannot fulfill the conditions on which you gave it to him. You demand that he shall live in it, but you won't give him anything to live on. He has nothing."

"What? He has an estate."

"He has no such thing! You haven't given us anything, and you won't. Your deeds of gift, as you call them, are not valid; you can take from us tomorrow what you have given us today. Yes, and why all this bother? The estates are yours. Everything is yours. Simply tell us that you don't want to give us anything, and you will not hear a word from us. But why this farce?"

"You are mad!" cried Varvara Petrovna. "You forget to whom you are speaking!"

"But I never wanted to speak. I wanted to be silent.

Do you think it was easy for me to say this? I asked you to drop it," and there was such distress in his voice that it seemed as if tears were choking him.

"I am sorry for my brother," he continued, after a short silence. "Why have you ruined him? You allowed him to marry, compelled him to give up the service and remove here with his family. Before this he did manage to live, he lived by his own labor, he didn't ask you for anything, and he was comparatively comfortable then. But here, from the day he came, you have condemned him to a life of misery—you are always tormenting him in one way or another."

"How do you mean? Tell me how?" Varvara Petrovna was aroused.

"In every way!" Ivan Sergeyevich was desperate and could not help shouting. "Do you not tyrannize over everybody? Who can breathe freely near you?"—and he strode up and down the room. "I felt that I ought not to be saying this—I beg of you, let us stop!"

"So that is your gratitude for all . . ."

"Again, Mamma, again, you will not understand that we are not children, and that your behavior is insulting! You are afraid of giving us anything! You think that it would lessen your power over us! We have always been dutiful sons, but you have no faith in anything or anybody. You believe only in your own power! And what has that given you? The right to tyrannize over everybody!"

"So you think that I am wicked?"

"You are not wicked, but I do not know what is going on in your mind, why you should behave in this way. Do examine yourself and remember what you have done."

"What, exactly? To whom have I done wrong?"

"To whom? Who is happy with you? Remember

only Polyakov and Agatha [the two servants whose children had been suppressed]—all whom you persecute, exile. They would all love you, all be ready to lay down their lives for you, if—but you make them all miserable. Yes, and I myself would give half my life if I did not know all this and did not have to say it. They are all afraid of you, and they could love you. . . ."

"Nobody loves me! Nobody has ever loved me! Even my children are against me!"

"Do not say that, Mamma: we are all ready, your children first of all. . . ."

"I haven't any children!" suddenly shouted Varvara Petrovna. "Go away!"

"Mamma!" Ivan Sergeyevich ran to her.

"Go!" repeated Varvara Petrovna still more loudly, and with this word she herself left the room, slamming the door behind her.

The next morning she was handed a letter in which Nikolai announced that Ivan and he were about to move in on their father's estate, the village of Turgenevo. They had obtained a legal authorization and believed that their mother could not dislodge them. Ivan attempted to see her, but, when told that he had presented himself, she "went to her writing table, seized Ivan Sergeyevich's youthful portrait, and threw it on the floor. The glass was smashed to pieces, and the portrait flew against the opposite wall. When the maid came in and wanted to pick it up, Varvara Petrovna cried, 'Leave it,' and so the portrait lay there from the beginning of June to the beginning of the next spring." It should be noted that Ivan was her favorite son, and that she had never been able to forgive him his infatuation with Pauline Viardot, the celebrated Spanish singer, his lifelong admiration and at one time mistress.

He now rescued his daughter from the household and sent her to stay with Mme Viardot, and he never saw his mother again. He and Nikolai moved into Turgenevo, which was only a few miles from Spasskoye. One day, when his mother was absent, Nikolai brought his wife over and showed her around Spasskoye, which she had not seen. When Varvara Petrovna learned of this, she slashed Polyakov in the face with a riding whip, then collapsed and passed into a decline, from which she never recovered. When she was dying, Ivan was summoned, but she had died before he arrived. "May the Lord save us from such a death," he wrote to Pauline Viardot. "She was merely trying to stupefy herself. A short time before she died, she ordered her orchestra to play dance music in the next room. One ought to speak of the dead with pity and respect, so I shall not say anything further. But since I must tell you what I know and feel, I shall mention one thing more: my mother thought of nothing else in her last months except (I'm ashamed to say) of ruining us—my brother and me. In her last letter to the manager of her estates, she gave him clear and precise orders to sell everything for a song—if need be, to burn everything! . . . And yet I feel that it could have been so easy for her to have made us love her." And later, when he had read her diary: "What a woman, my dear friend, what a woman! I could not close my eyes all night. May the Lord forgive her for everything! But what a life! Truly I am deeply shocked. Yes, yes, we must be good and just, if only in order not to die as she died."

This story is told by David Magarshack in his recent biography, *Turgenev, a Life*—to which I am here much indebted—and in *The Turgenev Family,* by Varvara Zhitova, from which I have just quoted. It was published first in Russia in 1884, just after

Turgenev's death, and has recently been translated into English. Varvara Zhitova was supposed to be the child of poor parents, who had been adopted by Varvara Petrovna a few days after her birth.* Her picture of the Turgenev household is already bad enough, but it is made even worse when we learn from a letter of Ivan's to Pauline Viardot, written after his mother's death, that the girl was one of two "hangers-on" who had to be "removed from the house, where they were constantly creating discord . . . a regular Mme. Lafarge, false, sly, malicious and heartless. It would be impossible to tell you all the bad things that that little viper has done." He partly, however, blames her bad character on the influence of his mother. It had apparently been one of Varvara Petrovna's tricks to play the girl off against her slighted sons, yet at the same time Varvara was always furious when there was any suggestion that the girl was becoming a favorite with the servants.

Turgenev, entertaining the children of a friend, once made up the following story:

"A poor child had sick parents and did not know how to cure them, which gave him a great deal of unhappiness. One day somebody said to him, 'Somewhere there exists a cave, and in that cave every year on a certain day a drop of water oozes down from the roof— a miraculous drop of life-giving water. Whoever drinks

* I have now learned from the new Soviet edition of Turgenev that this girl was actually Turgenev's half-sister, the illegitimate child of his mother and the doctor A. E. Behrs, who was the father of Tolstoy's wife: *Complete Collected Works and Letters* of Turgenev, Volume I of the Letters, page 652. I have quoted her account of Turgenev's break with his mother from her memoirs, which were published under her married name of V. N. Zhitova. Turgenev's mother had given her her own family name Lutovinova and called her an adopted daughter.

this drop of water will receive the gift of being able to heal both the diseases of the body and the pains of the soul.' So a year passed, and then another year—I don't know exactly how long, but the child at last found the cave, and went inside. It had been hollowed out in the rock, and the stones of its vault were cracked. As soon as he had gone inside, the poor child was seized with fright; all around him crawled snakes and reptiles, each more horrible and repulsive than the other, which looked at him with evil eyes. But the brave boy did not want to go back without having got the drop, so he waited to watch for the moment when he would see it ooze out of the rock. After waiting a long time, very frightened, he perceived at last, on the roof, a something wet that glistened. Little by little, this liquid pearl grew round and was forming a drop as transparent as a tear. But hardly had the drop formed than all the reptiles strained up from below it and opened their jaws to catch it. At that moment, the drop, which was just about to form, disappeared back into the vault. The child mustered his patience and continued to wait. And again the reptiles and serpents stretched themselves up on their tails, and, almost grazing the little boy's face, they opened their jaws toward the vault. But the child was no longer afraid. It seemed to him at every moment that the snakes were going to throw themselves on him, to plunge their fangs into his flesh or to wrap themselves about him to strangle him. But he never forgot his purpose; he, too, stood with open mouth. And a miracle occurred! The drop of life fell between his lips—he swallowed it. The snakes all began to hiss, and they made an infernal racket, but, unwillingly, they had to give way and allow the boy to pass; they were forced to confine themselves to piercing him with envious looks. And it turned out that it had not been for nothing that the child had drunk the life-giving drop. It made him a great savant; he was able to cure his parents and came to be a famous man."

Here Turgenev stopped.

"What happened then?" asked the children.

"What more do you want?" he said. "Surely that's enough for today. I'll tell you something more tomorrow. But you must give me time to think."

II

And what was the rest of the story? Let us see what happened to the brave little boy who got away with the life-giving drop.

He did not, we may note as important, much care to revisit the cave. There was already, on the Lutovinov side, a tradition of horror behind the Turgenevs. Once, Varvara Petrovna took the girl Varvara to look in on her stepfather's place, which now belonged to her. The house, in which nobody lived, was almost in ruins. Some of the windows were broken, and the frames of the portraits, which were never cleaned, had become quite black. They walked through a long, dark and narrow hall and turned off into another corridor, where they were faced by a door boarded up with planks. There was, however, an old-fashioned latch, toward which the girl put out her hand. Varvara Petrovna snatched it away: "Don't touch it! You mustn't! Those rooms are accursed!" "I shall never," the daughter writes, "forget her accent and look, so much fear, hate and fury they expressed." It had been

Varvara's apartment, and it had revived some intolerable memory. It is quite evident that Ivan felt hardly less reluctance to return to the Spasskoye household. He had inherited eleven estates, including Spasskoye—in all, about thirty thousand acres. He had immediately liberated his household serfs, and he had tried to persuade his peasants to pay him rent for their land instead of compensating him by work on his. He was arrested in 1852, and exiled to his country place, for having written an article on Gogol's death, in which he had called Gogol "great." (It was as impossible for Nicholas I as for Stalin to brook the magnification of any other Russian, and Turgenev was already *mal vu* on account of *A Sportsman's Sketches*.) He was thus obliged at this time to spend sixteen continuous months at Spasskoye, and he had later to return at intervals in order to keep track of his properties, yet one feels that he was never much at home there, and—except in his literary treatment of them—not close to the people and their work. He sees them casually; he shuts himself up to write; he is much addicted to hunting. The supervision of his huge property is a task with which he cannot grapple, and he installs an uncle as manager. Ivan spends as much time as possible in St. Petersburg or Western Europe. But the uncle proves extremely incompetent, and Turgenev has to go back from time to time to straighten matters out. On one occasion—in 1867, seventeen years after his mother's death—the complaints of his uncle at his absence compel him to return to Russia, but he can hardly drag himself to Spasskoye. The situation is all the more trying because by this time Turgenev has decided to have the uncle replaced. His letters to Pauline Viardot have the sound of a journey to the Dark Tower on the part of a reluctant

Childe Roland who is equipped with no resonant slug horn to challenge the evil spirits. In St. Petersburg, business delays him from making the trip to Moscow. In Moscow, he expects to return to Baden in less than four weeks: "I am leaving tomorrow for Spasskoye. . . . I hope to be back in a week." But the train can take him only sixty miles. "We are in Russia at the time of year when, due to the melting snow, all communications cease." By the time he has travelled two or three miles by sleigh over roads that are full of appalling holes, he has developed "a violent cough, which is continually getting worse. . . . I passed a sleepless night in a wretched inn room, with my pulse at a hundred a minute and a cough that was cracking my chest, and at seven o'clock in the morning I was obliged, in that miserable condition, to subject myself again to the torture of the washout holes and to get back, more dead than alive, to the railroad line and Moscow. . . . If my uncle would only be reasonable and let things be arranged by mail!" In Moscow, he partly recovers: "Tomorrow I set forth again on the assault of Sevastopol." But he doesn't; three days later he is still in Moscow, with the iron ball of the journey still fastened, as he says, to his legs; and this iron ball turns into gout, which keeps him in Moscow till spring. "I have received not a letter but a novel from my uncle, who treats me as if I were a murderer because I don't come to Spasskoye. . . . My new manager has found everything literally in chaos—there are debts that I didn't expect." Turgenev never got to Spasskoye; he returned to St. Petersburg in April.

Two years after his mother's death, Turgenev wrote two short stories—*Mumu* and *The Wayside Inn* (Постоялый Двор) (1852), in which, for the first time in his fiction, he deals with his mother directly.

The first of these was based, he said, on actual happenings, and Varvara Petrovna appears in person as a tyrannical and cruel landowner who compels a deaf-mute serf to drown a little pet dog which he has earlier rescued from drowning and which is the only thing he has to love. The bitterness of the mistress at not being loved herself figures here as a motive, and we appreciate the story more if we have some independent knowledge of Varvara Petrovna's life: she has tried to make friends with the little dog, which has refused to come to her when called and then snarls at her when she tries to pat it. In the other story, the callous woman landowner is combined with the Force of Evil—unconquerable and inexpugnable—embodied in a masculine character. This demon in human form works on the lady's cupidity to induce her to sell him an inn that has been occupied and run for years by one of her most trusted serfs. This serf has had every reason to assume he could trust his mistress, but the scoundrel has moved in on him, seduced his wife and brought her to a point of infatuation at which she is ready, at his orders, to steal her husband's savings. The villain conceals his real plan, pretending he needs the money for another purpose, and when he uses it to buy the inn and turn her husband out, she is horrified at what she has done, whereupon he turns her out, too. He prospers and is lucky enough to sell the inn just before it burns down. His victim, who has lost his wife and his living, is driven to fall back on religion and spends the rest of his life in pilgrimages.

There is so little overt bitterness in Turgenev, and to his contemporaries his life seemed so easy, that they were likely to be puzzled by his pessimism. It moved Henry James to complain of his "atmosphere of unrelieved sadness. We go from one tale to the other in the hope of finding something cheerful, but we only wander into fresh agglomerations of gloom." And, what is more striking, even Mérimée—at the moment when he has just written *Lokis!*—begs Turgenev not to be so painful: *"Faites-nous donc une histoire qui ne finisse pas trop mal. Vous abusez depuis quelque temps de notre sensibilité."* But the stories of Mérimée, some of them practical jokes, are shockers. Turgenev's show the permanent stamp of an oppressive, a completely hopeless and a permanently harrowing experience.

He could not have talked very much of the uglier aspects of his early life, for no one appears to have thought of accounting in terms of this for the themes and the mood of his fiction. Nor could even his great Russian contemporaries, Tolstoy and Dostoevsky, when they reproach him for his love of the West, for his indifference to affairs in Russia, have quite understood the terrible weight, the lasting effect of Spasskoye—its implications for the whole of Turgenev's thought. Dostoevsky was a congenitally dislocated man; his family had gone to pieces even before his parvenu father had been murdered by his own peasants. Tolstoy had been an orphan, exhilaratingly self-dependent; he had inherited his estate at nineteen, with no hateful family memories, and during the years of his rather wild freedom and his service in the Crimean War, it had been kept for him as a home by an affectionate aunt whom he loved. When he married, he founded a family that was something completely his own. His property of Yasnaya Polyana was a romance he was always inventing, as he had invented—out of old family papers and legends—the idyll of *War and Peace*. And even in his latest phase of pretending to abdicate his status of landowner, nobleman and popular writer, he was reserving for himself *le beau rôle*. But Spasskoye for Turgenev was a block of his past; he had grown up in it, been maimed by it, escaped from it. In jeering at him for making himself comfortable abroad and shirking his duties to Russia, his contemporaries were mistaken in several ways—not least in regard to the degree of his comfort. As he had never been at home in Spasskoye, so he was never really to feel at home anywhere, and even in the freedom of Europe—as Mr. Magarshack and others have noted—he reëstablished Varvara Petrovna in the person of Pauline Viardot, a formidable Spanish gypsy—like his mother, not handsome, though magnetic—who carried her household with a very high hand and cost Turgenev a good deal of suffering. What was fatal in her hold on Turgenev was that she not only possessed a strong character but combined with it a remarkable voice, which enabled him to regard her as a great artist. Her manager was her husband, and Turgenev had adored her and paid court to her for years without her allowing him to become her lover. He did, however, eventually succeed— Viardot was twenty years older than she—and, in a more or less harmonious *ménage à trois,* he became a kind of member of the family. He lived, in fact, with Viardot on terms that seem to have been almost fraternal. A great deal of his time was spent in the house of the Viardots or near them; but his daughter, who had been put in the care of Pauline, coming eventually to understand her father's position in the household, strongly reacted against it and her, and refused to remain with the family. Pauline, in the long run, was unfaithful to Turgenev with Ary Scheffer, at a time when the latter was painting her portrait, and Turgenev, finding this out, broke with her. The next year she gave birth to a son, and the situation became even more painful—because, if the boy was his, Turgenev wanted to see him, but he could not be sure that he was and tormented himself with the suspicion that Pauline's love affair with Scheffer had already been going on for some time before he discovered it.

Turgenev resented his slavery, and in the story called *A Correspondence*—as Mr. Magarshack suggests—he is evidently caricaturing himself as an idiotic lover and Pauline as a stupid ballerina: "From the very first moment I saw her ... I belonged to her entirely, just as a dog belongs to his master; and if now that I am dying I have ceased to, that is only because she has thrown me over. To tell the truth, she never paid much attention to me." In his letters to her, you feel his awe of her, and that he is writing of his thoughts and imaginings to someone who will not listen and who he knows will not listen. Many of Turgenev's friends did not like Pauline Viardot and deplored his devotion to her; but if one does not know anything about her except in connection with Turgenev, it is difficult to estimate how far the unpleasant impression one has of her is due to Turgenev himself. Here is one outside piece of testimony—by Heine, in an article on the music season in Paris in 1844: "One regrets, at the Opéra Bouffe, the absence of Pauline Viardot, or, as we like to call her, La Garcia. There is nobody to replace her, and nobody can replace her. This is no nightingale, who has only the talent of her species and admirably sobs and trills her regular spring routine; nor is she a rose—she is ugly, yet ugly in a way that is noble—beautiful I might almost say, and which has sometimes stirred to enthusiasm the great lion painter Lacroix [evidently Delacroix]! La Garcia recalls, in fact, not so much the civilized beauty and the domesticated face of our European homeland as the terrible splendor of an exotic wilderness, and at moments of her impassioned performances, especially when she opens wide her great mouth with its dazzling white teeth, and smiles with such cruel sweetness and such delightful ferocity, you feel as if the monstrous plants and animals of India or Africa were about to appear before your eyes."

If one were to put together all of Turgenev's stories of the unappeasable Evil Force, and if one were to read only these, one might think him a one-theme writer—like Poe or Nerval or Bierce, the victim of a neurotic obsession. Actually, however, these stories make little impression on the ordinary reader. The reason for this is that the Evil Power with which Turgenev is dealing here is, in a sense, no part of Turgenev himself but something that has been forced on his unwilling attention. With Dostoevsky, the Devil is inside him, and we are made to enter as much into the perverse and malignant characters as into the saintly ones. But though Turgenev can describe from inside many varieties of masculine weakness, he is unable to identify himself with any kind of aggressive malice. Already, in his early stories—and even more in the later ones, which have an element of the supernatural—the demons always come from outside. The villain of *The Wayside Inn* walks in on the family he will ruin from a world that is never described and is never accounted for; in the end, he disappears. The story is presented entirely from the point of view of his victim.

Turgenev, in his personal relations, had nothing of morbid suspicion; he was likely to believe in people to the point of gullibility, and when their treachery or dishonesty was proved to him, he would refuse to have anything more to do with them. Short of this, he gave money, in France, to every Russian who asked him for it, and one finds in *Tourguéneff Inconnu,* by a Russian friend, Michel Delines, some curious stories about this. Two young men, just arrived from Russia and representing themselves as Nihilists who had served prison terms for their writings, were taken up and aided by Turgenev. "One would have thought that the appearance of these two young men was of a kind that might have excited the mistrust of a student of faces, but they elicited, on the part of the novelist, only benevolent feelings; he was convinced that he was dealing with honest fellows." Later, apropos of an article in which Turgenev had expressed his political opinions, one of these young men sent Delines a letter of vulgar abuse of Turgenev and declared that he would never have anything more to do with him; yet, still later, he persuaded Delines to borrow for him some money from Turgenev, without mentioning for whom it was wanted—he would pay it back in a month. Then, instead of paying it back, he went to Turgenev and told him that he had owed Delines two hundred francs and that the latter had repaid himself by collecting this amount from Turgenev. When he was told that he had behaved dishonestly, the young fellow only sneered.

Delines at once wrote to Turgenev to straighten the matter out and let him know about the abusive letter. Turgenev asked to see it, and when he had read it turned pale and was silent. "Gradually his face lit up and he said to me with a reassured air, as if with the satisfaction of a man who has just made a discovery: 'I was mistaken about that young man, but now I can predict with certainty what his future career will be ... [he] will become a collaborator with Katkov [the editor of a reactionary paper], he will desert the Nihilists, with whom he is now allied, and he will cover them with mud; after my death, he will write about me and pretend to have been my intimate friend!' . . . I began to protest at this, but with an angry gesture he interrupted. He was feeling the impatience of the artist who is not allowed time to finish his sketch. 'Wait, wait,' he said. 'I haven't finished. He will not die a natural death. He will be killed by a woman. He's a coward before the strong, and bold, very bold, against the weak. Women will have a good deal to suffer from him. But someday he'll fall into the hands of one of those strong and resolute Russian women, and she will blow his brains out.'" As for the other young Russian, continued Turgenev—"'He, too!' I cried with amazement." Turgenev went on to explain that he had got his young man a subsidy to pursue his chemistry studies, "because he promised me that he would then return to Russia to apply his science to agriculture, and to teach the peasants new methods. But now that he has finished his studies, he thinks about nothing but getting rich and regards a humble schoolmaster's duties as far beneath him. . . . Oh, you'll see that he'll raise hob with the muzhiks; he'll turn moneylender and rob our peasants of their last bit of earth; he'll become the terror of the village, and he'll be murdered in the end by a muzhik." The first of these men, adds Delines, did abandon his Nihilist associates and bring accusations against them, did write for a reactionary paper and did publish a memoir of Turgenev. He did exploit women, and brought one of them to misery and madness; he had not, at the date of Turgenev's prophecy, as yet been murdered by one. The other man did not return to Russia but became a planter in Africa, and was said to be a very harsh master. It was thus from observation of others that Turgenev had learned how such people behaved; his own character gave no key to their conduct, and it never at first occurred to him that there was anything sinister about them.

But in observation Turgenev is always extremely strong. He is the expert detached observer rather than the searching psychologist of the phenomena of Russian life, and when he tries to go inside his characters he is likely to be less satisfactory than when he is telling you merely what they say and do, how they look and what one feels about them. It is curious, in view of this, that he should so much complain, in his criticism of Tolstoy, of the ineptitude of the latter's account of what is going on in his characters' minds. It was surely one of Tolstoy's most conspicuous gifts that he could put himself in the place of other people; it seems scarcely even a question of "psychology" but a matter of living in another's skin. Whereas, when Turgenev is telling what his hero or heroine is thinking, what ordeals they are going through, he sometimes becomes— what is rare with him—a little bit labored and boring. His characters perhaps come out best when they are presenting themselves to other people—as in such masterpieces of irony as *A Correspondence* and *Faust,* in which the two ignoble men, in their letters, unconsciously reveal to the reader what they do not know about themselves.

What people show themselves to be in relation to other people is Turgenev's particular forte, and he is for this reason especially successful in the invention of social types. This is now the direction that his work is to take. He is embarked by the middle eighteen-fifties on a deliberate and scrupulous study of the social situation in Russia. The cool, clear and balanced intellect that was central to the character of Turgenev was expanding and taking over after the panics and

the repressions of Spasskoye. Turgenev, in his early
stories, had usually concentrated on a single character
or on his ever-recurrent two friends—one rather well-
off and timid, the other rougher and bolder, a pair
who almost count as a unit. This pair—with the ac-
companying girl, in whom, as a rule, they share—begin,
with *The Two Friends* of 1853, to represent more than
the intimacy of a personal relationship. Here the
youth who is more cultivated and sensitive marries a
much less well-educated wife, who charms him at
first and then bores him. He escapes to St. Petersburg,
promising to come back soon, but then goes on to
Germany and then to France, and in Paris, to which
he comes as a greenhorn, he is killed by a Frenchman
in a stupid duel. The cruder but more enterprising
friend takes over the uneducated wife, and they live
together in perfect contentment. A social dilemma
emerges: shall a cultivated Russian landowner remain
at home and be bored or shall he go to the West, where
he does not belong, and which may very well prove
fatal to him? But in the next story—*A Quiet Backwater*
(Затишье) of 1854—Turgenev's world opens out. We
have here, for the first time in his fiction—though it
had earlier appeared in his plays—the Turgenev country
house, with its full cast of characters. The men—as
is so common in Turgenev—let the women down, but
the St. Petersburg petty snob, the genial swaggerer who
comes to nothing, the correct unimaginative man of
property are all intended here to be typical, as are the
proud and serious girl, who, finding no one worthy
of her, throws herself into a pond, and her jolly attractive
friend, who has to content herself with a pretentious
but shoddy Pole. The weakness of the men in comparison with the women is here made, by implication,
to illustrate a theory of Turgenev's as to the relative

stamina of the sexes in Russia. This is followed the next year—after three of his weak-hero stories: *A Correspondence, Faust, Yakov Pasynkov*—by Turgenev's first novel, *Rudin*. The character of Rudin was partly suggested by Turgenev's friend Mikhail Bakunin, and Rudin is evidently impotent, as Bakunin is known to have been. He, too, disappoints the heroine.

These basic themes—the two friends, the inadequate man and the demanding woman—are present in the novels that follow, and they are always now made to figure as motifs in a large social picture. The more farouche and tough-minded of the two friends comes to the front as a new kind of hero: the Bulgarian patriot Insarov, who is awaiting, in *On the Eve,* the moment to go back to Bulgaria and fight for his country against the Turks; the humbly born young medical student Bazarov of *Fathers and Sons,* who, in performing an autopsy on a peasant in the primitive community where his parents live, cuts his finger and, having no means of cauterizing it, gets it infected and dies of blood poisoning. But Turgenev's recurrent characters appear in a variety of guises. The women who demoralize or outclass the men may be selfish coquettes, like Irina in *Smoke* and Maria Nikolaevna in *The Torrents of Spring,* or noble zealots, like Elena in *On the Eve* and Marianna in *Virgin Soil* (Новь). These latter—along with Maria Pavlovna of *A Quiet Backwater*—are likely to be monsters of pride, and one remembers that one of the last entries that Turgenev read in his mother's diary was, "My mother! my children! Forgive me! And you, Lord, forgive me, also, for pride, that deadly sin, was always my sin." *On the Eve* is a significant example of the author's familiar pattern, for, though Insarov is tenacious and dedicated, he is tubercular and not up to his mission, and thus weak in relation to Elena, who runs the poor patriot ragged in insisting that he take her to Bulgaria as truly as Irina does Litvinov in breaking up his relations with his fiancée and then backing down on elopement. It is Elena who gets to Bulgaria; Insarov expires in Venice. But these principals have foils and opponents. The characters about them multiply; whole new milieux appear.

A brilliant satirical element now comes to life in Turgenev's work: the expatriate Russians at the beginning of *Smoke,* all rallying around their empty great man and alternately, among themselves, denouncing and fraternizing; the wonderfully caricatured family of Sipyagin in *Virgin Soil,* an official in smart society, who is ostensibly and smilingly liberal but in a pinch unrelentingly conservative. Each of these books is designed to throw light on some general situation and to suggest certain conclusions about it. *A House of Gentlefolk* (Дворянское Гнездо) (1858) develops on a larger scale the theme of the as yet unbridgeable gulf between Russia and Western culture: Lavretsky, who has been studying agriculture abroad, has to become aware that conditions at home are too primitive for him, and his unreliable wife, who has been making a fool of him in Paris and whom he has left and believes to be dead, turns up to prevent him from marrying the serious little girl at home. Elena, in *On the Eve* (1860), cannot find any Russian she respects and runs away with a foreign insurrectionist. Bazarov, in *Fathers and Sons* (1861), has really been training himself for a technical and classless society that does not as yet exist, and in the meantime he cannot survive in the contemporary Russian world, where he is bound to be out of place and which has no faith but science to offer him. In *Smoke* (1867), again, as in *A Quiet Backwater,* the simple old Russian virtues, enduring though a little dull, are betrayed by international sophistication; and in *Virgin Soil,* Turgenev's last novel (1876), the radicals of the Populist movement, who have been trying to "go to the people," are shown to be as powerless to make contact with it as the landowner Lavretsky has been with his up-to-date methods of agriculture or as the medical student Bazarov, who has sprung from it but is quite out of touch with it.

Turgenev—in the teeth of the Populists, the mystical Slavophils and the official reactionaries—remained firmly a "Westernizer." He never ceased to compare Russia with Europe, to see it in the perspective of history, to estimate Russian possibilities in terms of the preliminary conditions that had made Western institutions possible. He was not in the least susceptible to the visionary excitements of his countrymen: he tried to look at everything in Russia with the same self-possession and realism that one brings to a foreign country, and to judge it with the same common sense. Turgenev was always proud to believe that he had contributed—through *A Sportsman's Sketches,* by which Alexander II was supposed to have been influenced— to the emancipation of the serfs, but in politics he was not optimistic. He could never lose sight of the discrepancies, the disparities so impossible to reconcile, that he was occupied with dramatizing in his novels. He did not approve of Russian feudalism, so he was hated by all the conservatives, but he could not believe in the imminence of a genuine revolution, since he could not make out any forces that were as yet far enough developed to put a revolution through, so he antagonized the more advanced Leftists. He was publicly opposed to violence and declared that he looked to the government to introduce the needed reforms; yet in his work insubmissive violence does certainly play a role. In a later edition of *Rudin,* six years after its first publication, he made his hero die on the barricades, but in Paris, in 1848; in *On the Eve,* we have an intransigent rebel, but a rebel against the Turks in Bulgaria, who has no involvement in Russia and who has, in consequence, seemed to Russians a more or less unconvincing character. Turgenev's last novel, *Virgin Soil,* however, is all about revolutionaries at home. He still believes at this point that the Populist agitation is premature, and he makes one of his characters predict that there will be no revolution for thirty years. This was said as of 1876, and twenty-nine years later the 1905 revolution occurred, to be followed twelve years afterwards by the Kerensky revolution, so Turgenev was not far out.

In the meantime, Turgenev had no religion, so he could not delude himself with the light of Russian Christianity, by means of which Tolstoy and Dostoevsky were able to console themselves and which led them to condemn him so readily as a frivolous man of the world. No delusion and no emotion could fantasticate his strong conviction of the wretched situation of Russia or obscure his lucid perception that the remedy would be a long time coming. He was taken in by fraudulent idealists; he was stirred to bursts of sympathy by real ones. He was constantly under fire from both sides, and he sometimes answered his opponents back. He had always, on the one hand, to be careful of arousing the censorship and, on the other, to resist the clichés that his editors tried to impose on him. But through his casual blowings of hot and cold, his professions of belief in reforms from above and his secret contributions to radical papers; through his sometimes hysterical

encounters with Tolstoy and Dostoevsky, his glowing
amours and his slumps of gloom, his shuttling between
Russia and Europe—like the man in his strange story
Phantoms, who flies back and forth between them
without ever being satisfied with either—he sticks
to his objective judgment, his line of realistic criticism,
his resolve to stand free of movements, to rise above
personalities, to recognize all points of view that have
any sincerity or dignity, to show Russia how to know
herself. In this he is truly heroic, and the time has come
now to thank him for an effort that in Turgenev's own
day would seem to have been sometimes most thankless—since he had constantly to offend his countrymen
and since foreigners who admired his writings could
have had no idea of the pressures that Turgenev was
obliged to withstand or even of the significance of what
he wrote. It is as if his sense of justice, his magnanimity,
his instinct to see things in their proper proportions
had been prodded to especial stubbornness, in the
household of Varvara Petrovna, by injustice, vindic-
tiveness and outrageous pretensions. And if Pushkin,
"my idol, my teacher, my unattainable model," had
taught him how to pack social meaning into the simple
presentation of incident, it is probable that the Germany
of Goethe (another of his admirations), the Germany
of his student days, had inspired him with the high
conception of the writer's responsibility that was to
win him his peculiar authority, an authority all the
more striking because many of his countrymen would
not admit it. It is, in any case, true that by Turgenev's
time—as Annenkov tells us in an eloquent passage—
the imaginative writer, since he could comment on
society as other people could not do, had come to
play a role of unique importance.

Turgenev explains his ideals as a writer and defends

the integrity of his literary career in a preface—composed at the end of his life for the collected edition of 1883—which seems to me particularly worth quoting since it has not been included by either Isabel Hapgood or Constance Garnett in their complete translations of Turgenev's fiction. He has been, he here tells us, reproached "with abandoning my former direction, with apostasy, etc. To me, on the contrary, it seems that I might be reproached more properly for having stuck to my position too consistently and, as it were, having followed my direction in too single-minded a way. The author of *Rudin,* written in 1855, and the author of *Virgin Soil,* written in 1876, are obviously one and the same man. I have been aiming, from beginning to end, in the measure of my strength and intelligence, dispassionately and conscientiously to describe and incarnate in appropriate types both what Shakespeare calls 'the body and pressure of time' and the quickly-changing physiognomy of Russians of the cultured class, which has served chiefly as the subject of my observations." He runs through the series of his novels and shows that his critics, in the long run, have more or less cancelled one another out, and he triumphantly ends by telling of the reactions to *Virgin Soil* : first people had said that Turgenev had been living so long out of Russia that he knew nothing about what was going on there and that no such persons existed as the woman revolutionary Marianna; then, hardly a month later, there had been a sensational arrest of a group of revolutionaries which included eighteen women, and Turgenev was immediately accused of having been affiliated with them, since otherwise how could he have known about them? He goes on, in an admirable paragraph, to point out the then current confusion of Russian literary criticism, which cries up the ideal of the "unconscious creator," the "poet" who "thinks in images" and always chooses subjects from "real life," yet who actually, nevertheless, is likely to treat his subjects with a perceptible political bias. You may deal with nature, they say, you may deal with the life of the people; but the moment that he, Turgenev, ventures to touch on the muddled, the psychologically complicated, the morbid, that lies below the surface of society, they shout at him: "Stop! That won't do—that is speculation, preconceived ideas; that is politics! the work of a publicist!" Yet are not such phenomena as these as susceptible of being represented "in images" as those of external nature? "You assert," Turgenev answers these critics, "that the publicist and the poet have different tasks. Not at all: in both cases their tasks may be exactly the same; but the publicist regards them with a publicist's eyes, the poet with the eyes of a poet. In the department of art, the question how? is more important than the question what? The fact that what you will not accept—in images, mind you: in images—exists in the soul of the writer is no reason for impugning his intention. . . . Believe me, a genuine talent never serves any alien ends, and it finds satisfaction in itself; its content is supplied by the life about it—it is a concentrated reflection of this; and it is as little capable of a panegyric as it is of a pasquinade. The point is that that kind of thing is beneath it. To subordinate oneself to a given thesis or to carry out a program— this is possible only for those who cannot do anything different and better." A wariness of the censorship here no doubt somewhat shrouds the contours of Turgenev's actual thought: surely something is smuggled in when he slips into his argument the statement that the tasks of the publicist and the poet may be exactly the same; yet the novels that Turgenev is defending have themselves been given their shape by the censorship. Their technique is a further extension of that of *A Sportsman's Sketches*: the noncommittal which is none the less committal. Turgenev got a good deal farther with the challenging social problems of Russia than either Tolstoy or Dostoevsky. Yet he satisfied the same kind of aesthetic ideal as Mérimée, Flaubert and their school. It was an art that was continued by Chekhov, who observed "the life about him" with equal detachment and had even less of hope for the immediate future.

But now that we know the immediate future, both Turgenev and Chekhov are relevant to the present situation of Russia, because many of the old elements and problems are still there in the Soviet Union, and a reading of these two great Russian writers will do much to dissolve the mirages that the Soviets have projected for the rest of the world and that seem to float still before the Russians themselves. It may be worth while to note here some passages in Turgenev's novels which have acquired a special interest in the light of what has happened since.

One of the most amusing characters in *Smoke* is a man named Sozont Ivanich Potugin, whom Litvinov meets in Baden and with whom he has long conversations. Potugin is worried and depressed about Russia and disgusted with the delusions of his countrymen. They boast about "Russian inventiveness," but the Russians "have invented nothing"; they boast of their architecture, art and music, when none of these really exists (this did not long remain true of music); they even boast that nobody in Russia starves. In an earlier conversation, Litvinov has asked Potugin about another expatriate in Baden, whose prestige seems to be immense, though Litvinov does not find him interesting and cannot, in fact, get anything out of him:

"Tell me—how do you account for the unquestionable influence of Gubaryov on everybody around him? He's neither gifted nor able, is he?"

"No, of course not; he has no abilities."

"Is it character, then?"

"He hasn't got that either: what he does have is a strong will. We Slavs in general, as everyone knows, are not much endowed with that virtue, and when it does appear, we give up before it. Mr. Gubaryov wanted to be a leader, so everybody acknowledges him as one. What can you do about it?! The government has freed us from our dependence on serfdom, and we are grateful to it for that, but the habits of slavery are rooted too deep in us; we shan't get away from them so easily. In everything and everywhere, we have to have a master. This master is usually some active person, though sometimes some so-called tendency takes possession of us—just at present, for instance, we have all bound ourselves over to the natural sciences. But why—convinced by what sort of reasoning—do we give ourselves into bondage, that's the mysterious thing; it's evidently just in our nature to. The great point is that we must have a master. Well, we get one—which means he belongs to us, and we spit upon everything else! We're just naturally underlings! And the pride of being underlings and the underlings' abasement! Then a new master comes along—away with the old. Before it was Jacob, now it is Sidor; give Jacob a box on the ear and fall at the feet of Sidor! Remember how many such tricks we have played! We talk about non-compliance as if it were a peculiar characteristic of ours, but we don't make our refusals as a free man does, laying about him with his sword; we make them like a lackey, hitting out with his fists—and what is worse, if you

please, this lackey does his thrashing by his own master's orders. And yet, my good sir, at the same time
we're soft; it's not difficult to get us into one's hands.
And that's how Mr. Gubaryov has achieved his present
domination; he keeps chiselling and chiselling at the
same spot and finally he chisels through. People become
aware that a man has a high opinion of himself, that a
man believes in himself, that he gives orders—that's
the main thing, he gives orders; consequently, he is
bound to be right, and one is compelled to obey him.
All our schismatics, our Onyphrites and Akulinites,
established themselves in just this way: the man who
takes the staff is the corporal.

"Such leaders have nowhere to lead the people, and
in the meantime the Slavophils bemuse themselves with
a groundless belief in the 'masses':

"According to them [the Slavophils], everything is
always *going to be*. Nothing ever takes place in the
present, and Russia through ten whole centuries has
failed to produce anything of her own—not in government or jurisprudence or in science or in art or even
in the crafts. . . . But wait a bit, be patient a bit: everything is going to come. And why should it be going to
come?—if I may be so curious as to ask. Why, they
answer, because we educated folks are trash; but the
people—oh, that great people! Do you see that peasant's overcoat?—that's where everything is going to
come from. All the other idols have been destroyed:
let's believe in the peasant's overcoat. But suppose the
overcoat fails us? No, it will not fail us—read Kokha-
novskaya and roll up your eyes. [Kokhanovskaya was
a woman novelist who wrote about rural life.] Really,
if I were a painter, this is the picture I'd paint. An educated man would be standing before a muzhik and
making a low obeisance: 'Cure me, little father muzhik,'
he says. 'I'm deathly ill.' But the muzhik, in turn, bows

low to the educated man: 'Teach me, little father master,' he says: 'I'm dying of ignorance.'"

The leader who was actually to impose himself on the demoralized Russia of fifty years later had more character and brains than Gubaryov, but his faith in the peasant's overcoat went somewhat beyond what was warranted. Turgenev—as Mr. Irving Howe has noted in a paper on him—anticipated the solid side of the Bolsheviks, something of the character of Lenin, as Dostoevsky, in *The Devils* (Бесы),* anticipated the fanatical side. Solomin, the factory manager of *Virgin Soil,* with his long-range view of Russia, who realizes the natural docility and the ignorance of peasants and workers and tries to make a beginning of training them by instituting a workers' school, goes on to a coöperative factory of his own when his hastier would-be allies have come to grief through precipitate action. "He's a really splendid fellow," someone says of him, "and the great thing about him is that he doesn't pretend to be any quick healer of our social ills. Why, pray, are we Russians the way we are? We're always waiting for something: something or somebody, we tell ourselves, is going to come along and fix everything up in a moment, heal all our sores, pull out all our diseases as if they were aching teeth. Who will that magician be? Darwinism? Country life? Arkhip Perepentev? A foreign war? Whatever you like! Only, little father, do please pull out the tooth!! It's all laziness, flabbiness, inadequacy. But Solomin's not like that, no—he's not going to pull any teeth—he's really a splendid fellow!"

But they did expect Lenin to pull the tooth, and they continued to imagine he had pulled it long after their leader was dead, a victim of the monstrous discrepan-

---

* *The Possessed* in Constance Garnett's translation.

cies that Turgenev had insisted on facing. What the
Russians were getting instead of Lenin was something
that was at first close to another of Turgenev's characters—the secretary of the Senate, Kurnatovsky, who
appears in *On the Eve*. Elena is writing to Insarov, the
Bulgarian patriot whom she loves. Her father has
asked Kurnatovsky to dinner with the idea of having
Elena marry him, and she describes him in a letter to
her lover. He is short, she tells Insarov, with flat wide
lips and hair cropped close, and he wears a constant
smile—as it were, official, as if smiling in this way were
a duty.

"He conducts himself very simply, conducts himself
with precision, and everything about him is precise:
he walks, laughs, and eats as if he were performing a
duty. . . . There is something iron in him, and dull and
empty at the same time—and honorable; they say that
he *is* very honorable. . . . He almost gave up his civil
servant's job to take charge of a big factory. . . . He said
he knew nothing about art, as if he meant to imply
that he thought art unnecessary, but that a well-con-
ducted government might, of course, permit it. Rather
indifferent, however, to Petersburg and the *comme il
faut:* he once even referred to himself as a proletarian.
'We're common workmen!' he said. I thought to myself: If Dmitri Insarov had said that, I shouldn't have
liked it, but let this fellow talk, let him boast! With
me he was very polite; but it seemed to me that I was
talking with a very very patronizing superior. When he
wishes to praise someone, he says that So-and-So has
principles—that is his favorite word. He must, I am
sure, be very self-confident, industrious and capable to
the point of self-sacrifice (you see I am quite impartial);
that is, of the sacrifice of his own interests, but he is
certainly a great despot. Woe to anyone who falls into
his hands. At dinner they started talking about bribes.

"I know," he said, "that in many cases the man who takes a bribe is quite innocent; he couldn't have acted otherwise. But, if he's caught, we have to break him just the same.'

"Break the innocent!"

"Yes—for the sake of principle."

"What principle?" Shubin asked. Kurnatovsky seemed to be surprised or to find himself at a loss, and replied, 'That needs no explanation.'"

On the subject of Russian mendacity—one of the most serious national failings, which has been carried, since Turgenev's time, in the Soviet propaganda and purges, to such incredible lengths—Turgenev has a great deal to say, for it was evidently much on his mind. Henry James, who knew him in Paris, reports with characteristic litotes his dwelling on the subject in conversation. Of the failings of the Russian character Turgenev, he says, "was keenly conscious, and I once heard him express himself with an energy that did him honor and a frankness that even surprised me (considering that it was of his countrymen that he spoke) in regard to a weakness for which a man whose love of veracity was his strongest feeling would have least toleration." And lying is one of the vices against which Potugin rails: "One day, with my dog and gun, I was making my way through a forest . . . I am aiming for a bog in which there are supposed to be snipe. I look about me, and there, sitting in the meadow in front of his little house, I see a timber merchant's clerk, as fresh and as plump as a filbert. He's sitting there and grinning—about what I don't know. So I asked him, 'Where is that bog around here—are there any snipe in it?' 'Please, please,' he replied at once, as if I had given him a ruble: 'Fortunately for us, a bog of the very first quality; and as for gamebirds of every kind— why, good God!—in wonderful plenty you'll find them.'

I proceeded on my way, but not only did I find no game, even the bog had been long dried up. Now, will you please tell me: why does the Russian lie? Why does the political economist lie?—and even about gamebirds?" Of Solomin and Marianna in *Virgin Soul,* he writes: "A man who told the truth—that was the great thing! That was what had made such an impression on her. Something which is very well known but not altogether understood is the fact that, although the Russians are the most incorrigible liars in the whole world, there is nothing they respect so much as the truth—to nothing do they respond so readily." There is an entry in the Goncourt Journal which may be added as a supplement to this: "He [Turgenev] said that, music apart, of all the peoples of Europe the Germans had the least correct response to art [the assumption evidently is that the Germans are scrupulous in other ways], and that the kind of little false and stupid conventionality which made us [the French] reject a book seemed to them the amenity of perfection applied to the truth of things. He added that, on the contrary, the Russians, who are a lying people, as is natural for a people who have long been slaves, liked truth and reality in art." In view of all this, it is striking that his respect for a friend of his youth, Nikolai Stankevich, was partly inspired by his feeling that the latter had cured him of lying. Even Tolstoy, who so liked to bait him, paid a tribute to Turgenev's exceptional truthfulness.

It is impressive to see how the authority of Turgenev was felt by the non-Russian world. Taine praised him, and George Sand wrote to him, apropos of *A Sportsman's Sketches,* "*Maître, nous devons aller tous à votre école.*" For Mérimée, the courtier of Napoleon III, forlornly dying of asthma and the imminent collapse of the Second Empire, Turgenev, who had helped him with his Russian studies and with whom he had corresponded for years, seems to figure at this point in his life as a kind of last moral support in the serious practice of letters. Mérimée is always hoping that Turgenev will come to see him—as is Flaubert, in his different way also so dreary, in the provincial isolation of Croisset, breaking his back, in his final years, over the desolating and thankless ironies of *Bouvard et Pécuchet*. "Courage!" Turgenev had written him, from Weimar, when his friend had been disappointed by the reception of *L'Education Sentimentale*. "After all, you are Flaubert!" and he tried to make him known in Russia by translating his *Hérodias* and *La Légende de Saint Julien l'Hospitalier*. Conversely, he sent to Flaubert a French translation of *War and Peace*, which was one of the last books the latter read, and passed on to Tolstoy the high praise of it—accompanied by certain reservations—in a letter that Flaubert had written him. Turgenev knew most of the important writers who were making of the novel, in that period, the great literary form of the nineteenth century, and he followed the work of all of them. He arranged to have Zola and Maupassant translated into Russian, and he was a pillar of the Goncourt dinners. The Goncourts admired him up to the moment when, after his death, Edmond discovered from a memoir by a friend of Turgenev's, Isaac Pavlovsky, that Turgenev had not really cared much for their novels. For Henry James— like Turgenev himself, never much at home among the French and dissatisfied with the ideals of French fiction—he provided the model of a more humane art not inferior in formal distinction, as well as an encouragement to James to develop his own point of view and to deal with his own people, who, like the Russians, were so little known in Europe and did not fit into the European categories. Even in England, Turgenev's name was known by the sixties. On a visit there in 1858, he was

invited, at Mérimée's suggestion, to a banquet of the
Royal Literary Fund, and, in aid of a similar Russian
fund, founded the following year, he wrote a description
of it, in which he dwelt on the effectiveness of the English
in making such organizations work. He paid his respects
to Carlyle, who had found *Mumu* very affecting but
who rather surprised Turgenev by laughing immod-
erately when the visitor was telling him that he suffered
from spots before his eyes and had once, on a hunting
trip, mistaken one of these for a rabbit; and
to Thackeray, who had never heard of him and who
also roared with laughter when, after inviting his visitor
to recite for him something in Russian, he was unable
to restrain himself, at the outlandish sound to his English
ears of one of Pushkin's loveliest lyrics. For Renan,
who delivered, at the Gare du Nord, a speech over
Turgenev's coffin, when his body was being sent back
to Russia, Turgenev was a mind like his own, which com-
prehended the most diverse points of view and which
contemplated their ultimate harmony: "The repellent
aspects of things do not exist for him. Everything in him
becomes reconciled: the most opposed parties unite
to admire him and to praise him. In the region to which
he transports us, the words that rouse the vulgar lose
their venom. Genius achieves in a day what would
otherwise require centuries. He creates a higher atmosphere of peace, in which those who were formerly
adversaries discover themselves in reality to have
been collaborators; he opens the era of the great am-
nesty, in which those who have fought in the arena of
progress clasp hands as they sleep side by side."

This conception by Renan of Turgenev must, I
think, derive from a passage in the latter's lecture on
Hamlet and Don Quixote, which, though still little
known in English, had been early translated in France.
Though very characteristic of Renan, it does not really

quite fit Turgenev. It was easy enough for Renan to look ahead to the ultimate resolution of conflicts; he was accustomed to dealing with movements that belonged to the remote past. The conflicts in Turgenev are not truly—or only rarely—resolved, any more than the forces they represent were resolved in his contemporary Russia. The Paris of the mid-nineteenth century was quite ignorant of Russian affairs, and for this reason the Russian Turgenev was largely invisible to it; what it knew was the distinguished visitor, the good Russian giant of the Goncourts, the correct and well-balanced and modest friend, the cultivated foreigner who spoke all the languages yet who always was somewhat exotic, and so could charm without discommoding. Turgenev thus came to present in his Western and in his Russian connections two distinct and contrasting faces. For George Moore and Henry James, his stories are beautiful idylls: the Irishman and the American adore his high-souled young women, and they sympathize with his weak young men; they admire the descriptions of forest and field as if they were Corot landscapes, and the peasants, with the fantasy of their folk tales, the devotion of their touching attachments, are a people, almost like the pixies, that appropriately inhabit these landscapes. Turgenev must, of course, have been aware of this, and he exhibited a great deal of skill in managing his double life. This is a problem that has to be dealt with by every Russian exile. The Russian assumes, as a matter of course, that no foreigner can really know Russia, since one cannot imagine it correctly in any terms supplied by the West, and nobody but a Russian, he thinks—not entirely without justification—can have the freedom of the Russian language. But the Russians, wherever they are living, carry with them the Russian world, to which, when they gather together, all the other worlds become peripheral. That this world is

unlike the West, that it poses unique problems, that
the people of their half-primitive country are innumerable and the country is vast, and that those Russians
who are properly civilized are immeasurably more
versatile and brilliant and learned than the intelligentsia
of any other nation—all these considerations are
bonds of solidarity and sources of pride. Yet when
Russians come together and talk, nobody else can
hear them, and even if the outsider *could* hear them,
he would not in the least understand. Their movements,
their groupings, their feudings, their scandals, their
benefit performances and their domestic vicissitudes,
discussed passionately wherever there are Russians—
among whom every word or event seems communicated
instantaneously throughout the whole Russian circle—
pass unnoticed by the foreigners about them. But to
this alien world the Russian—unlike the average
Englishman, Frenchman or German—deliberately
adapts himself; he speaks its language, gets the hang
of its attitudes; and the usual educated Russian is so
easy to get along with, so amusing and so good a story-
teller, so apparently outspoken and spontaneous, though
at times perhaps a little evasive, that the foreigner
has no way of gauging the immense amount of reserve
behind this. Turgenev was a typical example. What
Turgenev's friends in the West could hardly have
guessed about him was that each of his delightful novels,
which, in form and in sensibility, could stand up beside
anything of the kind that the West itself had produced,
was, from the moment it appeared in Russia, an occasion
for passion and polemics, that for Turgenev himself to
return meant attacks and entreaties and ruptures,
putting his head in a hornet's nest, as well as an opportunity for sudden reprisals by the government.

We are struck by this piquant contrast between
the two faces of Turgenev when we compare his letters

to foreigners—rather formal, in perfect taste, always respectful to the recipient and his country—with his letters to his Russian friends. The voice of the Turgenev who at thirty-eight addresses the twenty-eight-year-old Tolstoy seems to proceed from a different person: "I shall never cease to love you and to value your friendship, though—probably through my fault—each of us, in the presence of the other, will be bound for a long time yet to feel a certain embarrassment. . . . Whence this embarrassment arises . . . I believe you yourself understand. You are the only person in the world with whom I have misunderstandings, and this comes precisely from the fact that I have wanted not to limit myself to simple friendly relations—I have wanted to go further and deeper, but I have been doing this in an indiscreet way: I hooked on to you, made demands on you, and then, becoming aware that I had made a mistake, relinquished you, it may be, too hastily; that is what has caused this 'gulf' between us." And he goes on to analyze the situation. He is worrying, in another letter, about Tolstoy's opinion of his work: "I know you did not care for my last story [*Asya*], and you were not alone; many of my best friends are not enthusiastic about it; I am sure you are quite right; and yet I wrote it at white heat, almost in tears—so we never know what we are doing." In Paris, he complains to Tolstoy of the French, a line that was likely to please him: "I have met only one nice girl—and she is a Russian; only one intelligent man—he is a Jew. I don't really care much for the French; they may be splendid soldiers and administrators—but in their heads there is only one alley, along which they push always the same ideas, ideas they have accepted once for all. Everything that isn't their own seems to them outlandish and silly: *'Ah, le lecteur français ne saurait admettre cela!'* Once he has said these words, the Frenchman cannot even imagine that it is possible for you to make any reply—well, let us leave them to God!" To another Russian friend, Turgenev expresses himself with equal frankness on the subject of *Anna Karenina*. What has here put Turgenev's back up is the issue raised by Tolstoy in his novel between good old honest Russian Moscow and wickedly Westernizing St. Petersburg— which is one of those matters of perennial interest to Russians, since the competition between these two centers has gone on even under the Soviets and was involved in the rivalry of Kirov with Stalin, of which the non-Russian is hardly aware. "I haven't yet," Turgenev writes, "read the last instalment of *Anna Karenina,* but I can see with regret the direction that this whole novel is taking. However great the talent of L. Tolstoy, he will not be able to extricate himself from the Moscow bog into which he has got himself. Orthodoxy, the gentry, Slavophilism, gossip, Arbat [a then aristocratic section of Moscow], Katkov [the reactionary editor], Antonina Bludova [who had a Slavophil salon in Moscow], bad manners, conceitedness, feudal customs, officerdom, hostility to everything foreign, sour cabbage soup and absence of soap—chaos, in a word. And in this chaos so gifted a man must perish. That's the way it always is in Russia." One feels here, on Turgenev's part, a certain impulse to assign to Tolstoy the destiny of a frustrated Turgenev character, to bury him in the old Russian swamp that Turgenev had come out of and dreaded.

Turgenev's relations with Tolstoy as well as with Dostoevsky were intensely dramatic and comic. In the case of both his great contemporaries, when, on visits to that Western Europe which they made such a point of disdaining, they had lost all their money gambling— Dostoevsky lost even his watch—Turgenev would lend them money. Dostoevsky rewarded him for this by denouncing him on every occasion, but, fleeing, two years later, from his creditors and making a stay in Baden, at the time when Turgenev was living there, Dostoevsky reasoned with himself that just because he had not paid Turgenev back he ought not to fail to call on him. Dostoevsky, in his account of this interview, an anonymous memorandum of which he wanted to have put in the official archives, reported that Turgenev had been outrageous; that the bad reception of *Smoke* had caused him to inveigh against Russia, declaring that if the Russians were totally destroyed, it would be no loss to human thought; that "we must grovel before the Germans" and that he now regarded himself as a German. Dostoevsky had advised him, he said, to acquire a telescope so that he could see what was going on in Russia. It is not implausible that Turgenev should have let himself go à la Potugin of *Smoke* and declare, as Dostoevsky reported, that "there was but one universal and inevitable road—that of civilization, and that any attempt at a policy of Russianism and independence was pigheaded stupidity and folly." But Turgenev does not elsewhere appear as a slavish admirer of the Germans, and in his own account of this interview—sent to Petersburg when he learned of the memorandum—he asserts that Dostoevsky's visit had lasted no longer than an hour, in the course of which he had bitterly attacked the Germans and had stormed against Turgenev and *Smoke* in tirades to which Turgenev "had had hardly the time or the wish to reply." He regarded Dostoevsky, he says, on account of his epileptic attacks and for "other reasons," as "not in full control of his intellectual faculties" and had "behaved with him as he would with a sick man." Dostoevsky was again gambling madly and as usual ruining himself. A few years later (Turgenev's loan still not repaid), he put his creditor into *The Devils* as the exquisite and silly Karmazinov. But at last, in 1874, nine years after the loan had been made, hearing that Turgenev had returned to Russia, Dostoevsky sent him the money. His explanation for not having done so before was that he had not been able to remember whether it was fifty or a hundred thalers—Dostoevsky had asked for a hundred but Turgenev had given him only fifty—and that it had been only a few days before, when he had come upon a letter from Turgenev, that he had been reminded of the correct amount.

With Tolstoy, who was also opposed to Turgenev's Westernizing policy, Turgenev had a disagreeable quarrel in the course of a conversation in which he was telling with complacency of the new English governess he had found for his daughter. Turgenev the next morning sent apologies, but he misdirected his letter and soon received from his friend a challenge—not, Tolstoy fiercely declared, to the usual literary duel of the kind that concludes with the adversaries drinking champagne together; they would have to shoot it out with rifles. Turgenev apologized again, but later heard that Tolstoy was circulating the story and calling Turgenev a coward. Turgenev now challenged Tolstoy, but said that he was just going abroad and couldn't be bothered to fight him till he came back to Russia again. Tolstoy in his turn now apologized, and seventeen years later, when he had publicly become a Christian, wrote Turgenev proposing a reconciliation. Turgenev went to visit him in the country—their estates were not far apart—but said afterwards that he felt rather nervous when he beat the new saint at chess. Immediately after this, when Turgenev was in Paris, he received from Tolstoy a letter in which the latter tried to pick a quarrel with him, expressing doubts of Turgenev's "sincerity." Later, in 1881, when Turgenev was visiting Spasskoye again, Tolstoy, at one o'clock in the morning, suddenly descended upon him, dressed in a peasant's costume, and put on such a performance of Christian humility that Turgenev was rather impressed. What, Turgenev said, showed that Tolstoy was actually making some progress as a Christian was that, instead of simply laying down the law, he allowed his opponent to do some of the talking. When Turgenev returned this visit, there was a birthday party in progress. Turgenev took off his coat and danced the cancan with a twelve-year-old girl. Tolstoy noted in his diary: "Turgenev—the cancan. Sad."

Turgenev did sometimes lose his temper; with Russians he was rather touchy. Is it entirely Dostoevsky's parody—ascribed to the absurd Karmazinov—that makes the elegiac *Enough* sound perhaps a little petulant and mawkish? And yet it is impossible not to feel, as Mr. Magarshack suggests, that Turgenev, the atheist, was a good deal more successful at practicing the Christian virtues than either the holy man of Yasnaya Polyana or the creator of Alyosha Karamazov.

One result of assimilating Turgenev to the school of writers, either French or influenced by the French, of the late nineteenth and early twentieth centuries—to Mérimée, Flaubert, Maupassant, George Moore, Henry James, Joseph Conrad—has been that till recently it has not been thought worth while to translate his non-fictional writings, which are mainly concerned with Russian affairs. It was no doubt assumed at the time of Turgenev's great foreign reputation that the men and the movements with which these writings dealt were quite unknown in the West and that they would not be of interest abroad. Yet Turgenev's explanation of his literary aims—such as the preface already quoted —would, for example, have been salutary reading for our writers of the "Art is a weapon" thirties, when Russia had become so much more real to us but was sending us inferior literary products. And the *Literary Reminiscences* of Turgenev—which, in Mr. Magarshack's translation, appear now for the first time in English—is certainly of Turgenev's best, comparable in beauty and interest to Yeats's *The Trembling of the Veil,* which in some ways it rather resembles. In the case of the common run of such books of literary memories, we are mainly impressed by the author's having managed to see at close range so many distinguished people without finding anything interesting to report of them; but a Yeats or a Turgenev is able—as in the latter's two brief glimpses of Pushkin—to make of a remark or an anecdote the revelation of a whole personality. The dominating figure in these memoirs is Vissarion Gregorovich Belinsky, the great Russian critic of the eighteen-forties, who, seven years older than Turgenev, took an interest in his work from the first and with whom he became close friends. At a time when the young Turgenev paraded his affectations and was often considered an ass, Belinsky discerned his sincerity in his earliest published work, a long poem called *Parasha,* and, despite Belinsky's humble origin, his harsh manners, his limited learning and his ignorance of the world, Turgenev came not only to admire him but even to find inspiration in his candor and moral nobility, his passionate interest in letters (which was finely aesthetic as well as moral), his vigorous and earnest efforts for the development of a great literature in Russia, at a time when, as Turgenev says, the Tsar was doing everything possible to discourage not merely literature but even higher education. To call on his friend, he remembered—in that atmosphere of spies and suppression—was enough to set one up for the day. This intimacy with Belinsky was undoubtedly one of the most important influences of Turgenev's life. It is obviously reflected in his fiction in the constantly recurrent motif of the two contrasting friends—though, in the years before he knew Belinsky, he had already had a somewhat similar friendship with another intellectual, Nikolai Stankevich, already mentioned above, which makes one think that he must have been predisposed to this kind of relationship. Stankevich died in 1840, and Turgenev first met Belinsky in 1842; and the first of the stories that exploit this theme—*Andrey Kolosov*—was written in 1844. Later on, the description of Yakov Pasynkov in the story of that name is so similar to the description of Belinsky in the *Reminiscences* that it is evident that the latter had sat for Yakov, who dies of an injury to the lung, as both Belinsky and Stankevich died of tuberculosis. Now, *Yakov Pasynkov* is also a kind of preliminary study for the large-scale *Fathers and Sons,* and when we come to *Fathers and Sons,* we find that it is dedicated to the memory of Belinsky—who had died thirteen years before—and that its hero, like Belinsky himself, is the son of a poor army doctor and has a pitiful premature death. Turgenev had spent two months with his friend, not long before the latter's death in 1848, in a hotel at a German spa, where it was hoped that his health might improve. Turgenev pointed out to Pavlovsky that Bazarov, of *Fathers and Sons*, was blond, "like all my sympathetic heroes," like "Belinsky, Herzen and others." (It is also worth noting that the *Literary Reminiscences* contain Turgenev's account of the execution of the French murderer Troppmann, as great a piece of writing in its way— prosaic, circumstantial and somber—as any of Turgenev's stories.)

III

The work of Turgenev has, of course, no scope that is comparable to Tolstoy's or Dostoevsky's, but the ten volumes collected by him for his edition of 1883 (he omitted his early poems) represent a literary achievement of the concentratedly "artistic" kind that has few equals in nineteenth-century fiction. There are moments, to be sure, in Turgenev novels—*On the Eve* and *Virgin Soil*—when they become a little thin or unreal, but none can be called a failure, and one cannot find a single weak piece, unless one becomes impatient with *Enough,* in the whole four volumes of stories. No fiction writer can be read through with a steadier admiration. Greater novelists are more uneven: they betray our belief with extravagances; they bore or they fall into bathos; they combine poetic vision with rubbish. But Turgenev hardly even skirts these failings, and he is never mediocre; his texture is as distinguished as his temperament.

This texture barely survives in translation. Turgenev is a master of language; he is interested in words in a way that the other great nineteenth-century Russian novelists—with the exception of Gogol—are not. His writing is dense and substantial, yet it never marks time, always moves. The translations of Constance Garnett are full of omissions and errors; the translations of Isabel Hapgood do not omit, but are also full of errors and often extremely clumsy. Neither lady seems ever to have thought of taking the indispensable precaution of reading her version to a Russian following the Russian text, who would at once have spotted the dropped-out negatives and the cases of one word mistaken for another. The translations of Turgenev into French—though some are by Mérimée and Turgenev himself—have a tendency to strip him down to something much barer and poorer. The task of translating this writer does present some impossible problems. "What an amazing language!" wrote Chekhov on rereading the story called *The Dog.* But this language will not reach the foreigner. How to render the tight little work of art that Turgenev has made of *The Dog,* narrated by an ex-hussar, with his colloquialisms, his pungent sayings, his terseness and his droll turns? And the problems of translating Turgenev are to some extent the problems of translating poetry. There is a passage in *The Torrents of Spring*—a tour de force of onomatopoeia—that imitates in a single sentence the whispering of leaves, the buzzing of bees and the droning of a solitary dove. This is probably a conscious attempt to rival the well-known passage in Virgil's First Eclogue and Tennyson's imitation of it:

> *The moan of doves in immemorial elms,*
> *And murmuring of innumerable bees.*

«Изредка, чуть слышно и словно не спеша, перешёптывались листья, да отрывисто жужжали, перелетывая с цветка на соседний цветок, запоздалые пчёлы, да где—то воркова́ла горлицка однообразно и неутомимо.»

But it would take another master to reproduce Turgenev's effects, just as it took a Tennyson to reproduce those of Virgil, and a Turgenev to compete with these.

Since I am going to go on in this section to call attention to the principal themes that run all through Turgenev's work and to relate them to his personal experience, I must emphasize here the solidity and the range of Turgenev's writings. It is only in the later stories which deal with the supernatural that these underlying themes emerge as obsessions or hallucinations. They are otherwise usually embodied in narratives, objectively presented, in which the backgrounds are always varied and in which even the individuals who belong to a constantly recurring type are always studied in a special context and differentiated from one another. Turgenev is not one of the great inventors, as his two colleagues and Dickens are, but in his tighter, more deliberate art he is perhaps the most satisfactory of the company to which he belongs, for he never oppresses, as Flaubert does, by his monotony and his flattening of human feeling, or fatigues, as Henry James sometimes does when his wheels of abstraction are grinding, or makes us nervous, as Conrad may do, through his effortfulness and occasional awkwardness in working in a language not native to him with materials that are sometimes alien. The material of Turgenev is all his own, and his handling of it is masterly. The detail is always amusing, always characteristic; every word, every reference, every touch of description has naturalness as well as point; the minor characters, the landscapes, the milieux are all given a full succulent flavor. The genre pictures—the funeral supper at the end of *An Unhappy Girl*, the transference of the property in *A Lear of the Steppes*— are wonderfully organized and set in motion, although that exhilaration of movement that Tolstoy is able to generate in such episodes as the hunt in *War and Peace* and the races in *Anna Karenina* is quite beyond Turgenev's powers, as is the cumulative fun and excitement of the town celebration in Dostoevsky's *The Devils*. But neither can fill in a surface, can fit language to subject like Turgenev. The weather is never the same; the descriptions of the countryside are quite concrete, and full, like Tennyson's, of exact observation of how cloud and sunlight and snow and rain, trees, flowers, insects, birds and wild animals, dogs, horses and cats behave, and yet they are also stained by the mood of the person who is made to perceive them. There are moments, though not very many, when the affinity between

natural phenomena and the emotion of the character
exposed to them is allowed to become a little melo-
dramatic in the old-fashioned romantic way—the
volcanic sunset in *Faust* when the heroine is herself on
the verge of eruption—but in general Turgenev is
protected from the dangers of the "romantic fallacy"
by his realistic habit of mind.

Let me here, also, call attention to a story that seems
to me a masterpiece and that sounds a different note
from those I shall discuss later: *The History of Lieutenant Ergunov,* of 1867. This Lieutenant is a heavy and
clumsy and extremely naïve young man who is highly
susceptible to women and who regards himself as something of a dandy. Stationed in a provincial town, he becomes involved with a household that purports to consist
of an elderly woman living with two nieces. They are of
mongrel and dubious origins; one of them, who calls
herself Colibri, is semi-Oriental, exotic. The Lieutenant
never discovers that the two girls are prostitutes and
that their bully is lurking in the background. His
suspicions are not even aroused when he has dropped
off to sleep on a couch one day and been awakened by
the efforts of one of the girls—he is carrying government
money—to detach from his belt his wallet. He becomes
so fascinated by Colibri that it is no trouble at all
for her to drug him. They rob him, bash in his head
and, assuming he is safely dead, throw his body down
a ravine. It is only his exceptional vigor that enables
him in time to recover from this. The thieves have,
of course, made their getaway, but he presently receives
a long letter from the girl who tried to steal his wallet,
in which she tells him that though she has "a bad
morality" and is "flighty," she is not really "a villainess." She is terribly sorry about the whole thing; the
others had induced her to lend herself to luring him
to the house and then sent her away for the day. "The

old villainess *was not* my aunt." She begs him to answer, but he never does. Ergunov all the rest of his life tells the story at least once a month.

It is typical of Turgenev's art that the anecdote in itself, as I have sketched it, cannot convey Turgenev's point. Nothing could be more different from a story, say, by Maupassant. There are no tricks of the professional raconteur, no sudden surprise at the end. We follow a steady narrative, built up with convincing detail. It closes calmly enough with Ergunov's shaking his head and sighing, "That's what it is to be young," and displaying his terrible scar, which reaches from ear to ear. And it is only after we have finished the story that we grasp the whole implication of the triumph of good faith and respect for the innocent over the brutal violation of human relations. Ergunov is the side of Turgenev himself that never could believe at first that the people who exploited him were not honest. It is a question in *Lieutenant Ergunov* not of one of the author's obsessive themes but of a feeling that, for all his demons, all his ogresses and their helpless victims, continues to assert itself almost to the end of his work —Gemma's letter of forgiveness to Sanin, in the later *Torrents of Spring,* reversing the roles of the sexes in *Ergunov,* embodies the same moral—and a feeling that he shares with the creator of Myshkin as well as with the creator of Pierre. This instinct sets the standards for Turgenev's mind, and it is the basis of his peculiar nobility. It is the essence of the life-giving drop that he has rescued from the cave of the reptiles.

But this story is almost unique. The positive force of honesty, even the survival of innocence—though they sometimes occur in the novels: Solomin in *Virgin Soil,* Tatyana and her aunt in *Smoke*—are excessively rare in these tales. There are examples of religious dedication—*A Living Relic* in *A Sportsman's Sketches,*

A Strange Story, A Desperate Character (Отчаянный).
—but, especially in the last two of these, you feel that
they are simply cases, included with the other cases,
of the unhealthiness of Russian life. In general, the
ogresses and devils continue to have the best of it,
and the timid and snobbish young men continue to
disappoint the proud women. To return to the series
where we dropped it—in 1857, ten years before
Lieutenant Ergunov—this has happened to the heroine
of *Asya* and to Gemma of *The Torrents of Spring,* and
is to happen to the heroine of *An Unhappy Girl* (two
of these the illegitimate daughters of gentlemen and one
the daughter of an Italian confectioner). It is only
in *First Love* that the girl under a social shadow is
allowed to have a passionate love affair, and I am sure
that it is partly to this, the exceptional element of sex
interest, that the story owes its special popularity—
along with, for the same reason, *The Torrents of
Spring*—among Turgenev's shorter fictions. Yet note
that it is not the young boy but his father who enjoys
Zinaida's love, and that Turgenev explained that the
story was based on an experience of his own youth.
The figure of the elder Turgenev plays no such role in
his work as that of Varvara Petrovna, but the aloof and
dashing father of the narrator of *First Love,* who fasci-
nates Zinaida and slashes her arm with his riding crop,
evidently has something to do with the diabolic brother
of *The Song of Triumphant Love,* who mesmerizes and
rapes his sister-in-law. If the heroes in Turgenev are
inhibited from going to bed with the women and do so
only, still with inhibitions, when—as in *Smoke* or *The
Torrents of Spring*—they, the men, are themselves
seduced, the man who prevails over women is likely to
treat them with violence and to become an embodiment
of the Evil Force.

In the meantime, Varvara Petrovna is reappearing

in *Her Ladyship's Private Office* (Контора) (originally intended as a chapter in an early attempt at a novel, but first published in the *Literary Reminiscences*), and in *Punin and Baburin,* and the Lutovinova grandmother who killed the little serf boy turns up as a variation of the Varvara Petrovna character in Agrippina Ivanovna of *The Brigadier*. The masculine Force of Evil, after lying in abeyance since *The Wayside Inn* of 1852, reappears five years later in *A Tour in the Forest* (Поездка в Полесы), and it is here for the first time invested—at least in the minds of the peasants of the story—with supernatural implications. This piece was added by Turgenev to a new edition of *A Sportsman's Sketches* published in 1860, but afterwards presented by the author—in a collected edition of 1865—in its chronological place. For it does not belong with the *Sketches*—it is more philosophical and more complex; it shows the development of Turgenev's art. I agree with Dmitri Mirsky in his admiration for *A Tour in the Forest*—with its wonderful descriptions of pine forests, its feeling for the non-human life of trees that both embraces and isolates human beings, that oppresses at the same time it calms. And in the forest the demon is found—Efrem, a bad peasant who fears nobody, who stops at no outrageous act and whom his neighbors can do nothing about. He makes his living through robbery and brings up his son as a thief. It is no use to arrest him and put him in jail. The only good thing one can say of him is that he usually will not injure anyone who comes from his own settlement. Sometimes he will shout from a distance if he sees a fellow-villager, "Keep away, brother! I'm a killer! The forest demon is on me!" "But why do you mind what he says?" the narrator asks the man who is telling the story. "Can't the lot of you deal with a single man?" "That seems to be the way it is." "But he's not a magician, is he?" "Who knows?" And the forester goes on to tell of the chanter in the church who had thrashed Efrem in the dark when he did not know who he was, but then, when he recognized him, had fallen on his knees before him. Efrem had punished the chanter by putting a spell upon him and causing him to waste away. "That chanter must be an idiot." "Do you think so?" the peasant replies. Once an order goes out to catch Efrem. They have a smart chief of police, and he leads ten men into the forest. Efrem comes out to meet them. "Grab him! Tie him up!" someone cries. But Efrem, looking hideous and frightful, breaks off a big club from a tree and threatens them. "On your knees!" he commands them, and they all fall down on their knees. They have had to get a new chief of police. "But why did they all obey him?" "Why? That's the way it is." But though Efrem connects himself with the *leshi,* the Russian forest goblin, and though, on one of his marauding exploits, he successfully masquerades as a devil, the element he represents has not yet come to wear the aspect of something quite outside the natural world. He is identified also with the bear; the foresters regard him as a kind of bear. And Turgenev here succeeds in assigning him to a role in a partly comprehensible world. When the narrator first came into the forest, he fell to brooding, in a moment of solitude, on the profound disappointment that had been his life. He has always been expecting happiness, and he has never been able to find it (Turgenev had just broken with Pauline Viardot at the time this story was written). On his second day in the forest, he and his peasant guides run into a forest fire deliberately started by Efrem—apparently, out of sheer *Schrecklichkeit.* The foresters console themselves in noting that it is only the kind of fire that runs along the ground and so does not burn the trees. They retreat from the flames to rest. The narrator lies under a tree and watches a dragonfly, who is also taking a rest on a branch. He reflects that it is wrong to complain. What is normal is to live like this insect in a state of tranquil equilibrium: whatever rises above or sinks below this level is automatically rejected by nature. If one suffers through one's own fault or through that of others, one can only keep silent about it. The bad peasant—in his own way normal, as normal as his brother the bear—seems now to fade into the background as a part of the order of nature. The revery is interrupted: "What's the matter with you, Egor," cries one of his guides to the other. "What are you brooding about?" He explains to the narrator that Egor has just lost his last cow. As Egor drives them off in silence, " 'There,' I thought to myself, 'is a man who knows how not to complain.' " We are as far from the conception here of the inimical nature of Vigny— *"Vous ne recevrez pas un cri d'amour de moi!"*—as from the sympathetic Nature of the "romantic fallacy." There are here no romantic poses, no rhetorical affirmations or negations. There is not even any attempt to develop a clear point of view: only a moment of experience, two days in the woods, human consciousness and animal life and the life of strong vegetation.

In reading *A Tour in the Forest,* it occurs to one that this indigenous demon, against whom the people of the forest feel themselves utterly helpless, against whom they can have no redress, represents a constant factor in Russian life, an ever-recurring phenomenon of history: the bad master whom one cannot resist, Ivan the Terrible, Peter the Great, Stalin. The masculine Force of Evil reappears in *An Unhappy Girl* (1868) as Susanna's horrible stepfather, and in *A Lear of the Steppes* (1870) you have one male and two female villains, all more or less unaccounted for. In *Lear,* the two daughters of old Kharlov, who destroy him, no doubt dominate the son-in-law, but there is nothing to explain why both of them should have risen to such positions of power save the example of Varvara Petrovna, on whose character they present variations. Maria Nikolaevna in *The Torrents of Spring*—another strong and cunning peasant—is a still further variation. And thereafter, as Turgenev nears sixty, both the female and the male evil powers not only cease to wear the aspect of noxious products of the social system or even of elements of animal nature; they become supernatural beings, who prey upon and take possession, who swoop in on us from outside our known world. This development on Turgenev's part synchronizes—despite the fact that during the seventies he wrote, in *Virgin Soil,* his most ambitious social novel—with a haunting and growing sense of the nullity of human life and the futility of his own endeavors. This feeling first breaks out in *Enough* of 1864. The title of *Smoke* is inspired by it: "He sat alone in the train," he writes of Litvinov at the end of this book. "There was nobody to disturb him. 'Smoke, smoke!' he several times said to himself [he is watching the smoke of the train]. And suddenly everything seemed to him smoke, everything, life itself, Russian life—everything human, especially everything Russian. It was all smoke and steam—he thought—everything seems constantly changing; always new shapes; appearances fly after appearances; but actually it is always the same and the same; everything is hurrying away, everything is speeding off somewhere—and everything vanishes without a trace, without ever achieving anything; a different wind has blown, and everything has been driven in the opposite direction, and there you have again the same ceaseless agitation, the same movement that results in nothing." In the late *Poems in Prose* (1878–82), this despondency has reached its nadir. You have, for example, the discouraging dialogue between the Jungfrau and the Finsteraarhorn, which, waking or drowsing in the course of their millennia, see the human race, far below them, come to life, stir about for a little, and eventually die out like vermin. And at the same time the Force of Evil seems to rush in to fill this vacuum. These *Senilia,* as he calls them, are full of nightmares— the nightmare of the giant insect that fatally stings the young man, the nightmare of the end of the world, in which people in a country house are surrounded and swallowed up by a raging and icy sea.

These nightmares have begun in *Phantoms* of 1863, and this is followed, thirteen years later, by *The Dream.* The element of the supernatural first appears in *The Dog* of 1866. This very curious story associates itself with *Knock! . . . Knock! . . . Knock! . . . ,* which follows it in 1870. Both deal with mysterious destinies, one fortunate, the other unfortunate—a suggestion of which is also to be found in *The Torrents of Spring* of 1871. In *The Dog,* the Force of Evil wears the aspect of the gigantic mad dog which persistently attacks the hero and from which he is only saved by his heaven-sent protector: a setter which has come to him first as an invisible but audible presence. The canine guardian angel is again, like the Lieutenant's innocence, a form of the life-giving drop. But this angel in the subsequent stories grows weaker and at last gives way before the Demon of Evil: the diabolic baron of *The Dream;* the priest's son, possessed by the Devil, of *Father Alexey's Story;* the sinister Renaissance sorcerer of *The Song of Triumphant Love.* I do not agree with Mirsky that the realistic setting of these stories prevents them from being successful. They *are* certainly less compelling than the diabolic tales of Gogol, from which they may partly derive, for the reason that the world of Gogol, being always distorted and turbid, is more favorable for this kind of horror, but they are nonetheless creepy enough and can hold their own with any such fantasies. The fault that one

would find with them is rather that they are not merely
horrible but hopeless. The forces that battle with the
goblins are too feeble; they do not have a chance of
success. Compare Gogol's vampire story *Viy* with
Turgenev's *Clara Milich,* which fundamentally it somewhat resembles. It is not only that the rude village church
in which the young student of Gogol keeps his terrible
vigil with the girl in the coffin is closer to peasant folklore
than the "small wooden house" in Moscow where
Turgenev's student lives with his aunt and has his rendezvous with the dead Clara; Gogol's hero arouses more
sympathy, puts up a better fight than Turgenev's, who is
actually, like Sanin in *The Torrents,* more attracted than
frightened by the vampire.

This story—of 1882, the last that Turgenev published
—is, in any case, the culmination of the whole morbid
side of his work. Clara Milich is a talented young girl as
to whom people cannot be sure whether she will turn
out "a Rachel or a Viardot." She is not really beautiful;
she has a swarthy complexion, coarse hair and a mustache on her upper lip. She is very much the gypsy type;
one would imagine she was bad-tempered and capricious
—a passionate, self-willed nature, hardly even particularly intelligent. "What tragic eyes!" someone says.
Clara fixes upon the student Yakov, a somewhat
feminine and frail young man, with whom she has
hardly exchanged words at a party, and she sends him
a mysterious and urgent message begging him to meet
her in a certain street. When she meets him, she tells
him, with tears in her eyes, that she feels a great need
to talk with him but does not know how to go about it,
and he behaves in such a priggish way—he thinks her
not respectable, too forward—that she gibes at him
and runs away. He soon hears that she has committed
suicide. Performing in a provincial theater, she had
drunk poison just before going on and had played the

first act with unusual feeling and warmth, then, the moment the curtain fell, had dropped writhing in convulsions to the floor. "What strength of will! What character!" people said. Yakov fears that he is to blame, and he looks up her family and reads her diary and finds that—for reasons not clear—she had counted on him to "decide her destiny," and had then written, "No! no! no!" in evident disillusionment and despair. Clara begins to haunt him in dreams and hallucinations (she is rather like the female spirit who carries Turgenev around in *Phantoms*). At one of their meetings he kisses her—he feels her burning nearness and her cold moist lips—and he wakes his aunt with a cry. What can come of such a love? he wonders. When he remembers that kiss from the dead, a wonderful sensation of cold runs quickly and sweetly through all his limbs. "Such a kiss," he says to himself, "not even Romeo and Juliet exchanged. But the next time I shall hold out better. . . . I shall possess her." The next time he throws himself upon her: "You have conquered! Take me!" he cries. His aunt finds him on his knees, with his head on the armchair where the ghost had been sitting. In a delirium, he declares he is Romeo, who has taken the poison on Juliet's death, and he dies with a smile on his face.

Spasskoye, the prison of his childhood, is closing in on Turgenev, but though his progress in nightmare has brought him to surrender to Clara Milich, he finds courage, in a strange last story, to strike back at the Evil Force. Turgenev in his earlier phase had hoped, as has already been said, that the feudal social system of Russia might be reformed from above by the Tsar. It is the Bulgarians, not the Russians, to whom, in *On the Eve,* Elena devotes her life. Bazarov, in *Fathers and Sons,* though he does not believe in institutions, is by no means a revolutionist. But the implication of *Punin and Baburin* is certainly revolutionary. Even after

Fathers and Sons, the theme of the two friends persists, but in this story of 1874 the stronger of the pair is no longer a Nihilist: he is a republican who is sent to Siberia. The story ends, however, with the good news of the emancipation of the serfs. In *The Watch,* which follows *Punin and Baburin* in 1875, the two friends appear again, with the same Bazarov-Arcady relationship. In this ingenious parable, the narrator is given a watch by his godfather, a corrupt official who has lost his job but who still always powders his hair (it is the beginning of the nineteenth century). He is delighted by the present at first, but a cousin, whose father had been sent to Siberia for "agitational activities and Jacobin views," carefully examines the watch, declares that it is old and no good, and, learning that it was given the boy by his godfather, tells him that he should accept no gifts from such a man. The narrator worships the cousin, and the rest of the story consists of his efforts to get rid of the watch by burying it or giving it away. But he always—under pressure of his family or of his own insurmountable pride in it—is compelled to get it back again. What does this watch represent? The antiquated social system? The corruption of old Russia? The father and the godfather are crooks; the watch, though the boy does not realize it, has evidently been stolen. It is only at last expelled from their lives when the tough-minded Jacobin cousin hurls it into the river at the cost of falling in himself and of almost getting drowned. *Virgin Soil* (1876), as we have seen, is occupied entirely with a revolutionary subject. Though the agitational activities of the Populists are regarded as premature and shown here as coming to grief, it is implied at the end that the movement is quietly going on and may eventually result in something. And among the *Poems in Prose,* there is one, *The Threshold* (1878), that Turgenev did not publish and that was not known till after his death, when a Populist paper printed it, which was inspired by the attempt of Vera Zasulich to assassinate General Trepov: " 'O you who want to cross that threshold, do you know what awaits you there?' 'I do,' the young girl replies. 'Cold, hunger, hatred, ridicule, scorn, insult, jail, illness, and death itself.' 'I know it.' . . . The young girl crossed the threshold, and behind her fell a heavy curtain. 'Fool!' snarled someone after her. The answer came from somewhere: 'Saint!' "

"I once," Pavlovsky reports that Turgenev used to say in his later years, "believed that the reforms would come from above; now I am entirely disillusioned. I should have joined the youth movement if I had not been so old and if I could have believed in the results of a movement that came from below. The new social type whose existence I have put on record, the literate peasant who reads the papers and despises and robs the other peasants, is a hundred times worse than the old-fashioned landlord."

In *Old Portraits* (1881), a cruel and unscrupulous landowner takes advantage of a technicality to reclaim from another landowner a serf who has spent twenty years as the latter's devoted servant. The serf promises to kill his new master, bides his time for a favorable moment, and then splits his head with a hatchet. Two weeks before Turgenev's death, in 1883, he carried this theme further. He was dying of cancer of the spine and in such pain that a little later, when Maupassant came to see him, he begged him to bring a revolver. But he managed to compose one more story, which he dictated to Pauline Viardot in a mixture of French, German and Italian, and asked her to put into French. When she asked him whether he would not rather use Russian, he replied, with tears in his eyes, that he did not feel strong enough to bother about style as he would have to do if he phrased it in Russian. The title of this

story—which will be found in French in the new
Soviet edition mentioned above—was originally called
Une Fin. Here the Russian landowning gentry, whose
emergence from a barbarism of brigands has been shown
retrospectively in *A House of Gentlefolk* and whose
origins recur as a horror in the *Stenka Razin* episode
of *Phantoms* (Stenka's Cossacks had drowned in the
Volga a seventeenth-century Turgenev), returns to its
original brutality in a now degenerate form. Talagaev—
talagai means an obstinate lout—belongs to an old country family, of which he is very proud. His father was famous for his hunting, for his turnouts with silver trim-
mings, and for once having ordered his coachman to
blindfold the eyes of a horse and plunge into an ice-
covered river. This father and his generation have
squandered the family money, and the surviving
Talagaev, though reduced to peddling poultry, makes a
point of keeping up his appearance so as not to be taken
for a peasant, a sacristan or a merchant: "Why shouldn't
I go in for trade? What if I do belong to the gentry? What
if my ancestor did wear the brocaded gold cap that was
given him by Tamburlaine?" When an innkeeper refuses
to buy, he insults him and shoots off a gun that he carries
—"Do you think it's not loaded?" he jeers—and goes
away singing *Stenka Razin* in a voice "neither pleasing
nor true." "He wants to be a bandit," one of the men at
the inn mutters, "but he can't even sing the bandits'
song!" Having lost caste with his own social group, he
succeeds in luring away from home, with the promise
that he will show her the Kremlin, the fifteen-year-old
daughter of a neighbor of good standing but small
property, and makes his usual insolent scene when her
father comes to take her back. When we next see Talagaev, he has just been detected in cheating a peasant on a
horse deal and is mobbed in the market place. At last,
during a bitter snowstorm, when the narrator is battling

the weather on his way to dine with a neighbor and has been suggesting to his coachman that the latter might well marry the girl whom Talagaev has tried to abduct (a bridging of the social gulf which the coachman cannot accept: "Oh, but she's a lady," he says), the horses shy suddenly away from something dark in the road. It is the body of Talagaev, lying in a pool of blood, his forehead split with a hatchet and a thick rope around his neck. The narrator remembers having said once in the presence of the murdered man that it was sad to think he might end his life in a brawl, and that Talagaev had answered, "Oh, no, my good sir! The Talagaevs don't die like that!" So the Evil Force of Turgenev is again given a social role and—never defeated before—is finally brought to a reckoning.

The last important event of Turgenev's literary life was his well-known letter to Tolstoy, written not long before his own death, in which he tells his uncomfortable friend how glad he is to have been his contemporary and urges him to return to literature. It is a good deal more moving than anything on record in his letters to Pauline Viardot. He had had a *rapprochement* with her when she was aging and had lost her voice, and she had joined Turgenev in Baden. Unable any longer to sing, she now began to compose and teach singing. Her ambition was to have a music school and a concert hall of her own, and Turgenev actually built her one. He wrote the librettos for the operas in which her pupils performed and himself pumped the bellows for the organ. He even acted comic parts in these operas. When a Russian friend tried to remonstrate, he only answered that Anton Rubinstein and Clara Schumann had thought so highly of *Le Dernier Sorcier* that they had advised Mme Viardot to orchestrate it; but he wrote to a German friend, "I must confess, however, that when I lay stretched out on the floor in the part of the Pasha and saw a cold sarcastic smile of disgust play on the haughty lips of your Crown Princess, something went cold inside me. You know how little I care for my dignity, but even I could not help thinking that things had gone a little too far." Undoubtedly a latent resentment is expressed, in *The Torrents of Spring,* through the picture of the bondage of Sanin to the terrible Maria Nikolaevna, the daughter of a millionaire peasant, who combines irresistible attraction with merciless love of power. In the delirium of his last days, he called Pauline Lady Macbeth and railed against her for having denied him the happiness of married life. On one occasion, when she entered the room, he—symbolically—threw his inkwell at her. (One of her few recorded comments on Turgenev was that he was *"le plus triste des hommes."*) Later he sank into a coma and emerged from it only to say, *"Venez plus près ... plus près. Le moment est venu de prendre congé ... comme les tsars russes. . . . Voici la reine des reines. Que de bien elle a fait!"*

His body was transported to Russia and buried, by his orders, beside Belinsky's.

October 19, 1957

Translations. A good deal of the Russian Turgenev goes dead in our English translations. Of our only complete versions of Turgenev's fiction—those by Constance Garnett and Isabel F. Hapgood—one cannot give a brilliant account if one has used them, like the present writer, as a crib for perplexing passages or to check on a passage one has translated oneself. One is all too likely to find, in Constance Garnett's case, that she has evidently been equally puzzled, since she has simply dropped the problems out. Turgenev did not possess the Russian genius for impersonation to quite the same degree as Tolstoy, the voices of whose characters one hears almost as if they were present in the room; but he cared, in a literary way, much more about language than

Tolstoy did and—where the latter makes his people speak spontaneously—Turgenev likes to compose little parodies and to compile, as it were, groups of specimens of how different kinds of people write or speak. (In this he sometimes sounds like Proust. See the little disquisition in *An Unhappy Girl* on the very special relation of the vulgarisms in Russian of Ratsch, the Czech, to the deliberate vulgarisms of the poetry of Prince Vyazemsky.) Mrs. Garnett makes little attempt to grapple with this side of Turgenev. She does not try to reproduce the illiteracy of the old princess's letter in *First Love* or the ecclesiastical turn of that of the old priest in *Smoke*. In the latter book, where a good deal depends on the point of the witticisms, ineptitudes and allusions of clever people or people who think themselves so, she, in many cases, either skips them, leaves them unexplained or, missing the point herself, improvises something clumsy. It is, for example, quite evident that the creature which is supposed to be mesmerized in the fifteenth chapter of *Smoke*—referred to as *rak* and *écrevisse*—is some kind of large crawfish, but Mrs. Garnett makes it a crab, which may also be called a *rak*—and Miss Hapgood repeats her error. When Sipyagin in *Virgin Soil* shows off to the schoolboys by stumping them with the Russianized Greek words for *ostrich* and *monkey,* Mrs. Garnett makes things even more difficult for them and for the reader by substituting—one cannot imagine why—*ornithorhyncus* and *wendaru;* and in the tirade of Potugin I have quoted from *Smoke,* she translates *scepticism* for отрицание, which really means *negation, denial,* with in this case an implication of defiance. Miss Hapgood—confusing it, no doubt, with отречение—gives it as *resignation*. Both ladies, in view of what follows, make obvious nonsense of the passage. You cannot contend "with a sword" or one's "fists" for either scepticism or resignation.

And, in general, of the style of Turgenev Mrs. Garnett gives little idea. He was, as I say, especially interested in language: he uses an enormous vocabulary, is strong on the innumerable nuances of the volatile Russian verbs and composes his long well-stitched paragraphs— which the translators often break up—in a dense and substantial prose which is never allowed to be tedious. Now, Mrs. Garnett handled all this with a facility that makes it seem flimsy. Miss Hapgood is more conscientious—she is a good deal less distinguished than Mrs. Garnett, who has something of a literary gift, an agreeable style of her own, which runs on in its light English way and makes all her translations readable. But Miss Hapgood does take the trouble to try to reproduce the prose word for word, or at least phrase for phrase, preserving the variety of Turgenev—unlike Tolstoy, he rarely repeats a word—and his effect of architectural solidity that does not impede narrative progression, and she shows how the names are pronounced and explains the allusions with footnotes which make her edition helpful to the foreigner reading Turgenev. Where Miss Hapgood completely fails is in her handling of Turgenev's dialogue. She has adopted the absurd policy of translating the pronouns of the second person singular with English *thou*'s and *thee*'s with results as grotesque as any that would be produced by a similar practice in rendering the conversation of a French or a German novel of modern life. Here is a specimen of Miss Hapgood's method—a master is speaking to his servant: " 'Fool',— said I to him,—'what art thou grinning about? When thou didst open the door, the dog probably took and sneaked out into the anteroom. But thou, gaper, didst notice nothing, because thou art eternally asleep. Can it be that thou thinkest I am drunk?' " The "took and sneaked out" here is not a lapse into vulgarism: it is a literal translation of the Russian which has, in this case,

the same idiom that we have; but it is misplaced
here nevertheless—the narrator does not talk like a
peasant, and it is, besides, quite incongruous in a
passage which suggests an historical novel set somewhere in the seventeenth century—a suggestion itself
incongruous with Turgenev's contemporary subject.
The story from which this speech is taken, *The Dog,* is,
however, a formidable example of the difficulties of
translating Turgenev. The narrator is a small landowner, a bachelor, who has formerly served in the
hussars, and his way of expressing himself is idio-
syncratic and racy. Tolstoy would have picked up his
vein and would have made him talk more fluently and
freely; but Turgenev has made of his colloquialisms, his
droll turns, his stock sayings, his terseness, a medium
that characterizes him but that is also a literary exploit, a
textured and tight work of art: "What an astonishing
language!" wrote Chekhov, who particularly admired
this story. But what aroused the admiration of Chekhov
will often leave the foreigner blank and set traps for the
foreign translator. Mrs. Garnett, in the matter of dialogue, takes the opposite line from Miss Hapgood. She
makes the characters talk like well-educated and well-
bred English people—with results, if not equally queer,
at least rather unlike the original. Bazarov in *Fathers and
Sons* sounds more gentlemanly than Turgenev quite
means him to be: he seems to have come from English
Cambridge rather than from the Petersburg medical
school. Yet one has to strike some kind of tone which is
recognizable—Miss Hapgood's is not—as natural
human speech, and Constance Garnett's "great swells"
and "splendid fellows" and "queer fishes" and "comical
old chaps," though they do not seem right if one knows
the original, are certainly defensible in versions intended
for English readers.

There is no question, then, that Turgenev is more

difficult to turn into English than any other of the Russian prose classics—with the possible exception of Gogol, whose grotesquerie, however, is laid on so thick that it cannot help but carry through into a version in a different language.

But, even allowing for this, the performances of these two ladies are extremely unsatisfactory. They seem both to have worked rather rapidly and to have done very little checking. Constance Garnett perhaps knew Russian somewhat better than Miss Hapgood, but they both make many mistakes so obvious and rudimentary that they betray an astonishing negligence on the part of two accomplished women who were certainly not hacks. We do owe Mrs. Garnett a debt for making so much Russian literature available, but she translated many texts so fast that none of her versions is very dependable. In a desultory examination of these two English versions, I have, for example, noted two passages in which Miss Hapgood, and one in which Mrs. Garnett, have carelessly dropped out negatives, and thus made the author appear to have written the opposite of what he intended. Miss Hapgood makes the strange mistake of transforming into "a bitch" the male puppy of *The Dog,* though it is given a masculine name and referred to by masculine pronouns and masculine verbs throughout; and in *A Tour in the Forest,* with a verb in the neuter impersonal form, she supposes that разгулялась means "I've been on a spree," instead of "it [the weather] has been clearing up." Mrs. Garnett, in *Fathers and Sons,* mistakes дворец, *palace,* for дворецкий, *butler.* It is evident that neither has taken the precaution, indispensable for the foreign translator, of reading her version to a Russian who is watching the Russian text.

Since many of the translations of Turgenev into French were supervised by Turgenev and Mérimée and some of them actually made by them, one might

expect them to be more reliable. When I looked up
Potugin's speeches in an anonymous French version of
Smoke, which has a foreword by Mérimée and which I
assumed to be one of those that Turgenev and he had
passed, I found something stripped and dry, in which, to
be sure, no reference had ever been left in doubt—
the text had all been rewritten so that nothing could
puzzle the reader or blur his impression of anything;
but hardly a trace was left of Turgenev's rich descriptions or his idiomatic style. The explanation of this is to
be found in Mérimée's letters. He had, on first reading
Smoke, expressed to Turgenev misgivings as to whether
the book would be acceptable to the French. They would
not understand its problems; they would fail to be
interested in the opening: the soirée of émigré Russians
chattering about their leader Gubaryov. Better begin, he
says, with the scene in which the hero Litvinov receives
from his old love Irina the unexpected bunch of helio-
trope. This, he thought, would establish the sex interest
and lead the French reader on. Mérimée had thought at
first of translating the novel himself, but he had to give
up this project, and relinquished it to a Prince Golitsyn
who, Turgenev informed him, did not know Russian
and who, as Mérimée later informed Turgenev, did
not have any grasp of French grammar. The Prince
turned out also to be a prude who tried to expurgate the
principle love scene and to omit any mention of those
immoral characters doing business at Baden-Baden
whom Turgenev calls Mademoiselle Zizi and Mademoiselle Zozo. He wanted to change the title to "La Société
Russe Contemporaine." "I have just run through his
translation," Mérimée writes Turgenev. "It is extremely
free, very much, and too much abridged, even for me
who have often reproached you with your excessive use
of adjectives and your putting too many ideas and
images into a single sentence." Mérimée did his best for

Golitsyn's version, but it is hardly the book Turgenev wrote: it is no longer a brilliant chapter in the social history of Russia; it is an adaptation, a love story, designed to entertain the French. The translations of his stories into French which were made by Turgenev himself are curious: in purging them of his rich language and removing unfamiliar allusions, he virtually produced new and somewhat different stories.

But the problems of translating Turgenev are to a great extent the problems of translating poetry. Here is a description of a starry night—from Section XX of *The Torrents of Spring*—which shows him at his best in this vein:

Уже совсем «вызвездило,» когда он вышел на крыльцо. И сколько—ж их высыпало, этих звезд, больших, малых, жёлтых, красных, синих, белых! Все они так и рдели, так и роились, наперерыв играя лучами. Луны не было на небе, но и без нее каждый предмет четко виднелся в полусветлом, безтенном сумраке. Санин прошел улицу до конца ...

And here are two English translations of it—the first by Constance Garnett, the second by Ivy and Tatyana Litvinov in *Three Short Novels* by Turgenev (published in Moscow):

"It was bright starlight when he came out on the steps. What multitudes of stars, big and little, yellow, red, blue and white, were scattered over the sky! They seemed all flashing, swarming, twinkling unceasingly. There was no moon in the sky, but without it every object could be clearly discerned in the half-clear shadowless twilight. Sanin walked down the street to the end."

"All the stars were out when he stepped on to the porch. And oh, the innumerable hosts—great, small,

yellow, red, blue, white! All of them glowed and shim-
mered, twinkling incessantly. There was no moon, but
even without a moon every object stood out distinctly in
the thin, shadowless dusk. Sanin walked to the end of
the street."

Now, one of the most important words in the third
sentence above is наперерыв, *vying with one another*.
The так и рдели, так и роились suggests a bright dot-
ting of stars, and the наперерыв makes them twinkle.
But both these translators have mistaken this word
for the somewhat similar-looking непрерыв, which
means *unceasing* and which is quite inappropriate here.
Miss Hapgood has here got it right:

"The sky was studded with stars when he emerged
on the steps. . . . They were all fairly glowing and
swarming, vying with one another in darting their rays."
Miss Hapgood has too many present participles, but
Mrs. Garnett is even clumsier: she writes "unceasingly"
after three other -*ing*'s, and she has twice used "the
sky" in an awkward way at the end of a sentence or
clause, where Turgenev has used it but once. In the
sentence that follows about the moon, which is designed
to give a different effect, the sound and the placing of
четко are important, and the Litvinovs, with their
"stood out distinctly," have handled this somewhat
better than Mrs. Garnett with her "could be clearly
discerned."

Here is an even more difficult passage, already
spoken of above, from Section XXIV of the same story
—a tour de force of onomatopoeia.

Mrs. Garnett and the Litvinovs render this respectively as follows:

"Gemma was sitting on a garden-seat near the path,
she was sorting a big basket full of cherries, picking
out the ripest, and putting them in a dish. The sun was
low—it was seven o'clock in the evening—and there was

more purple than gold in the full slanting light with which it flooded the whole of Signora Roselli's little garden. From time to time, faintly audible, and as it were deliberately, the leaves rustled, and belated bees buzzed abruptly as they flew from one flower to the next, and somewhere a dove was cooing a never-changing unceasing note."

"Gemma was seated on a bench beside the path, selecting the ripest cherries from a great basket and putting them on a plate. The sun was low—it was nearly seven—and there was more crimson than gold in the broad slanting rays it flung all over Madame Roselli's little garden. Every now and then the leaves whispered, gently and almost inaudibly, belated bees flew from blossom to blossom with staccato buzzes, and a turtle-dove cooed monotonously and indefatigably."

Turgenev's description of the leaves and the bees is full of sighing and buzzing: it contains almost every sibilant in the much-sibilating Russian language, is all a play of з's, с's, ч's, ш's and ц's. But these translators have been led by the inevitability of rendering запоздалые *belated* and its juxtaposition with *bees* into alliterating on *b,* a sound quite irrelevant to the subject, which does not once occur in the Russian till Turgenev gets to the dove —for whose monotonous sobbing he finds other combinations. It will be noted that, in dealing with the dove, Mrs. Garnett has resorted to her irritating strings of participles; and, after all, неутомимо does not really mean "unceasing." Here again Isabel Hapgood, though not brilliant, is more faithful to the Russian.

We get, however, even further from the original in a French translation I have found in a book called *Pages Choisies des Grands Écrivains: "Le soleil déclinait, il y avait plus de pourpre que d'or dans les rayons obliques qu'il dardait sur le jardin. Parfois, les feuilles murmuraient doucement. Quelques abeilles attardées bourdonnaient de fleur en fleur. Une tourterelle invisible roucoulait inlassablement.''*

Here an elaborate sentence of twenty-seven words has been reduced to three short sentences which together contain eighteen and which leave out most of the detail.

But it would take, after all, a master to reproduce the effects of Turgenev; and in view of all these literary inadequacies, broken meanings from linguistic pitfalls and international incomprehensions, it inspires a kind of awe to realize that Ivan Sergeyevich has been recognized throughout the West as a virtuoso of literary form and an authority on human behavior, whose honesty and poetry and pathos—if not entirely his humor—have come through from even his clumsiest translators. He would have for us today much more interest as a social critic of Russia than he did for his Western contemporaries. Would there be a real public for a new translation? Macmillan six years ago began issuing the whole of Turgenev in the Constance Garnett translations, but since the other volumes have not followed, these cannot have found a very large market. The best possible thing, no doubt, would be an omnibus edition in three or four volumes, containing the most accurate available translations, supplemented by corrected Garnett, with the most important gaps filled in, and a selection of the most interesting letters—the kind of thing the French Pléiade Series has been doing with such distinction. Certainly the new translations of *First Love* and *Rudin* by, respectively, Sir Isaiah Berlin and Mr. Alec Brown, recently published by Hamish Hamilton in one volume of his Novel Library, would be eligible for such a collection.

SUKHOVO-KOBYLIN:
«Кто убил француженку?»

The plays of the nineteenth-century Russian dramatist Alexander Sukhovo-Kobylin are one of the curiosities of literature, and the story of his life is even stranger. This life and his writings together, though they are hardly known outside Russia, have for nearly a hundred years supplied the Russians with a subject for speculation and argument.

Let us first explain the personal problem. Alexander Vasilevich Sukhovo-Kobylin belonged to an extremely old and very ancestor-proud Moscow family who boasted of having distinguished themselves under Ivan the Terrible. He was at once a dashing social figure and an unusually cultivated man, who had studied at the University of Moscow, where he won a gold medal, and afterwards pursued his favorite subject, philosophy, at Berlin and Heidelberg. On a visit to Paris, he made, in a restaurant, the acquaintance of a French girl, a Mlle Louise Simon-Dimanche, who was not much older than twenty, by simply sitting down at the table where she was dining with an older woman and engaging her in conversation. When he returned to Russia, he induced her to follow him, and he set her up first in a millinery shop, then in a wine shop, and then in a shop that sold flour and treacle produced on one of his family estates. But she had

no talent for trade, and none of these businesses pros-
pered. Her lover, however, kept her in style, and she was
liked and accepted by his mother and sister, though she
could not be received socially, and for Alexander to
marry her was out of the question. She lived for eight
years in Moscow, but she made very few friends there,
and eventually Alexander began paying court to a
cleverer woman, Nadezhda Ivanovna Naryshkina, who,
though said not to have been a beauty, "was fascinating
by reason of her special kind of grace, her witty conversation, and by that assurance and even audacity which
were characteristic of the ladies called 'lionesses.'" She
"fell passionately in love with Kobylin," (I am quoting
the account by Leonid Grossman, in his book on
Sukhovo-Kobylin.)

On the ninth of November, 1850, the body of Alexander's French mistress was found in a snowdrift near a
cemetery just outside Moscow. She was dressed as if to
go out for the evening. Her throat had been deeply cut,
the carotid arteries severed, and three of her ribs broken.
That a struggle had taken place was shown by a black
eye and bruises and scars on one of her arms from the
shoulder to the elbow. Nearby there were the tracks of a
sleigh and the prints of horses' hoofs. No weapons were
found. The body had evidently been brought from
somewhere else.

Four serfs—two men and two women—who had
waited on Mlle Dimanche at the expense of Alexander
(it is such a nuisance that two of the chief actors should
have hyphenated names that I am going henceforth to
abridge them) confessed to having murdered the French
woman on account of her harsh treatment of them and
her niggardliness in paying their wages. They said that
they had attacked her when they found her asleep in bed
and had tried to smother her with a pillow, then beaten
her with their fists and a flatiron, and cut her throat with

a knife; they had dressed her and left her in the snow. But this story did not seem very plausible. Why should they have gone to the trouble of decking her out in all her finery?—she was found with rings, earrings and a brooch. It was true that before the liberation of the serfs by Alexander II domestic servants did sometimes kill their masters: Dostoevsky's father was murdered by his, and Tolstoy could never be sure that his own father had not been poisoned. But Mlle Dimanche had announced that she was going back to France, and could they really, on account of hard usage, have hated her enough to kill her? They, however, were condemned to from sixty to ninety lashes and from fifteen to twenty years at hard labor or factory work. The men were also sentenced to be branded.

But it now began to appear that the confessions had been extorted—Alexander is supposed to have paid for them—by dint of bribery and torture, and by causing to be invented the answers to questions which had been put by the investigators but had elicited quite different answers. The servants were examined again, and they now told another story, which left Kobylin under heavy suspicion of having committed the crime himself. The new version of the murder was that Mlle Dimanche, in a jealous rage, had descended on Kobylin when he was with Naryshkina, that he had cut her throat with a candlestick—presumably one of the old-fashioned kind that has a spike to stick the candle on—and had the servants take the body away and dump it in the snow. The serfs were released, and it was stipulated that they were not to be returned to Kobylin. Alexander was put in jail for six months. The proceedings, from the time of the murder, dragged on for seven years. Naryshkina got out of Russia and lived for the rest of her life in France, where she married Alexandre Dumas *fils*. Kobylin eventually went to Paris, too, and renewed his friendly relations with her. She had already had an illegitimate daughter by him, who lived with her and Dumas. She and Kobylin named this daughter after Louise Dimanche. Kobylin dropped out of society, and, on returning to Russia, lived much on his country estates and continued to study philosophy. His family were, however, uncomfortable so long as he was under suspicion and at last appealed to the Empress, who managed to have him cleared. If it had not been for this special intervention, he said, he would probably have ended in Siberia. He devoted himself to study and made a translation of Hegel, which was lost when his country house burned down. He died in March, 1903, in a villa on the French Riviera.

In 1928, Leonid Grossman, well-known as a writer on Dostoevsky, published *The Crime of Sukhovo-Kobylin,* the result of what I take to have been the first thorough research into the documents of the case and the history of the Sukhovo-Kobylin family. Grossman attempted to show that the murder was unquestionably committed by Kobylin. His case is derived, however, from evidence which is not necessarily conclusive. He is able to show that on his mother's side Kobylin had a bad heredity. An ancestor, Ivan Dmitrievich, who had had with his brother an iron foundry on his property, is reported by a friend of the family to have treated his serfs with much harshness and to have been in the habit, if he wanted more land, of boldly moving in on his neighbors'. Against his encroachments they had no redress, since he had been able to buy all the officials to whom they could have had recourse. A descendant of his—inconsistently described by Mr. Grossman first as Alexander's mother's cousin but later as her father—came to be known as "the Nero of the Ardatovsky district." He

had a bandmaster of his household put to death when
the man had been sent a note by one of his actress
mistresses, and he was known for his "uncontrolled
propensity to outbursts of cruel anger." On one occasion, when he had come to believe that the steward of his
estate had been cheating him, he punished him in a
hideous way. The man, who had "been living very
decently" and "was creating for himself a respectable
situation," had made a point of sending his son to
school in Moscow. "The boy had just come home on
vacation, and he was made a victim of Ivan
Dmitrievich, who subjected him to a very cruel
lashing in the presence of his parents" because the
master knew "that they adored him, and that the
suffering thus imposed on them was more painful than
any punishment which he might have contrived for
themselves." The mother of Alexander loved poetry and
novels—"especially tragedy." She liked to be fashion-
ably dressed, says one of her daughters, "danced remarkably well, loved the theatre, and never missed a chance
to dance or engage a box." As a young girl, she had liked
to ride and to hunt with a rifle; in her old age, she
smoked cigars and read Schelling in French translation.
She intimidated her servants by cuffing them. In all this
history of the Sukhovo-Kobylin family one is made
aware in what seems to us a rather shocking way of the
discrepancy between the barbaric life that these
landowners were able to lead at the same time that they
were cultivating, as Alexander and his mother did, the
flowers of Western thought and art.

   When a distinguished young professor, under whom
Alexander had sat at the Moscow University, was
brought into the Sukhovo-Kobylin household as a
tutor for his sister and he and the sister fell in love, the
snobbish Sukhovo-Kobylins regarded the infatuation

as an insolent threat by the tutor, and Alexander, in one of his rages, declared he would kill the young man if the matter went any further. The people who knew Alexander, according to Mr. Grossman, had admired him but not much liked him, and they believed he had murdered his mistress. Some bloodstains were found on the wall of his apartment, and there were spatterings of blood on the back stairs, which had been imperfectly rubbed away, and Kobylin could not satisfactorily explain these on the grounds that an aunt, who had lived in the rooms, had once applied leeches to her daughters; that his valet had had a nosebleed; and that the cooks had been killing poultry. His alibi at the time of the murder—he claimed to have been elsewhere at a party —seemed to depend on unsatisfactory evidence. Then Mlle Dimanche's cook deposed that to force him to confess to the crime he had been imprisoned in a "secret room," where he suffered "inhuman tortures," administered by the police—horrible beatings and hangings on a hook—at the same time that he was deprived of anything to drink and given nothing to eat but salt herring.

In 1936, however, another writer named Grossman— in this case Viktor—published a book called *The Case of Sukhovo-Kobylin,* in which he tried to refute the other Grossman. He prints side by side the two versions of the murder, and neither of them is convincing. If Kobylin was the culprit, why was it necessary for him to struggle with his mistress so brutally and to cut her throat with a candlestick? Can one really cut a throat with a candlestick? And why did he have Louise's picture hanging over his bed all the rest of his life and visit her grave every year. Leonid Grossman believes that, his theatrical instincts being highly developed, his grief was all acting. But why did he and Naryshkina

name their illegitimate daughter Louise Dimanche?
Leonid Grossman calls attention to Kobylin's looking
forward longingly to the time "when the Lord God
will allow my sinful soul to find peace in my blessed
penitence [любезное покаяние]." "Penitence for
what?" asks Grossman. But not even this is definite
evidence, for Kobylin may be speaking simply of his
wasted years of dissipation. One cannot tell what
actually happened. It is one of those Russian puzzles
that never get properly solved. The Russians, with their
vagueness about actual events and their ready imagina-
tions, perhaps prefer to have them like this. Is it true
that the Tsar Alexander I had not died when he was
supposed to have died but arranged for himself a false
funeral and stole away to the East, where he lived as a
holy man for more than a quarter of a century and was
twice recognized by people who knew him? When,
sometime in the late eighties, Alexander's tomb was
opened, it is said to have been found empty, and the
Communists, when they opened it later, reported that it
contained only a bar of lead. Had the body, as some
have said, been secretly moved in the meantime by the
order of Alexander II? Is it true that the Grand Duchess
Anastasia escaped from the massacre of the Royal Family and, after many ordeals and investigations, is still alive
in Virginia? This last legend does not seem probable,
but many Russians have been ready to believe it.

To return to the case of Kobylin: His plays, two of
which were censored by the Tsar, were never, though a
trilogy, performed in sequence until 1901, when Kobylin
was eighty-three; but the great director Meyerhold produced them in 1917 and 1922, and these books record
three other performances, the latest in 1964. They have
been reprinted at least twice in the Soviet Union, most
recently in 1969. In this same year, a new book, *The Fate*

of Sukhovo-Kobylin, by Isador Kleiner, appeared, and one gathers from the line it takes that the continued popularity of Kobylin as a dramatist has prompted the Soviet Union to justify him in more or less "Marxist-Leninist" terms. The murder is rather brushed aside, and a brief is made out for Kobylin as a somewhat tragic case of a landowner caught between the "contradictions" of belonging to the feudal system yet foreseeing the future of a better Russia and being capable of criticizing his own situation. Now, it is true, as we learn from Leonid Grossman, that Kobylin did prophesy the economic ruin of the landed gentry as a result of Alexander II's reforms, such as the emancipation of the serfs. But he calls Alexander "senseless," and the articles he wrote were all in defense of the old regime, upholding its privileges and rights. "He did not love or trust the Russian people," said one of Grossman's informants. "He regarded the Slavs as an inferior race, who needed to be kept under tutelage."

And now, knowing Alexander Vasilevich's history, let us examine the sequence of plays, on subjects so very ungentlemanly and almost entirely lacking in refinement, by this elegant and fastidious gentleman. His three dramas deal more or less with the same characters and have a certain disjointed continuity. When Kobylin published them together in a volume in 1869, at a time when the first play was already a success but the performance of the two others was still forbidden, he called them *Pictures of the Past,* presumably in order to forestall the possibility of their being taken as criticisms of the present. The first of these, *Krechinsky's Wedding,* was written to pass the time during the six months when Kobylin was in prison. He had always admired the French theater, and this first piece is a "well-

made" play on the model of those of Scribe. But in the
trilogy as a whole, the influence of Gogol predominates
—the Gogol of *The Inspector General*. Krechinsky is a
well-born rascal, who has squandered his inheritance
and is hoping to marry for her property the daughter
of the respectable landowning Muromsky family. He
sustains the pretense of still being well-to-do, and he
staves his creditors off by tricking the girl—Lidochka—
into lending him a diamond solitaire, which he offers to
a pawnbroker at its actual value and for which at the
last moment he exchanges a paste substitute. He is
exposed as a swindler and impostor, and one expects
a conventional ending, with the engagement of the
unwise Lidochka to a decent young man from the
country who is congenial to her landlord father. But the
girl remains loyal to Krechinsky and saves him from
prosecution. She appeases the indignant pawnbroker
by turning over to him the genuine diamond which he
thought he was buying from Krechinsky.

At the beginning of the second play, *The Case,* the
decent young man, Nelkin, comes back from five years
in the West and finds the family distraught by a new
situation. Krechinsky is trying to blackmail the Muromskys by coöperating with the local authorities, who are
threatening to circulate a rumor that the daughter
herself was implicated in the swindle of the diamond,
that she has been seduced by Krechinsky, and that she
has even had a child by him. He does not let his own
hand appear but asserts that the scheme is a plot of the
officials and advises the father to buy them off. This
drives the old gentleman frantic: he has fought at Boro-
dino with Suvorov and his career has been in every way
honorable; he will not allow any doubt to be cast upon
his daughter's honor. He is, however, eventually bullied
into raising the sum demanded—though this violates his

sense of his dignity—to meet the demands of the bureau-crats, who range from corrupt *ronds de cuir,* eager to rake in some money, to a perfunctory privy councillor—a prince who is suffering from hemorrhoids, the result of eating too many strawberries. A high functionary takes the money while pretending to reject it with scorn and denouncing the old gentleman for attempting to bribe him. The father, in an outburst of indignation, says, "My blood inside me is speaking, and blood doesn't ask what it can say and what it mustn't. . . . What are they torturing me for, what for? For five years I've been enduring sufferings which there are no human words to describe!" But nothing he can say or do makes any impression on the cold-blooded bureaucrats, and he suddenly dies of a stroke caused by shock and chagrin. His peasant steward has tried to advise him to resign himself and to leave it all to God, Who will sometimes see that justice is done, but old Murom-sky will not accept resignation. Nelkin fiercely swears vengeance on Muromsky's persecutors but confesses his own impotence and hopelessness. He is last seen kissing Lidochka's hand and vowing eternal love, but we feel that in spite of what has happened she has still not entirely been purged of her fatal *tendresse* for Krechinsky. The cynicism of Kobylin is thorough-going. Leonid Grossman calls these unpleasant come-dies "tragedies without catharsis."

In the last play, *The Death of Tarelkin,* this cynicism is intensified by the complete elimination of all the honest people—who have always been made very stupid—and the evocation of a cloud of corruption that becomes quite suffocating. One of the lesser conspira-tors, Tarelkin, has been cheated by his superior of his share of the money of the bribe, and he contrives a device for retaliating. He gets possession of some compromising papers with which he can blackmail this superior, and in order to evade his master and the creditors who are making his own life miserable he steals the card of identity of a next-door neighbor who has just died and pretends that it is he himself who has died. He removes his toupee and false teeth and impersonates the other man. He puts a dummy in a coffin in his house and creates the illusion of a decomposing corpse by producing a stench with dead fish. The dummy is buried with ceremony, but Tarelkin's boss, who is trying to retrieve the damaging stolen papers, appears in disguise as a creditor and claims the right to search the dead man's effects. He finds the toupee and teeth in a drawer, and at once has Tarelkin arrested as an impostor. Tarelkin is reduced to helplessness by being tied up, imprisoned and entirely deprived of water—an ordeal which, Leonid Grossman points out, is similar to those inflicted to obtain a confession from Louise Dimanche's cook—and he gives up the compromising papers. He is accused of being a wizard or werewolf who can change his shape at will, a vampire who sucks people's blood, and this motif is made by Kobylin a symbol for the practices of the bureaucrats: "I am now of the opinion," says one of the scoundrelly characters, "that our whole country is a great pack of wolves, snakes and hares, which have suddenly been turned into people, and I've come to suspect everybody, and so we have to go on the principle that everyone is to be arrested." At the end of the play, Tarelkin, exposed and denounced as a monster, robbed of his only weapon, again assumes the disguise and the identity of the neighbor he has been impersonating and, turning at the end of the play to the audience, begs someone to give him a job as manager of an estate: he knows all about agriculture and, as for his honesty, "you've seen yourselves how I've suffered for the truth!" He can be reached in care of his former boss. He bows and runs out, and the gloating official shouts after him, "I'm telling you, go to Hell. They won't refuse you there—they'll take you in!"

These plays grow continually more turbid, and something like a real stink arises from them, as if set off by the putrefying fish in the opening scene of *Tarelkin*. I do not know anything in literature quite like them. The nearest examples I can think of are the Ben Jonson of *The Alchemist* and the Henri Becque of *Les Corbeaux*. But the grotesquerie of the incidents, the transformations of the characters (inspired by the transformations of a lightning-change artist in Paris by whom Kobylin had been much impressed) have lent themselves, as photographs show, to such modern productions as Meyerhold's, which exploit their possibilities for fantasy. One of the characters, Rasplyuev, who first appears, in *Krechinsky's Wedding,* as a disreputable rascal but then turns out in the following play to have become a district police inspector, is a kind of Falstaffian clown, who seems to have been a favorite in Russia.

Now, what light is thrown by these plays on the innocence or guilt of Kobylin? There seem certainly to be echoes of the murder: the author's preoccupation with death, the hopelessness of contending with imperturbable crooked officials. One can interpret them in either of two ways: one can assume that they constitute the blast of an honest and much wronged man, like the outburst of old Muromsky, giving vent to an accumulating resentment—was the persecution of Kobylin also an attempt to extort blackmail money from a rich man under suspicion?—or one can think that their gruesomeness and evil odor are due to the bad memories and bad conscience of Kobylin, the results of a horrible act.

This trilogy had never been translated until recently: *The Trilogy of Alexander Sukhovo-Kobylin,* by Mr. Harold B. Segal, associate professor of Slavic Literatures at Columbia University. I know that a Russian woman who had previously been asked to translate these plays refused, on the ground that they were untranslatable. She was right: they are written in a language which, besides being very colloquial, is dense with humorous invention of a special grotesque kind. The problem is somewhat similar to that which would be presented by an attempt to transfer into another language the comic quips and turns of phrase of an Elizabethan or Jacobean dramatist. Mr. Segel, however, has plunged right in, regardless of these literary fantasies—which was probably the only way, if one undertook the task at all. He is himself not particularly sensitive to style, as is shown in his introduction, where he varies from such yesterday's slang as "and then some" to today's official jargon, such as "the Muromskys arrive to finalize plans for the wedding." For the language of the characters he sometimes resorts to the former of these ("Some find!" "Some case!"), sometimes to Yiddish ("With a dagger yet!"). As for "I prefer it better," that is not English at all. The shrinking and vanishing of the honorifics, so important to the Russian bureaucracy, is inevitable in an English version. But Mr. Segel's translation and introduction are valuable in making it possible for the reader of English to form some idea of these very odd plays and the story of their author, both of which convey so much of that old barbaric Russia that still lives in our own day. One wonders whether the recent popularity of Kobylin may not be mainly due to the conscienceless stupidity of his bureaucrats.

March 18, 1971

NOTES ON TOLSTOY

An English translation has now been published of
Henri Troyat's *Tolstoy*. This version by Nancy
Amphoux seems competent, but it is smoother in the
French, which makes the conflicts and vicissitudes of
the tumultuous Tolstoys run off at a very rapid pace—
although the French version, as a piece of bookmaking,
is of a clumsiness quite foreign to the French tradition.
One would have expected a paperbound two volumes
like Troyat's biography of Pushkin, but what we get
is a hardbound monstrosity, six by almost nine inches
and almost three inches thick, which is nearly impossible to handle without a reading rack.

This huge volume is introduced on the jacket as
follows in a blurb signed Jean Bassan: "Tolstoy and
Troyat suggest an easy parallel: two names that begin
with T, two Russians at least in origin [Troyat is actually Armenian], two stout and solid fellows (*deux
gaillards solides et larges*), two mountains of blackened
paper, two authors of *romans-fleuves,* of historical novels, two great novelists of the Russian land, the same
classical predisposition for simplicity and work well
done. All this goes without saying." The writer then
goes on to point out certain differences, among them
that Tolstoy was born in 1828, whereas Troyat was not

born till 1911. This idiotic ballyhoo should not, however, prejudice one against M. Troyat's book, which is, so far as I know, the best presentation of Tolstoy's whole career that is at present available in English. Aylmer Maude's *The Life of Tolstoy* is still an indispensable work—I am sorry to see that it no longer appears in the list of the World's Classics—because Maude was one of Tolstoy's secretaries as well as a trusted translator, and is able to give a first-hand account of Tolstoy's domestic relations and of the difficulties caused by the interference of Chertkov, the old man's tyrannical disciple.

What M. Troyat has put together is a record of Tolstoy's life from the copious letters, diaries and memoirs of Lyov Nikolaevich himself, his wife, his children and his friends. Has ever an eminent writer been so documented by written evidence? The number of members of the family who kept diaries seems from our point of view incredible. One of the daughters, Tanya, started hers at twelve. The conflict between Tolstoy and his wife over Chertkov, against whom she developed—not, it would seem, without cause—a mania of jealousy, over the right to publish her husband's writings, on which she was partly dependent for the income to support the family, and over the possession of his later diaries, in which she felt she had been maligned—all this has been pieced together in a depressing but absorbing narrative.

The comic aspects of Lyov Nikolaevich's life from the moment of his religious conversion are too obvious and too well known to need to be described here at length. While preaching chastity, poverty and the inescapable obligation to share the manual labor of the muzhik, he continued to give his wife pregnancies, most of them resulting in children, up through the age of seventy; to live comfortably among his family, with a secretary and a doctor in attendance; and although he did learn to make shoes and sometimes worked in the fields, to occupy himself chiefly with the production, subject to Chertkov's censorship, of his innumerable religious tracts.

In all this, despite his profession of humility, there was certainly a fair amount of vanity. "Once for all [he had written at twenty-five] I must accustom myself to the idea that I am an exceptional being, one who is ahead of his period, and who is by temperament absurd, unsociable and always dissatisfied. . . . I have been lying to myself in imagining that I have friends, that there were people who understood me. A mistake! I have never met a single man who was morally as good as I am, who has always in every situation been drawn, as I have been, to the good. Who, like me, is always ready to sacrifice everything for this ideal. It is on this account that I find no society in which I feel at home." He was later to speak much of his imperfections, but, even discounting the stock reproaches that women make to their husbands, it is possible to sympathize with the Countess, Sofia Andreevna, when she complains of Tolstoy's "vanity, his desire for glory, the need to have himself talked about as much as possible." "He unloads everything on me [she writes in her diary], everything without exception: the children, the management of the properties, his relations with people, his business affairs, the household, the publishers. He scorns me for taking care of all that, he shuts himself up in his egoism and constantly criticizes me. And what does he do himself? He goes for walks, he rides, writes a little, does whatever he pleases, does nothing whatever for the family and enjoys the profits of everything:

of his daughter's help, of his comfort, of the adulation that is squandered on him, of my submission to him and the trouble I take for him. And the glory, this insatiable thirst for glory to which he has sacrificed everything and continues to sacrifice everything!"

In all this, on the part of Tolstoy, there was evidently a certain perversity. He liked to make people uncomfortable by reminding them at the dinner table that not everyone could enjoy these luxuries. "Why," he demanded in the course of one of their parlor games, "must Ustyusha, Alyona, Peter, etc. [the servants] cook, prepare things, sweep, clear away, serve, while the gentlemen eat, stuff themselves, go to the water closet and eat again?" One of the relatives he liked best and who interested him most was a cousin, Alexandrina Tolstoya, who was a maid of honor to one of the grand duchesses. When he made his discovery, by revelation, of what he regarded as the true Christianity, he harangued her insultingly for her Orthodox faith: "Whether rightly or wrongly, I consider your faith as a work of the Devil, uniquely conceived to deprive humanity of the salvation promised by Christ." He recalled this letter after sending it, but wrote another in a not very different vein: "I understand that any woman can desire her salvation, but then, if she is a true Christian, she will begin by dissociating herself from the Court, from the world; she will go to matins, she will fast, she will save herself as best she can. How has a courtier's situation come to be a diploma of theology? It is comic in the highest degree!" It is as if he had discovered only late in life that the church depends on the state and the state on the police and the army, and that hence all run counter to the teachings of Jesus; and as if he were reprobating other people for not having always known and acted on this.

Is it Tolstoy's notion that Alexandrina, rather remarkably intelligent though she evidently was, would be ready to give up her social position and the Orthodox ritual she had been practicing all her life for the extremely subversive doctrines of her now fanatical cousin? And how much of his gospel of asceticism and his gesture of stripping himself of his property may not have been due to the impulse to worry and exasperate his wife? When he was asked to give land to his peasants, he was able to protest that he was powerless, since everything now was in the name of the Countess. When people wrote him complaining that he was not living up to his principles, he would reply that he was sorry, that he was deeply embarrassed, but that he was fatally caught in the web of his family and other obligations.

At the time of the terrible famine of 1891–92, not far from the Tolstoy estate, he at first took the attitude that there were plenty of people who were ready to feed the starving out of pride in the name of benefactors and in order to prevent them from revolting; whereas the fundamentally important thing, for the purpose of combatting the famine, was not to give the people food, but "to love the hungry as well as the fed." And yet as the misery grew worse and more people were dying of hunger, he was unable to remain indifferent and, contrary to what he thought were his principles, he undertook to organize effective relief and in this he was aided by the Countess and his daughters. He fought for and financed the Doukhobors, who were then being persecuted for their refusal to serve in the army; and though he would not take part in political and social reforms, he was in general opposed to suppression by the government and insisted on the paramount importance of obeying one's individual conscience. He was perhaps a kind of Protestant at the same time that his aspirations to saintliness were quite those of a Russian holy man.

It is evidence of his great vitality, of his extraordinary insight into other personalities, and of his genuine if intermittent efforts toward nobility of moral character that he should have been able to command, to the end of his long life, so much reverence as well as admiration. All this M. Troyat has got into his book compactly and without much commentary. (It should be mentioned that a translation has only recently appeared of *The Last Year of Leo Tolstoy* by V. F. Bulgakov. Bulgakov was Tolstoy's last secretary, and he shows how, up to the agonies of the final moments, the family went on performing the familiar rituals of Russian life, the celebration of days sacred to the saint after whom the Count had been named, the amusements such as "post office" and chess, the enjoyment of music and the discussion of literature, and the entertainment of guests on a scale which to us seems quite staggering.)*

What follows are more or less detached notes for which these books provide a pretext.

In college I read translations of *The Kreutzer Sonata* and *Master and Man,* and although I was rather impressed by the latter, the absurdity of the former and

* Tolstoy's daughter Alexandra has published a pamphlet, *The Real Tolstoy* (Henry S. Evans, Morristown, New Jersey), protesting against Troyat's book. Most of her criticisms are matters of detail, which, however correct, are not particularly important or are matters of her own interpretation of the behavior of her father. After all, Tolstoy's inconsistencies are a matter of record on the part of a good many witnesses; and Troyat's general picture of Tolstoy does not seem to me, as it does to her, disparaging. Her only point that may have a certain importance is her assertion that her sister Maria informed her before her death that their mother, in order to correct the impression produced by Lyov Nikolaevich's account of her conduct, had concocted a retrospective diary designed to refute his complaints.

the bleakness of both discouraged me from further reading of Tolstoy. When, however, I was studying Russian after a trip to the Soviet Union, I sat down to *War and Peace*. I came to it under favorable circumstances. I was then living alone in the country in Connecticut beside the small Mianus River. I was buried in a fairly large forest with not another house in sight. I would begin to read or write after dinner and not go to bed till four in the morning. It was winter, and the only drive was covered with snow. I could imagine myself perfectly in the country house of the Bolkonskys, when the smooth and worldly official, Prince Kuragin, is coming to present his worthless son for the hand of the Princess Maria, whom he wants to marry for her money, and her father, the laconic old Prince, whose attitude toward the Kuragins is anything but cordial, makes his servant put back on the road, in order to obstruct their arrival, the snow that has just been removed in their honor.

I was surprised to find the book so amusing: the scene at the death of Pierre's father and the episode of debauchery with the bear. The atmosphere was anything but bleak. And the vitality of the characters was amazing. Tolstoy is perhaps—in a less caricatured way from those of either Dickens or Proust—the greatest mimic in fiction, and this is something that cannot be brought over in translation. Though I did not always know which syllable of a Russian word should be stressed and could not have read a page aloud correctly, the voices of the characters, in my winter solitude, seemed to come right out of the pages and to animate my little house: the dry brusquerie of the old Bolkonsky, compelling his son, Prince André, to acknowledge the failure of his marriage: *"Plokho delo, a?"* *"Chto plokho?"* *"Zhena!"* ("Bad business, eh?" "What is bad?" "Wife!"); the wheedling diplomacy of the old Kuragin, who tries to reassure the grasping elder princess by calling her "*Moya golubushka*" ("my dear little dove"); the girlish high spirits of Natasha, more or less transformed by Constance Garnett into a proper little English girl such as one finds in the drawings of Du Maurier, with her gay and rather infantile family. "*Smotrite na papà*" ("Look at papa"), cried Natasha for all the ballroom to hear . . . "(completely forgetting that she was dancing with a grown-up), bending her curly head to her knees and filling the whole room with her ringing laugh. . . . '*Batyushka-to nash! Orël!*' ('Our Father! An eagle!') exclaimed the nurse loudly from a doorway." And the invidious often comic contrast between the characters when they are speaking their formal French, and when they relapse into their good old blunt Russian. There is always the imputation of a kind of dishonesty of sophistication to the use by these Russians of French: it is only by resorting to French that Rostopchin, fleeing from Moscow in flames, is able to justify his behavior, even though he is only explaining it to himself. The cool tone of the comment on what the characters are doing is the tone of Tolstoy himself, of the personality of the author, who always remains aloof almost to the point of irony, the tone of the aristocrat, who, though not without admiration for certain of his imagined aristocrats and though proudly patriotic as far as the war with the French is concerned, is reluctant to admit any stake in anything that is going on. His enthusiasm for the peasant Karataev who appears toward the end of the book, is rather a giveaway of the comparative unreality of this all too wise and simple character.

The only possible objection to *War and Peace* has been made by Dmitri Mirsky: that it is something of an idealized idyll of the life of the old nobility, of the author's grandparents and parents, the mother whom he never knew, the father who died while he was still a child. The closer he comes to his own experience the more he is bound to be biased by the moral problems he is forced to confront.

(I recommend *War and Peace* to anyone learning Russian. The frequent conversations and correspondence in French afford an occasional relief; the vocabulary and style are not difficult; and since the novel is very long, the foreign reader will find, when he has finished it, that he has learned quite a lot of Russian.)

The carelessness of Tolstoy's style is a part of the aristocratic tone. He insists upon descriptive accuracy at any cost of clumsiness of language. This results in a piling-up of modifiers and a needless repetition of words that evidently made Turgenev shudder. So the nonchalant grammatical constructions of Proust— caught over, I suppose, from St. Simon—were taken to task, rather pettily, by Gide. Here is a phrase from *War and Peace* (II, 18), literally translated: "Repulsing the with surprised but dry eyes regarding her Natasha". . . ; and here is the arrival in the station of the ominous railroad train at the beginning of *Anna Karenina* (I, 17): "Actually, the locomotive gave a whistle from the distance. In a few minutes the platform shook, and puffing with the weighed-down by the frost steam, rolled past the locomotive, with the slowly and rhythmically bending and straightening-out shaft of the middle wheel and the saluting bundled-up frost-covered engineer; after the tender, always more slowly and more strongly shaking the platform, a wagon began to go by with baggage and a yelping dog; at last, vibrating to a stop, the passenger cars arrived."

That Tolstoy was not at all concerned about these constructions is shown in *Hajji Murad,* written very late, which is full of such sentences as the following: "On a cold November evening, Hajji Murad rode up late into the smoking with fragrant dung-straw brick smoke ["*kizyachuyin*"] Chechen unpacified village Machket." In English we should take care of many of these modifiers by making them into relative clauses; this overdependence on participles seems to be a weakness of the Slavic languages. Yet such are the pace and suspense of the stories that Tolstoy is telling that these clotted phrases do not impede them.

I do not know how much the foreign reader of Tolstoy is aware, in *Anna Karenina,* of the issue that Tolstoy is raising between the life of the Karenins and Vronskys in St. Petersburg, and that of Levin and Kitty in the country outside Moscow. For young people, especially young women, the shade of contempt that the author feels toward the people of Petersburg may not be perceptible at all. The affair of Anna and Vronsky may seem simply a romantic though tragic love story. Yet it is plain that Anna's creator does not take a lenient view of Anna, so beautiful but so immoral: she is damned by the Biblical epigraph; and Vronsky is made little short of ridiculous. Through a reckless desire to excel, he has broken the back of his mare in the races, as he is later to do with Anna; he bungles an attempt at suicide in which it seems evident that he has only half wanted to succeed; and, after Anna's effective self-destruction, he goes off in the train with nothing worse than a toothache, to the war against the Turks, of which Tolstoy did not approve. A stern moral judgment is half-hidden in this partly seductive story.

Childhood, Adolescence, and *Youth,* all written when

Tolstoy was in his twenties, are in the main autobiographical, but are mixed with elements of fiction. They are remarkable and very interesting but in certain ways rather unsympathetic. Yet what is unsympathetic is due to Tolstoy's instinct for telling the truth about himself. His characteristic traits are seen to have emerged very early. His reaction to being made to speak French—bound up with his reaction against mere elegance—when he is reprimanded by his sister's governess for speaking Russian instead of French, makes him want to chatter in Russian; and he loathes a later French tutor, who disapproved of him and punished him severely. "In our country, the people of a certain class [he writes in *Youth*], who love in a *beautiful* way, not only talk to other people about their love, but invariably, talk about it in French. It sounds strange and absurd to say so, but I am sure that there have been many people of a certain society, especially the women, whose love for their friends, their husbands, their children would be quite annihilated if they were forbidden to talk about them in French." This prejudice against the French was probably reinforced later as a result of the Crimean War, in which Tolstoy as a young man took part, when the Russians were beaten by the French and the English.

A certain exhibitionism in Tolstoy's religious attitude is illustrated thus early in his story of his first confession, which has taken place in the narrator's home, but which he feels obliged to supplement when, after lying in bed at night and remembering a sin which he has failed to acknowledge, he gets up early and goes to the monastery in order to discharge the duty of confessing it. The priest is at morning mass and cannot attend to him at once, and while waiting in a rather bare and shabby anteroom, "which spoke to me clearly of some new and up to now unknown life, of a solitary life of prayer and quiet and peaceful happiness, 'The months pass, the years pass,' I thought, 'he is always alone, he is always at peace, he always feels that his conscience is clean before God and that his prayers are heard by Him.' " This impulse toward asceticism continues to be felt but it has always kept a certain dramatic character, a certain desire to be known as acting out these gestures of humility. One may note here also the scene in one of the uncontinued beginnings of the projected novel on the Decembrist conspirators, in which a man of fifty-two, going to church on Maundy Thursday, remembers how once, at the age of twelve, he had felt a temptation to interrupt the mass by crowing like a cock and is obliged to make an effort to dismiss such buffooneries, which even now haunt him as impulses, and to recognize his sins and pray. It is this kind of impious self-assertion, later masked as apostolic vocation, that is seen to develop to immense proportions in the later years of Tolstoy's life and that makes the appalling discrepancy between his professions and his actual behavior so troublesome to his wife. His opinions caused his excommunication; but he was obviously disappointed at never being penalized by the government, which for once in his case showed good sense. He longed to be imprisoned, a martyr.

There is a story of Chekhov's which has all the appearance of having been inspired by Tolstoy. The connection seems further emphasized by its being called *A Story without a Title.* Mr. Ronald Hingley, the author of *Chekhov: A Biographical and Critical Study,* says that it was written at the time that Chekhov was most

under the influence of Tolstoy but that in this story he
was "attacking asceticism," "one of Tolstoy's cardinal
propositions." There is, however, I think, something
more to the parable than this.

The abbot of a monastery, so remote from the centers
of civilization that the only exciting events were occasional glimpses of a tiger, loved music, wrote Latin
verses and played the organ so beautifully that even
the deaf old monks were moved. One night, when they
had been living like this for decades without seeing any
other human beings, a hunter who had got drunk and
lost his way knocked at the gates of the monastery.
When the monks took him in, he reproached them for
leading such a withdrawn and tranquil life while the
people of the cities were headed for Hell: "Some are
dying of hunger, while others, not knowing what to
do with their gold, are drowning themselves in debauchery and are perishing like flies stuck in honey."
Is it not the monks' duty to save them? The drunken
words of the city-dweller were audacious and quite
improper; but they had a strange effect on the abbot.
He decided he must visit the city, and on the next day
started out with his staff. He did not return for three
months. The monks, who had much missed his music
and his sermons, threw themselves on his neck and
overwhelmed him with questions, but he bitterly
wept and would not speak a word. He had evidently
had a grueling experience. Without either eating or
drinking, he locked himself in his cell for seven days.
When at last he emerged, he told them that he had
started out gaily enough, seeing himself as a soldier
going forth to battle and certain of his victory. But what
he found in the city was such as he could never have
dared to imagine. By an unlucky chance, the first dwelling he entered turned out to be a house of debauchery.

There half a hundred men were squandering their money, getting drunk and using language such as no God-fearing men would dare. They feared not God or the Devil or death, but were happy and felt free to do whatever they pleased. And the wine, which was as clear as amber and which gave off golden sparks, must have been powerfully sweet and fragrant, because everyone who drank it smiled blissfully and wanted to drink more. In that sweetness lay the Devil's enticement. The old man became more and more inflamed; he wept with anger and went on to describe what he had seen. On the table, in the midst of the roisterers, stood a wanton half-naked woman. It would be hard to imagine anything more wonderful and captivating. He described her with all her charms. She seemed to be saying, "Look how naked and how beautiful I am!" She drank wine and sang songs, and let anyone do what he liked with her. He told them also about the races, the bull fights, the theaters, the artists' workshops where they depict and mold naked women from clay. He told them how beautifully and harmoniously and with what marvelous inspiration they played on invisible strings, and the monks listened to him hungrily and began to sigh in rapture. Having described all these temptations, the old man cursed the Devil and went back to his cell and shut the door.

When he came out the next morning, the monastery was empty. All the monks had run off to the city.

This was rather Tolstoy's situation when, in the interests of his religion, he denounced his early novels, which had given his public so much pleasure.

What confronted Tolstoy now that he seemed to have disposed of all other obligations and to have attained all personal goals was the degraded position of the muzhiks. And then there was the question of salvation. The gulf between the peasants and the educated classes in Russia was so wide that it presented to the Russian intellectuals and Westernized landowners a problem that, if they tried to think seriously about it, made them reformers or revolutionaries, or filled them with despair or stunned them. From Chernyshevsky, with his novel *Chto Delat'?*, to Lenin's political program with the same title, *What to Do?*, this question was reiterated through the nineteenth century and during the later revolutionary period. Tolstoy echoed it in *Tak Chto-zhe Nam Delat'?* in connection with his exploration of the misery of the Moscow poor. This question, as put by Tolstoy, sent a vibration through all the West from Gandhi to Jane Addams. There were poverty and degraded people everywhere, but in the West it was easier for the comfortable classes to be callous to this state of things or to contribute to occasional charities, and, except in the case of the American Negroes, the gulf was not so wide, even after the emancipation of the serfs, between the educated people and the peasants, as it continued to be in Russia.

One must always remember this appalling disproportion in connection with Russian literature and history. Among the great writers, Turgenev, abandoning his estates, left Russia, except for short visits, in order to live in the West and made fun of the Russian idealists who thought that the salvation of Russia was coming "out of the peasant's overcoat"; Chekhov, the grandson of a serf, was occupied mostly with the educated classes, but gave horrible pictures of the peasantry. Tolstoy tried to be a muzhik and denounced all art, including his own, which could not be understood by the peasant; the lower classes had to be gradually educated. Tolstoy, in his schools for his peasants, had of course tried to do this in a very small way. What a terribly long distance there was to go is shown by the slow results of education in the Soviet schools. Tolstoy's relapse into religion, in a belief, as the only hope, in the example of the virtuous and benevolent man, seems a throwing-up of hands in despair at the spectacle of so much evil, of which the abasement of so many human beings constituted a large part.

Tolstoy found himself now in the unusual, for a great writer perhaps the unprecedented, situation of having everything he could possibly want in a material way and having realized, in a literary way, all of his possible ambitions. He had a title and a distinguished ancestry and an extensive country estate, no adverse parental pressures, an attractive and intelligent wife, first-rate intellectual powers, and an imaginative genius which had enabled him to produce two masterpieces of fiction that were bringing in a good deal of money: when he heard of his former colleagues' receiving important official appointments, he would sometimes remark ironically that "though he had not himself earned a Generalship in the artillery, he had at any rate won a Generalship in literature." But he had served in the war against Shamil and had nearly been killed by a shell, he had fought in the Crimean warfare, and had declined or disregarded three crosses for valor; he had had innumerable women; he had seen all he wanted to see of Western Europe. He had acted as an Arbiter of the Peace, after the liberation of the serfs, with such an impartial justice as to infuriate many of his fellow nobles; he had instituted and directed a school for the peasants' children on a system of his own creation. He was, although sensitive, physically strong. It is no wonder—though so rare a phenomenon—that, having experienced and accomplished so much at a relatively early age, he should ask himself, as he does in *A Confession,* what there was to hope for and aim at next. Life at last has confronted him with a great blank. How is this blank to be filled? There is no further way to excel save through some effort of spiritual self-ennoblement.

The difference between Tolstoy's great early novels and his so much less satisfactory late ones is due to his having been able, in the former, to split up his own complicated personality into the several personalities of his characters—as in Pierre Bezukhov, Prince André, and Nicholas Rostov—each true to its own laws and each more or less of a piece. When he falls back on dramatizing his own mixed nature in an attempt to reduce it to something more easily acceptable, he produces such relatively implausible creations as Ivan Ilyich, Father Sergius and Prince Nekhlyudov.

The best way to get an idea of the drama created in the Tolstoy household by the conversion of Lyov Nikolaevich is to read his play on the subject, *And the Light Shines in the Darkness,* begun in the early eighties and not continued till 1900, the interval having extended through the period of his domestic conflicts. Tolstoy's imagination for family relations had always been one of the most striking features of his fiction. There are in *War and Peace* the families of the Bolkonskys and the Rostovs, in *Anna Karenina* the Karenins and the Levins. In his story of a horse, *Kholstomer* (sometimes translated as *Yardstick*), this imagination for the family extends even to the family of wolves who devour the horse's dead body: their physical characteristics are described, and we are told that the mother wolf makes a special point of feeding the smallest cub first. So in this play, Tolstoy is very well aware of the reactions to his proposed reforms of the other members of the family, and he actually makes these reactions seem far more sympathetic to the reader than the ideals professed by the reformer. He is trying here to dramatize the situation, and in assigning his own ideas to the moralist, he produces, as Mirsky says, a one-track fanatic who resembles his intolerable disciple Chertkov and who hardly does justice to his confused and torn self. The dramatic projection does not work in such a way as to justify the moralist. The balance becomes upset between him and his suffering dependents. There is not even the kind of balance that is preserved between Levin and Vronsky. And yet the reformer's position is fundamentally Tolstoy's own. This moralist refuses to defer to or to make any compromises with the army, the Church or the judiciary system. He will not take into consideration the problems that these institutions have been set up to deal with, or ask what would happen if they did not exist. (In his version of the Gospels, he had never hesitated to correct the words of Jesus as misreadings if they did not agree with his own opinions.) We are shown the man in the play arguing with the local priest and getting the better of it. But we also see the perplexities and convulsions of his family, confronted by a well-off father who wants to give away his property, to deprive his wife of her social position and his children of their inheritance. Tolstoy's present ambition is to announce his special revelation, regardless of consequences. He desires to figure as a voice of God. Gorky rightly said that Tolstoy and God were like two bears in one den. Tolstoy wrote four acts of this play yet got no further than notes for the fifth. But in the outline that he left, the reformer is shot by a princess whose son the prophet has inspired to resign from the army as a conscientious objector. (This ending is not included in the current twenty-volume *Collected Works* published in the Soviet Union.)

But in general, it seems to me that most of these post-conversion stories suffer from their being deformed by the moralistic bias. *The Death of Ivan Ilyich* has often been much admired; but I cannot believe that a provincial judge, even ill and on the verge of death, would have felt to an extent so demoralizing the futility of his life. Tolstoy would have had—he did have when he wrote *A Confession*—such broodings as he attributes to Ivan Ilyich, but I cannot believe that Ivan would have had them or that Tolstoy, in his early phase, would have invented so implausible a character.

In his other famous late story, *Father Sergius,* the main character becomes preposterous. Sergius is at first presented as a dashing young officer and man of the world who is about to marry a girl of his own class. But he finds out that she has been the Tsar's mistress, and since he has always aimed to excel in everything, and he cannot bear to be outranked, and since he cannot challenge the Tsar, whom he has previously adored, to a duel, he throws the girl over and decides, since he cannot in any other way hope to surpass the Tsar, to excel him in piety and penance. He therefore first enters a monastery but later goes on to live in a cave, where he devotes himself to prayer and self-mortification. In consequence of healing a sick boy, having been nagged by the boy's mother, he gets a great reputation as a healer, a *starets* or holy man, and soon he finds that people are flocking to him for cures and advice in their difficulties. But he comes to feel that this new position lays him open to the sin of pride. He now almost believes in his powers as a healer, and this is beginning to alienate him from God—since he has come to be working now not for God but for other people. He accordingly gives up his ministrations and devotes himself in solitude to worship. Confronted by a young woman who has made a bet that she will spend a night in his cell, he cuts off one of his fingers rather than succumb to temptation, and the woman goes into a convent. But when tempted a second time, he falls; and in order to expiate his sin, he becomes a vagabond and achieves his final victory over himself when he accepts twenty kopeks from some upper-class people who are travelling in a coach and on horseback and who among themselves are speaking French. He had been known, in his days in the army, for his outbursts of insubordination, but he has now got the better of his temper.

Now, Tolstoy was of course well qualified to understand the spiritual pride of Sergius, his ungovernable sensuality, and his equally ungovernable determination that no one should ever top him. But he is quite unable to imagine his hero's existence in the cave—which, to a non-Russian non-religious reader is equally unimaginable. What is the use of these endless sessions of prayer and worshipful meditation? Would they not certainly pall on a man who had enjoyed all the pleasures of society? The only attempt of Tolstoy to become a self-impoverished pilgrim was not at all like that of Father Sergius. He one day set out, disguised as a peasant, with two attendants, also disguised, and with a valise, which was carried by them, containing the indispensable conveniences, and after having arrived at his destination, a monastery, went to sleep on the floor of a flophouse. But his neighbor, a cobbler, kept him awake by snoring, and Tolstoy soon put a stop to this. The abbot of the monastery now found out who he was and immediately transferred him to a first-class hotel; he was passed before the common people who were waiting to see the *starets,* and entertained as a guest of honor. He could not face going back on foot, but returned by the train, though third class, and was met by his coachman with a carriage.

Resurrection is more impressive because it deals with actuality, a situation much less of fantasy. It seems to me an underrated book. It has become a critics' cliché to say that it is by no means equal to its more celebrated predecessors. *Resurrection* was begun in December, 1889, twelve years after *Anna Karenina,* but not finished till 1899, when the author made it ready to be published for the purpose of raising money to finance the journey to Canada of the heretical sect of the Doukhobors, who refused to serve in the army. Tolstoy said of the novel that he did not have time to make it what it ought to be; but what he seems to have meant was not that he did not have time to polish and prune it but that he ought to have brought it closer to his conception of the kind of thing that could be easily understood by an unsophisticated audience. Prince Nekhlyudov has to sit on a jury and finds himself in the position of judging a peasant girl with whom he has had a love affair and who has since then lapsed into prostitution and is now accused wrongly of having robbed and poisoned a merchant. Nekhlyudov offers to marry her, but she cannot take this seriously; and most of the rest of the story consists of his persistent attempts to rectify the judicial error. These take us through a whole panorama of tsarist officialdom, which gives Tolstoy an opportunity to exploit his inexhaustible interest in how different kinds of people behave and live. He even includes a group of young revolutionaries, of whose projects he disapproves but whose point of view he is able to understand. These judges and generals and rebels open up for Tolstoy a whole new department of contemporary life.

Resurrection takes you closer to the machinery of the government than anything he has written before. In the end, Nekhlyudov succeeds in getting his girl's sentence commuted—hardly a possibility under the present Soviet regime—but he insists on following her to Siberia. We get a vividly imagined picture of an elderly general and his wife who have been assigned to duty there—another instance of Tolstoy's success in presenting the life of a family existing under special conditions. Nekhlyudov's former love finds an admirer better suited to her than he is; and Nekhlyudov discovers the New Testament, which he borrows from one of the prisoners.

Tolstoy was contemplating a sequel which should show Nekhlyudov's subsequent struggles to lead a truly Christian life, but this sequel was never written. His own problems, one supposes, overwhelmed him. The title of this novel perhaps involves a kind of play on words that one is not aware of in translation. "*Voskresen'e*" means "Sunday" and *voskresenie* "resurrection"—the difference in spelling and pronunciation is slight; they are different forms of the same word—and the satirical accounts of the Orthodox services, one of them in a prison chapel, may be intended by Tolstoy to contrast with Nekhlyudov's real *voskresenie* when he is brought to it by the words of Jesus. It is easy to suppose one can fancy the scorn which Tolstoy must have felt on receiving from Turgenev's deathbed the famous last letter in which the older man begs him, addressing the professional moralist as "great writer of the Russian land," "to return to literary activity." Tolstoy had asked what the use was of making up tales about imaginary people when real ones were demanding attention to their problems. Yet something like a granting of Turgenev's request was eventually to take place.

The short novel *Hajji Murad* was produced in sporadic spells between 1896 and 1904, and it has the look of a holiday from the dutiful business of writing tracts and standing up as the prophet of a reformed religion. It is a kind of return to the methods and the point of view of *War and Peace*. Hajji Murad, a Caucasian chieftain, is compared to a wild thistle. He does not fit into civilization of the Western, even the Russian, kind. At first, an ally of Shamil, the formidable Chechen chieftain, who from the fastnesses of his mountains was defending his people against the armies of the Tsar, Hajji Murad, ambitious of leadership himself, betrays him and goes over to the Russians, with whom he hopes to coöperate in crushing Shamil. Shamil holds his family as hostages: his two wives and a son. The Russians treat Hajji Murad with respect, but they and he are aware that he can never really belong with them; and one day he gives them the slip and tries to rescue his family by a reckless raid. It is obvious that Tolstoy is able to identify himself with Murad more naturally than with Father Sergius. Hajji Murad is willful and intractable, alike as an ally of Shamil and as a protégé of the Russians. He is killed in a fierce battle by tribesmen who have taken the Russian side. But the story ranges very widely among characters not always directly connected with the passionate career of Hajji Murad: the Tsar's court, Shamil and his followers, the Russian officers, the death of a Russian soldier whose wife is relieved at having him killed because she has been got pregnant by a Russian clerk. It is here that we rejoin *War and Peace*.

Tolstoy's moral principles come into play in his treatment of Nicholas I, who is made a detestable figure: he acquires a respectable young girl as his mistress and, while enjoying a conviction of righteousness for having abolished capital punishment, thinks nothing of virtually condemning to death by making him run a gauntlet of beatings, a student who has struck his professor. But a fragment and an omitted chapter of the manuscript, unpublished at the time of Tolstoy's death, show how his preoccupation with the lives of different kinds of families led him away from this bitter portrait. He began to become interested in the Royal Family and he seems to be trying to explain how the Tsar got to be what he was.

This additional matter has also unaccountably been omitted from the selective Soviet edition. It is illuminating, by the way, to compare the texts published by Chertkov in Germany, which show in brackets what the censorship would not allow, with the recent English edition of Kuznetsov's *Babi Yar,* which shows omissions imposed by the Soviet censor. The effect is very much the same. In the one case, what is removed is everything derogatory to the Tsar; in the second, everything that unfavorably reflects on the recent procedures of the Soviet government.

In all Tolstoy's talk about love and God, it is a little hard to know what he means by either. He does not seem very much to love others; and what is his communion with God? He is more impressive when, at the time of the famine—though, as he said, in violation of his principles—he is saving the lives of the starving, or when he is compromising with his children and with Sofia Andreevna, to the last of whom he owed so much. For the rest, the cult of love and God seems often, as with Father Sergius, an arid self-directed exercise that simply raises the worshipper in his own esteem.

January 25, 1971

NOTES ON PUSHKIN

In 1821, when Pushkin was twenty-two, he wrote a long poem called *Gavriiliada,* which was circulated widely in manuscript but, on account of its impiety and indecency, never published during Pushkin's lifetime. It made trouble for him in 1828, when Pushkin was already in bad odor with the authorities. The servants of a Captain Mitkov complained that their immoral master had been reading them a blasphemous poem. The captain was arrested, and Pushkin was made to appear before the military governor general of Petersburg. He denied having written the poem, but this disavowal was not accepted, and he might well have been sent to Siberia if he had not addressed a letter to the Tsar in which he is thought to have confessed and expressed the deepest contrition. The *Gavriiliada* appeared in print only in 1861, when the poet Ogaryov had it published in London. Today it is included in all the Soviet editions of Pushkin; yet it still has so black a reputation among members of the old regime that I have found that a highly intelligent and otherwise well-read Russian friend has never been able to bring herself to face it.

The *Gavriiliada* was obviously prompted by the literature of the French eighteenth century, the mockery of the Bible by Voltaire and his follower Evariste Parny. It is directly indebted, in its comic treatment of the legend of the Immaculate Conception, to *Les Galan-teries de la Bible* and *La Guerre des Dieux* of the latter; and in Parny's version of the Garden of Eden, in which Satan in the guise of a serpent is made to play a liberating role, to his *Paradis Perdu*.

I have just reread the *Gavriiliada* and I found that it did not have the charm for me that it did when I first read it. But if one comes to it after Parny, graceful and well-turned though this is, but thin and dry in the eighteenth-century fashion, one is struck by Pushkin's faculty for making anything he touched humanly sympathetic. His Mary is successively ravished by Satan, who has transformed himself from a snake to a hand-some young man; by the Archangel Gabriel, who has been sent by the Lord to prepare the way for His holiday from the routine hymns and prayers in His praise, but takes advantage of the opportunity to make love to the irresistible Mary; and finally by the Lord Himself in the form of a quivering billing dove.

All these characters are brought to life much more vividly than Parny has been able to do. The first of the seductions leads Pushkin to remember wistfully his having aroused the desires of a correctly brought-up young girl; and the struggle between Satan and Gabriel is described in terms of his schoolboy wrestling with comrades. The serpent's account of the raptures of love to which he introduces Adam and Eve seems to me more attractive than those of either Parny or Milton:

> И не страшась божественного гнева,
> Вся в пламени, власы раскинув, Ева,
> Едва, едва устами шевеля
> Лобзанием Адаму отвечала.

This is an already masterly example of Pushkin's famous skill at alliteration, and the "Едва, едва" that follows

"Ева" is an example of Pushkin's power, later brought to such perfection, of making the language itself represent the thing described—in this case, Eve's mouth with lips open from being kissed. This is echoed, as it were, when Eve succumbs to Satan:

> Она молчит: но вдруг не стало мочи,
> К лукавому склонив свою главу,
> Едва дыша, закрыла томны очи,
> Вскричала: ах!.. и пала на траву...

But in general the vocabulary is a little repetitious in comparison with Pushkin's more mature and tightly economic style.

II

The Gypsies, of 1824, is a striking example of Pushkin's characteristic form. It concentrates in twenty pages a drama that seems to cover enough ground to have required many more. But I mention it because it seems to me to have been, even by Russians, rather imperfectly understood. Aleko, the central character, has fled cities and civilization in order to live with the gypsies, where he is able to enjoy a new freedom. A gypsy girl named Zemfira has found him in a waste place and brought him home to her father. Aleko loves her and lives with her; he stays with the gypsies two years. But she arouses his apprehension when he hears her singing a gypsy song in which a young woman defies her old husband and announces that she is now in love with a young man who is bold and hot-blooded. It presently becomes plain that Zemfira herself has taken a lover. Aleko wakes up one night and finds she is not by his side. He goes after her and stabs both the lover and her. The father rebukes him and orders him to leave. The gypsies live in lawless freedom; they will not tolerate murderers. Aleko, the old father says, is not fit for such wild life as theirs. He wants freedom only for himself. The gypsies depart like a flock of cranes and leave Aleko alone like a wounded bird on the steppe.

But in summarizing this story, I have failed to mention one very important circumstance that I find is often overlooked. When Zemfira brings Aleko back with her, she explains, at the very beginning, that he is being pursued by the law—"Его преследует закон." A later conversation with the old man, when Aleko is worried about losing Zemfira, makes it plain that the gypsies are pacific whereas Aleko is revengeful and violent. Zemfira's father long ago lost the woman he loved when he let her go off with a man who belonged to a different band; but Aleko protests that he would never stand for this: "I am not like that. No, I should never without fighting renounce my rights!" He would hound his enemy to his death and laugh fiercely when he had been destroyed. It is thus intimated, it seems to me, that Aleko was fleeing from the law on account of having committed a crime of violence and that he will inevitably commit another. The way that this is indicated, by a series of touches and never too explicitly, is entirely typical of Pushkin. The old man has already told Aleko the story of an outsider who had come among them but could never be at peace because he believed that God was punishing him for a crime. The fine Epilogue clinches this:

> Но счастья нет и между вами,
> Природы бедные сыны!
> И под издранными шатрами
> Живут мучительные сны,
> И ваши сени кочевые

В пустынях не спаслись от бед,
И всюду страсти роковые,
И от судеб защиты нет.

"But even among you there is no happiness, poor children of nature! And under the tattered tents there still dwell tormenting dreams, and your nomadic shelters in the wilderness provide no sanctuary from sorrows, but everywhere there are predestined passions, and from the fates there is no escape."

The last two lines show Pushkin at his most trenchant; in translation they can hardly seem anything but flat. But the snap of "судеб" and "нет" which follows the description of the gypsies roving peacefully away in the wilderness, chops off grimly the drama of Aleko. I have inadequately tried to render it by matching *escape* with *fates*.

III

In 1922, the poet Vladislav Khodasevich published a little volume called *Articles on Russian Poetry*, in one of which, *Pushkin's Petersburg Tales,* he discussed a curious production which seems of such interest and importance that one wonders at its not being better known. In a Russian paper called *The Day,* there was reprinted in December, 1912, by the Pushkin scholar P. E. Shchegolev, and again in the January, 1913, number of a magazine called *Northern Notes*, a story which had first appeared in 1829 in a miscellany, an almanac called *Northern Flowers*. This was *The Lonely Little House on Vasilevsky* [*Island*] (Уединенный Домик на Васильевском), signed Titus Kosmokratov.

One evening in 1829, at the Karamzins', Pushkin had

told a story which, according to the account of Pushkin's friend, Baron A. A. Delvig, considerably affected the ladies and made such an impression on a young writer named V. P. Titov, who was there, that he was unable to sleep that night and later wrote the story down from memory. He showed his version to Pushkin, who amiably made some corrections in it and gave him permission to publish it. Now, this strange story is quite plainly the original nightmare fantasy from which, as Khodasevich says, were to grow the three stories later written and published by Pushkin as *The Bronze Horseman, The Little House in Kolomna* and *The Queen of Spades*. These, it seems, have been known as the "Petersburg Tales," though there is no direct connection between them, and in *The Queen of Spades* the city "as such does not play any role." And yet a connection, although invisible, was felt to exist between them, "as astronomers are able to guess at the existence of a star which their optical instruments cannot yet reach." That invisible connection was the story written down by Titov and neglected for many years in the files of the 1829 miscellany in which it had been published.

This story is about a young man named Pavel. He is in in the habit of going to see a distant relative, a widow who lives in a little house in the suburb of St. Petersburg called the Vasilevsky Island. The widow has a daughter named Vera, to whom Pavel is "not indifferent." But he makes friends with a rather mysterious youth called Varfolomey, who never goes to church and who gets money from some unknown source. He exercises "over the weak young man an irresistible power" and persuades him to take him to see Vera and her mother. Varfolomey has designs on Vera, but her instinct is not to like him; she prefers Pavel. Varfolomey convinces Pavel that he ought to go into society and takes him to the house of a countess of his acquaintance, a beauty, to which her friends come in the evenings to gamble. These friends wear high wigs and baggy Turkish trousers and never take off their gloves. It is evident— though not to Pavel—that they are devils concealing their horns, hoofs and claws. In their company, Pavel forgets about Vera; but Varfolomey has been working on her, and Pavel finds that she now treats him with coldness. He demands an explanation of Varfolomey, and the latter now declares that Vera has fallen in love with *him*. Pavel makes a lunge at Varfolomey but is knocked down by a violent though painless blow. When he comes to, Varfolomey has disappeared, and Pavel hears ringing in his ears his last words, *"Be quiet, young man: you're not dealing with one of your own kind."* ("Потише, молодой человек, ты не с своим братом связался.") Going home, he finds a letter from the countess, giving him a rendezvous on the back stairs of her house for the following night.

When he goes there, the beautiful countess is alone, but just as he is about "to taste his bliss," the chambermaid knocks on the door and says there is someone to see the young gentleman. When Pavel goes down to the reception hall, he is told that the caller has left. He returns to the lady upstairs, but the same thing occurs again. There is nobody outside the door—nothing but the silent snowflakes. The third time, he sees a tall figure in a cloak, who beckons to him and vanishes in an alley.

Pavel is up to his knees in snow, and he signals to a cabby and orders him to take him home. Presently he comes to realize that he has been driven beyond the city limits and remembers the stories of cabbies who have cut their customers' throats. "Where are you taking me?" No answer. He sees that, in large figures, strangely formed, the cab is labelled "666"—which is, as he afterwards remembers, the number of the Beast of the Apocalypse. He strikes the driver with his stick and feels that he is beating not flesh but bones. The driver turns his head and reveals a grinning skull, which repeats, in a blurred voice, the words of Varfolomey, *"Be quiet, young man: you're not dealing with one of your own kind."* Pavel crosses himself; the sleigh overturns in the snow, and he hears a wild laugh; there is a terrible whirling gust of wind; and he finds himself alone outside the city gates.

Pavel comes to himself in his bed, and for three days is out of his mind. It now appears that Varfolomey is getting both Vera and her mother under his domination. Vera confesses she loves him. The mother falls ill and is sinking, but Varfolomey prevents them from sending for the priest on the pretext that the priest's appearance would convince the old lady she was dying and deprive her of her last hope. She calls Varfolomey and Vera to her bedside and with a wry smile tells Vera to kiss her bridegroom: "I'm afraid of going blind, and then I should not be able to see your happiness." The old lady dies. But Vera, who can still pray, rebels against the spell of Varfolomey: "Obey me, Vera, don't be stubborn," the demon tries to command her. "No force protects you now from my power." " 'God is the protector of the innocent,' cries the poor girl, in desperation, throwing herself on her knees before the crucifix." "If that's how it is," says the demon, biting his lips and with a face expressing impotent malignancy, "there's nothing to be done with you; but I'll get your mother to make you obedient." "Is she in your power?" asks the girl. "Look," the demon answers, fixing his gaze on the half-opened door to the bedroom, and Vera seems to see two streams of fire gushing from the demon's eyes and, in the glimmer of the guttering candle, the dead woman raises her head and with her withered hand she gestures the young girl to Varfolomey. Vera calls upon God and faints. Now a sound like a sudden shot wakens the sleeping maid, and she sees that the bedroom is full of smoke and that the curtains are burning with a blue flame. Attempts to put out the fire are vain; there is a storm that is spreading the blaze. The demon disappears. Vera wastes away, afraid that through her weakness she has been responsible for her mother's death and damnation. Pavel leaves Moscow and goes to live in the country. He is apparently half-insane, and the sudden appearance of a tall gray-eyed man throws him into convulsions; he becomes quite mad. His servant, coming in unexpectedly, finds him trembling and protesting, "I didn't cause her death." Very soon he, too, dies.

One can see how the three stories mentioned above— *The Little House in Kolomna* (1830), *The Bronze Horseman* and *The Queen of Spades* (the last two of which were written in 1833)—must have grown out of this sinister fantasy (published in 1829). In both *The Little House* and *The Bronze Horseman* as in the Vasilevsky *Lonely House,* you have a widow and her daughter living in humble circumstances, into whose household comes a young man; in *The Queen of Spades,* a young man comes to see an aunt and her niece. One recognizes in the countess of *The Queen of Spades,* with her evenings of gambling and her circle of friends, the gambling countess of the Vasilevsky story—though the former is an old lady and the latter, we are told, a beauty. One recognizes in the statue of Peter the Great that turns its head and terrifies Evgeni by asserting its despotic authority the cabby of the Vasilevsky story who turns his head with more or less the same effect. Pavel and Herman and Evgeni all go insane. All are threatened and finally ruined. But in the story written down by "Kosmokratov," the forces of Evil are everywhere. The presence of the Devil is quite explicit; in the stories that grew out of it a diabolical power is intimated only by the mention that the old countess is supposed to have known the Comte de Germain, the eighteenth-century adventurer who was rumored to have learned his arts from the Devil.

The most curious of these stories is *The Little House in Kolomna*. Here the widow loses her cook and engages a woman who is willing to work for whatever they choose to give her but who turns out to cook very badly. This cook is, however, an eager young man, whom the daughter has smuggled into the house. The old lady is horrified to find him shaving. He disappears, and that is the end. Pushkin tells you in the last stanza that the only moral of the story is that it is dangerous to engage a cook who is willing to work for very little, who was born a man, and to whom wearing a skirt is not comfortable or suitable, and who will give himself away by shaving his beard. "You won't be able to get anything more out of my story." But Khodasevich seems to believe that Pushkin is referring to the earlier story, which has in common with *The Little House in Kolomna* that both describe dangerous invasions of the modest homes of widows. I am inclined to think, however—I may have seen this suggested somewhere—that Pushkin, in the cramping conditions which Nicholas had imposed on him by making him a court official and by subjecting him to espionage and censorship, is expressing here, as in others of his works, his protest against this humiliation, which amounts to being made to pretend to a passive feminine role. He is warning of the inevitable dangers of forcing a spirited man of genius to play the part of a bad cook. So the Evgeni of *The Bronze Horseman* shakes his fist at the "idol" in the likeness of Peter the Great, who has founded his city on a swamp and exposed it to such floods as have destroyed Evgeni's sweetheart whom he was hoping to marry. Evgeni cries, "You'll reckon with me yet!"

The forces of Evil were closing in on Pushkin. They

dragged him down by the fatal noose of the insulting anonymous letters that spurred him to the duel with D'Anthès. But where do the devils come from that pursue their first victim as imagined by Pushkin, Pavel? What had Pavel or the widow or Vera done to incur their malice? Pavel is called weak, to be sure; and after the general catastrophe, both he and Vera feel guilt—she for having exposed her mother and having been the cause of her death and he for having caused the death of Vera. Old-fashioned Orthodox Russians seem to have felt the devils all about them. I have heard of the wife of a priest who, though living in the United States, always wore a scarf over her head and sat with her back to the wall to keep the demons out of her ears. In Turgenev, as I have said above, the Force of Evil, for no obvious reason, always seems to come in from the outside. In Dostoevsky, it exists in the men themselves. Which of the brothers Karamazov was guilty of the murder of their father? But in Бесы, *The Devils* (which Constance Garnett called *The Possessed*), the character based on Nechaev, the ruthless revolutionist who so hypnotized Bakunin, is an absolute force of Evil who could not conceivably be anything else.

(I have learned that "Kosmokratov's" story has now been included in Volume IX of a new edition of Pushkin —1956-1958—compiled by Boris Tomashevsky.)

IV

It is interesting to contrast two short personal poems by Pushkin and by Alfred de Musset which were composed in moments of melancholy:

Пора, мой друг, пора! покоя сердце просит,
Летят за днями дни, и каждый час уносит

Частичку бытия, а мы с тобой вдвоем
Предполагаем жить, и глядь, как раз умрем.
На свете счастья нет, но есть покой и воля.
Давно завидная мечтается мне доля—
Давно, усталый раб, замыслил я побег
В обитель дальную трудов и чистых нег.

> *J'ai perdu ma force et ma vie,*
> *Et mes amis et ma gaité;*
> *J'ai perdu jusqu'à la fierté*
> *Qui faisait croire à mon genie.*

> *Quand j'ai connu la Vérité,*
> *J'ai cru que c'était une amie;*
> *Quand je l'ai comprise et sentie,*
> *J'en était déjà dégoûté.*

> *Et pourtant elle est éternelle,*
> *Et ceux qui se sont passés d'ellé*
> *Ici-bas ont tout ignoré.*

> *Dieu parle, il faut qu'on lui réponde.*
> *Le seul bien qui me reste au monde*
> *Est d'avoir quelquefois pleuré.*

Pushkin's poem was written probably in 1834, three
years before his being goaded into fighting his fatal
duel with D'Anthès; Musset's when he was only thirty
and had still seventeen years before him. Musset's,
without his knowing it, had been picked up from his
bedside table by a friend with whom he was staying in
the country. Both are now among the best-known of
their poets' lyrics.

What is striking about these two pieces is that Musset
at thirty feels that he has lost everything, even his
belief in his genius, and that the only good thing now

left him is sometimes to have wept. Pushkin, being slowly crushed by censorship, by involvement in the life of the court (he was trying to resign from his official position), and by the incomprehension and indifference of his wife—is she the "friend" he addresses and begs to flee with him to a life of tranquillity, reminding her that every hour carries away a bit of existence and that although "we propose to live, behold, on the contrary, we shall die"?—nevertheless looks forward to escape and freedom for devotion to his work. Alfred de Musset already is saying farewell. Pushkin, although rather wistfully, on the eve of extinction, is still full of creative vitality and planning to find leisure for productions that, one assumes, like those of the past, will express something more than his sorrows.

V

It is ironic to find today among Pushkin's notes of 1830: «Шпионы подобны букве ъ. Нужны в некоторых только случаях, но и тут можно без них обойтиться, а они привыкли всюду соваться.» (Ѣ is an old letter identical in sound with *e,* which was abolished at the time of the Kerensky revolution.) "Spies are like the letter ъ. Needed only on certain occasions, though even then one could get along without them, but they are always sticking their noses in."

1970

A LITTLE MUSEUM OF
RUSSIAN LANGUAGE

Intended for Foreign Readers

The following are notes on language which I have made in the course of my reading. They represent conceptions for which we have no equivalents in English and which therefore may be of interest to inexperienced foreign readers. I do not notice the kind of oddities that will have been studied in the grammar or dictionary, such as the shift from one form, and occasionally one word, to another, beginning with the number five, or the fact that the same word is used for the hand and the arm (рука), and the same word for the foot and the leg (нога). (What exactly did Pushkin mean by the дамские ножки he so much admired?)

The vocabulary for snow, ice and frost is much larger and more varied than ours in English. The primary words are снег, *snow*; лёд, *ice*; and мороз, *frost*. But you have also the following special words (only a few of which have English equivalents):

сугро́б, snowdrift
сля́коть, slush
крупа́, sleet
и́ней   } hoar-frost
индиве́ть   } to cover with, or be covered
заи́ндевелый } with hoar-frost

и́зморозь, и́зморось, white frost, sleet, drizzling rain
льди́на, block of ice
гололе́дица, a thin layer of slippery ice
о́ттепель, thaw
ро́степель, general thaw in spring
полынья́ ⎫
про́рубь ⎭ hole in the ice

мете́ль ⎫
бура́н ⎬ blizzard (I do not understand the distinction,
вью́га ⎭ if any, between these three words.)

поро́ша, newly fallen snow
наст, frozen snow crust
зажо́ра, water collected under snow
прота́лина, place where the snow has thawed off

прищу́ривать, прищу́риваться, прищу́рить, прищу́-
риться; щу́рить, щу́риться (imperfectives); прищу́-
ривать, прищу́риваться (imperfectives); прищу́рить,
прищу́риться (perfectives); сощу́рить, сощу́риться
(perfectives).

This interesting group of words may mean simply to
half-close the eyes; but it is also applied to the peculiar
narrowing of the eyes characteristic of Russian women,
and indeed of most women in the east of Europe—which
is not practiced at all by our women—to indicate
apprehension and defense against what is apprehended
or the challenging invitation of flirtation.

When Pushkin, in Chapter VIII of *The Captain's
Daughter,* writes "Пугачёв смотрел на меня
пристально, изредка прищуривая левый глаз с
удивительным выражением плутовства и насмеш-
ливости," it is plain that Pugachev is simply half-
closing one eye.

When, in Chapters XVIII and XIX of Part Six of
Anna Karenina, Dolly notices that Anna has acquired

a habit which she has not noticed before, and in connection with which Tolstoy uses щурить and сощурить —"И ей вспомнилось, что Анна щурилась, именно когда дело касалось задушевных сторон жизни. 'Точно она на свою жизнь щуриться, чтобы не все видить,' подумала Долли." It is plain that Anna is half-shutting her eyes in order not to confront too closely the more intimate aspects of her life.

(Constance Garnett uses "dropping her eyelids" for щуриться and "screwing up her eyes" for сощуриться. A French translation by an anonymous translator gives quite wrongly for "сощурившись, точно вглядываясь во что-то далёкое," "*regardant fixement devant elle comme si elle eût cherché quelque chose dans le lointain*"; and in the passage quoted above, щуриться becomes misleadingly "*le clignement d'yeux d'Anna.*")

Turgenev uses щурить often to convey a variety of effects.

Coquetry: "'А я вот не курю,'—продолжала она, ласково прищурив свои бархатные глаза . . . Отстала от века.'" (*Virgin Soil*, VII)

"Её большие глаза глядели прямо, светло, смело, но иногда веки её слегка щурились, и тогда взор её внезапно становился глубок и нежен." (*Asya*, II)

"Странная усмешка слегка подёргивала её брови, ноздри и губы; полу-дерзко, полу-весело щурились тёмные глаза." (*Asya*, IV)

"Молодая девушка продолжала глядеть на меня с прежней усмешкой, слегка щурясь и склонив головку немного на бок." (*First Love*, IV)

A woman in front of a mirror: "то быстро поправляя перед зеркалом свои лоснистые волосы и чуть-чуть прищуривая свои дивные глаза . . ." (*Virgin Soil*, V)

Apprehension: ". . . но она, вероятно, угадала его

намерение и притаила дыхание, глаза ее прищу-
рились, точно она ожидала удара . . ." (*Song of
Triumphant Love*, VIII)

"'Ух, зти мне барыни! И улыбаются-то они вам,
и глазки этак щурят, а на лице написана гадли-
вость . . !" (*A Month in the Country*, Act IV)

I find here no mention of the blinking—except
gratuitously in the French translation above—that is
likely, on the part of Russian women, to accompany this
emotional narrowing, but I suppose it may sometimes
be understood.

Vladimir Nabokov, in *Ada*, and in his translated
books, has discovered a new and felicitous word for
rendering щурить and прищурить in English: "I ask
myself who that can be," murmured Mlle Larivière
from behind the samovar . . . as she slitted her eyes at
a part of the drive visible between the pilasters of an
open-work gallery." (*Ada,* Part One, Section 14)

An English reader must be struck by the weakness, in
comparison with English, of the verbs that correspond
to our *get*:

приобрета́ть, приобрести́, to obtain
достига́ть, дости́чь, дости́гнуть, to reach, attain,
   obtain
достава́ть, доста́ть, to obtain
доставля́ть, доста́вить, to supply, procure
добыва́ть, добы́ть, to earn

Get has a definite, physical, almost predatory and
aggressive sound; and it extends beyond getting money,
getting a new suit and being a go-getter to getting sick,
well, away, home, hurt, up, down, through, over, and
getting children (begetting). The definitions of *get*
occupy twenty-two columns in the big Oxford English
Dictionary. But the best the French can do is *obtenir*,

which is elegantly defined in Larousse as "*parvenir à se faire accorder ce qu'on désire*." The slogan about beating the Germans in the First World War took the moderate form of "*On les aura*." German has strong enough words for the various kinds of getting: *enlangen*, *erreichen*, *erwerben*, *kriegen*, *bekommen*, but no all-sufficing word like our *get*; Hungarian *kapni* seems to me to give a little more the impression of snatching something and keeping it. But the Russian words above are surely very mild, and they involve some suggestion of special effort. You cannot even ask somebody in Russian whether or not they have got something: you say "Есть ли у вас то-то и то-то?" or simply, with no verb at all, "У вас то-то и то-то?" The English-speaking peoples, on the other hand, "get" everything in a quick and decisive fashion.

Other recurring phrases which must strike the foreign reader of Turgenev as possessing a peculiar significance that they would not have in English are the решительный шаг, *a resolute step*, and пристальный взгляд, a *fixed* or *insistent gaze*. When you encounter one of these phrases on the part of a character of Turgenev's, you know that something special is about to happen, because either a resolute step or a direct searching look is exceptional, abnormal, for these people. But you find also in Tolstoy's *Adolescence*, "И с неописанным выражением твёрдости духа, Мими приказала всем посторониться, большими, решительными шагами подошла к рассыпанной дроби и . . . начала топтать её ногами." And in *The Cossacks*, "К постояльцу она привыкла и с удовольствием чувствовала на себе его пристальные взгляды." In this last case, we should say in English simply that she felt that the guest was staring at her; but an equivalent for the решительный шаг is hard to imagine in English.

приживальщик ⎫ (masculine)
приживалец   ⎬
приживалка (feminine)

This is someone, a friend or a relative, who comes to
live in your house and who has the privilege of staying
on indefinitely and of complaining about the arrange-
ments. This term is somewhat invidious but the phenomenon, with Russians, is extremely common. There
are some typical приживалки in Turgenev's *Mumu*.
They do not like it when the mistress of the house is in
particularly good humor because this means that they
have to make the effort to simulate good humor themselves and because they know that this mood will not
last and that it is likely to change very soon to a "gloomy
and sour" one.

It is difficult for the foreigner to understand the obligations of Russian hospitality and the inescapable duty
that Russians feel, at whatever inconvenience to themselves, to accommodate other Russians. It is strange,
in Chekhov's story, *The Duel*, to find people continually
lending money to the good-for-nothing nuisance Laevsky who considers himself a Tolstoyan idealist but runs
off with someone else's wife. An Anglo-Saxon would
flatly refuse; a French Laevsky would know better
than to ask for money. I once inquired of a Russian lady
whether, subjected to the demands of a Laevsky, she
would continue to lend him money. "It would be
difficult," she said, "to refuse." The only character in
the story who is able to resist Laevsky and becomes
indignant about him is a zoölogist with a German name.

The reader should bear in mind that слышать, which
usually means *to hear*, may also be applied to smelling.
"Он слышал ужасный запах . . ." (*Anna Karenina*,
Part Five, Section XVIII). "мамаша сидит подле

самого меня; она трогает меня; я слышу её запах и голос" (Tolstoy, *Childhood,* Chapter XV). Here you have the two senses combined.

нагляде́ться
наслы́шиваться
наслы́шаться
наслы́ха́ться

Of these verbs, the first has to do with looking at things, the other three with hearing things. Нагляде́ться may have either the meaning of feasting one's eyes on something or the meaning of being fed up with seeing it. So the other verbs may vary from a favorable to an unfavorable sense of hearing a good deal or enough. They belong to a class with the prefix на—наговори́ть, for example—which means to do something a great deal or thoroughly. These are interesting specimens of the changes in meaning which in Russian a simple prefix may make where we should have to use an adverb or an adverbial phrase.

Врёшь. This means literally *You lie*—second person singular from врать—but it has come to mean *You're crazy! You're talking nonsense!* I do not know of any Western language in which *You lie* would not be an insult, possibly provocative in the past to a duel. Now, lying has always been one of the worst Russian vices. Turgenev complains about it: many lies, he says, are perfectly gratuitous; and we have all had reason to complain of the lying propaganda of the Soviet Union. But the Russians take it very lightly, as the easy use of врёшь illustrates. The practice of lying is undoubtedly bound up with the exercise of the Russian imagination, which excels in the novel and drama. The myths about events in Russia that are put out by the Soviet government are the products, in degraded form, of the same imaginative genius as the works of the great Russian novelists and Stanislavsky's Moscow Art Theater.

1970

I have learned, since this was written, that a good deal more attention has been given to this subject than I was aware of at the time I wrote. The difference between врать and лгать, врун and лгун, враньё and ложь, the terms which represent the two varieties of Russian lying, has already been extensively discussed in *That's no lie, Comrade* by the Oxford Russian scholar Ronald Hingley in *Problems of Communism,* March–April, 1962. He refers the reader to an article by Dostoevsky, Нечто о враньё, in Number 35, 1873 of his Дневник писателя and an essay by Andreyev, Всероссийское враньё in Volume V of his Collected Works, St. Petersburg, 1913. The distinction is apparently clear between ложь, *a flat lie,* and враньё, for which French *blague* and Irish *blarney* have been suggested as possible equivalents. But враньё is distinctly different: it can go much further than either, and can easily become confused with ложь. "Отчево у нас все лгут, все до единого?" ("Why does everybody among us lie, all without exception?") Dostoevsky commences by asking. "I know," he proceeds, "that you will stop me and cry out, 'Why, that's nonsense, surely not all!' But you have no real argument, you're merely thinking of a way to begin effectively. . . . I have for some time been struck by the fact that, among the intelligent classes, it is impossible for a man not to lie. This is because, among us, even perfectly honorable men can lie. I am persuaded that in other nations on the whole only scoundrels lie; they lie for practical profit, that is, directly with criminal purpose. But with us it is possible for the most respected people to lie for most respectable ends." He proceeds to elaborate the occasions and ways in which Russians habitually lie: about things that have happened to them abroad, about subjects they know nothing about but on which, when travelling in trains, they do not hesitate to deliver long lectures. This last form of imposture, says Dostoevsky, is encouraged by a reciprocal attitude on the part of the impostor's listeners, who are always hungry for instruction and who will thank the liar for his pretended enlightenment, no matter how preposterous it may have been. One of the examples of the use of врать given in Louis Segal's Russian dictionary is "Ему сегодня что-то особенно врётся." ("He is today especially inclined to lie.") And I have discovered the remarkable verb, which I believe has no analogue in any Western language, завираться, which Mr. Hingley defines as meaning "to lie oneself into a trance," and Mr. Segal as "to get into a fit of babbling"; "Он завирается," says Mr. Segal, means "His mind is adrift." Robert Conquest, in an article in *The Listener* of January 21, 1971, says that Krushchyov was "a compulsive врун"—that is, the kind of romancer" who indulges in враньё, while "Stalin, a non-Russian, was a thoroughgoing, clear-cut liar." I have known only one accomplished врун. He once told me that Jean Paulhan, then editor of the *Nouvelle Revue Française*, had made him wait interminably in his office, then, on emerging, announced that his delay was due to the fact that a bomb had just gone off in the building. My friend had heard no explosion. "It's the kind of thing," he said, "that I might have done myself, but I was rather surprised at Paulhan's doing it." Mr. Hingley has some extraordinary stories about the lengths to which враньё can be carried. He quotes from Andreyev a story of a man who announces gratuitously that an aunt of his has died, though his hearers are well aware that she is going to appear in half an hour; and he cites from his own experience a case of a Russian who invented a story of the son of a man they both knew who he said had returned to the Soviet Union under an assumed name and written a book of which the exact title was given—in spite of the fact that Hingley knew perfectly well that this was all an improvisation.

In the Soviet Union, says Hingley, враньё and ложь have become fatally mingled. When they talk about something like the *sputnik*, though they are telling the truth, they make it sound like враньё; and when you know they are spinning fantasies, you must not try to trip them up. To do so would be bad manners. But if you pretend to believe them, become an accomplice, you find yourself a party to an understanding which is based on the acceptance of fantasy. The villages knocked together by Potyomkin to mislead Catherine the Great were an outstanding example of враньё—did Catherine even believe they were real? In the same way, the Soviet Russians were said to have constructed in Kiev an imitation, the famous Lavra, which had actually been destroyed by the Germans, in order to impose on visitors. Now, the Russian visitor to the West, who is accustomed at home to враньё, finds it hard to believe what he is told. A man I know who served under John Kennedy in some official capacity tells me that, when asked by a Russian official for the figures on the manufacture of missiles, the latter simply remarked, after glancing at the requested report, that he would like to know the real figures. Not that our figures may not sometimes lie; but it may indicate on our part a relative truthfulness that we have now been compelled in the long run to complain about a "credibility gap."

1971

II

THE STRANGE CASE

OF PUSHKIN AND NABOKOV

Vladimir Nabokov's translation of Pushkin's *Evgeni Onegin* is something of a disappointment; and the reviewer, though a personal friend of Mr. Nabokov— for whom he feels a warm affection sometimes chilled by exasperation—and an admirer of much of his work, does not propose to mask his disappointment. Since Mr. Nabokov is in the habit of introducing any job of this kind which he undertakes by an announcement that he is unique and incomparable and that everybody else who has attempted it is an oaf and an ignoramus, incompetent as a linguist and scholar, usually with the implication that he is also a low-class person and a ridiculous personality, Nabokov ought not to complain if the reviewer, though trying not to imitate Nabokov's bad literary manners, does not hesitate to underline his weaknesses.

Mr. Nabokov, before the publication of his own translation of *Evgeni Onegin,* took up a good deal of space in the pages of the *New York Review of Books* to denounce a previous translation by Professor Walter Arndt. This article—which sounded like nothing so much as one of Marx's niggling and nagging attacks on someone who had had the temerity to write about economics and to hold different views from Marx's—

209

dwelt especially on what he regarded as Professor Arndt's Germanisms and other infelicities of phrasing, without, apparently, being aware of how vulnerable he himself was. Professor Arndt had attempted the tour de force of translating the whole of *Onegin* into the original iambic tetrameter and rather intricate stanza form. Mr. Nabokov decided that this could not be done with any real fidelity to the meaning and undertook to make a "literal" translation which maintains an iambic base but quite often simply jolts into prose. The results of this have been more disastrous than those of Arndt's heroic effort. It has produced a bald and awkward language which has nothing in common with Pushkin's or with the usual writing of Nabokov. One knows Mr. Nabokov's virtuosity in juggling with the English language, the prettiness and wit of his verbal inventions. One knows also the perversity of his tricks to startle or stick pins in the reader; and one suspects that his perversity here has been exercised in curbing his cleverness; that—with his sado-masochistic Dostoevskian tendencies so acutely noted by Sartre—he seeks to torture both the reader and himself by flattening Pushkin out and denying to his own powers the scope for their full play.

Aside from this desire both to suffer and make suffer —so important an element in his fiction—the only characteristic Nabokov trait that one recognizes in this uneven and sometimes banal translation is the addiction to rare and unfamiliar words, which, in view of his declared intention to stick so close to the text that his version may be used as a trot, are entirely inappropriate here. It would be more to the point for the student to look up the Russian word than to have to have recourse to the OED for an English word he has never seen and which he will never have occasion to use. To inflict on the reader such words is not really to translate at all, for it is not to write idiomatic and recognizable English. Nabokov's aberrations in this line are a good deal more objectionable than anything I have found in Arndt. He gives us, for example, *rememorating, producement, curvate, habitude, rummers, familistic, gloam, dit, shippon* and *scrab*. All these can be found in the OED, but they are all entirely dictionary words, usually labelled "dialect," "archaic," or "obsolete." Why is "Достойна старых обезьян" rendered as "worthy of old sapajous"? Обезьяна is the ordinary word for monkey. In the case of the common word нега, Nabokov has surpassed himself in oddity. It is true that нега has two distinct nuances: voluptuous languor and simple enjoyment; but, instead of using any of the obvious equivalents, Mr. Nabokov has dug up from the dictionary the rare and obsolete *mollitude,* a word which his readers can never have encountered but which he uses for the first of these meanings; and for the second he has discovered *dulcitude*. One wonders how Nabokov would translate the last line of Pushkin's famous lyric "Пора, мой друг, пора" . . . "В обитель дальную трудов и чистых нег." "To a faraway haven of work and pure mollitudes"? "dulcitudes"? And what can one gather from Nabokov's statement that someone "had resolved in his lunes to exterminate all the Bourbons"? I find that *lunes* is an archaic word which may mean "fits of frenzy or lunacy"; but this statement will convey nothing to anyone who has not consulted a fairly comprehensive dictionary. There are also actual errors of English. I had never seen the word *loaden* before, and I have found, on looking it up, that it is "*Obs.* exc. *dial.*," and that it is not a past participle, as Nabokov makes it: the past participle, it seems, is *loadened*. The past of *dwell* is *dwelt,* not *dwelled; dwelled* has long been obsolete. "Remind one about me" is hardly English.

If it is a question of picking on Germanisms in Arndt, it is not difficult to find Russianisms in Nabokov. You cannot "listen the sound of the sea" in English; this is a Russianism: in English you have to listen *to* something. —Then *"Buyanov, my mettlesome cousin, toward our hero leads Tatiana with Olga . . ."* The natural English here would be *and* not *with.* If Tatyana had been telling about doing something with Olga, she would have said "Мы с Ольгой," meaning "Olga and I," and I suppose that we have here the same idiom, which Nabokov has translated literally. In the commentary, you find "a not-too-trust-worthy account that a later friend of Pushkin's . . . left us," where the English requires "has left"; but there is only one past tense in Russian where we have three, and Russians often make these mistakes. The handling of French is peculiar. The heroine of *La Nouvelle Héloïse* is given on one page as Julie and on the next as Julia; and he always speaks of "the *monde,*" instead of either "the world" or "*le monde.*" Also, why "his *sauvage* nature" when no French word exists in the Russian? As for the classics: his Eol and Zoilus ought to be Aeolus and Zoïlus; and his "automatons and homunculi" ought to be "automata," etc. And although he quotes Virgil in Latin, his speaking of the eclogues of "the overrated Virgil" as "stale imitations of the idyls of Theocritus" would seem to demonstrate that he cannot have had any very close acquaintance with this poet in the original, since Virgil, unlike Theocritus, is particularly accomplished in those qualities—tight verbal pattern and subtle effects of sound—which Nabokov particularly admires.

Then, too, there is the unnecessarily clumsy style, which seems deliberately to avoid point and elegance.

"The ache of loss chases Tatiana" (as he chooses to spell her)—why not "pursues," which would at least give a metrical line? "Well, this now makes sense. Do not be cross with me, my soul"—"makes sense" and "my soul" do not go together.

> *You will agree, my reader,*
> *That very nicely did our pal*
> *act toward melancholy Tatiana* ...

This is vulgarly phrased: "very nicely," "our pal," "act"—and so is "two-three pages." From the point of view of style, it was surely unnecessary for anyone with so fine an ear for words to write:

> *Although we know that Eugene*
> *had long ceased to like reading,*
> *still, several works*
> *he had exempted from disgrace...*

> *Farewell, pacific sites!*
> *Farewell, secluded refuge!*
> *Shall I see you?*

Nabokov translates literally "Увижу ль вас?" where the English would be, "Shall I ever see you again?" Such passages sound like the products of those computers which are supposed to translate Russian into English.

Since Mr. Nabokov is the least modest of men, I do not hesitate to urge my own rival claims against him. I once, for the purpose of an essay on Pushkin, made a version of three stanzas of *Evgeni Onegin*, which Mr. Nabokov is kind enough to include in his notes and to compliment as "well translated." He italicized, however, words and phrases of which he does not approve. Now,

these versions of mine were done, as is sometimes
Nabokov's version, in rhythmic prose with a strong
iambic base. I thus aimed to avoid padding, which is the
almost inevitable penalty of trying to put Pushkin into
English verse and which inevitably dilutes his quality.
I believe that I completely avoided this when I later
translated the whole of *The Bronze Horseman*. But in
these stanzas from *Evgeni Onegin*, I have put in a few
unimportant words in order to sustain the rhythm—such
as "farm girl" for "girl," "little boys" for "boys"—and
Nabokov has pounced upon these. But, aside from them,
my departures from the "literal" which have been obe-
lized by Mr. Nabokov (I hope he has had to look up that
word) were dictated by the desire to do justice to Pushkin
in preserving some poetic tone. When I say, for example,
that "the caravan of loud-tongued [крикливых] geese
stretched [тянулса] toward the south," it is almost as
literally accurate as and a good deal more poetically
vivid than Nabokov's "the caravan of clamorous geese
was tending southward." Again, with the description
of the horse becoming aware of the wolf—"Его почуя,
конь дорожный / Храпит"—I translated it "Snif-
fing him, the roadhorse snorts." Now, the primary
meaning of почуять is given by the small Müller-
Boyanus dictionary and two others that I have consulted
as *to scent, to smell*. Segal's larger dictionary gives *to
scent, smell, hear; to get, have in the wind;* Daum and
Schenk's *Die Russischen Verben* gives simply *wittern*.
The great Russian dictionary of V.I. Dahl gives one of
its meanings as нюхать, with an example, which is
precisely to the point, "Почуя серого [the wolf],
псы залились!" "Smelling the gray one, the dogs began
to bark." The Soviet Pushkin dictionary defines the
word as "to feel, to perceive by the senses, principally
by the sense of smell." This word is used three times in

Onegin in connection with the behavior of horses. Besides its occurrence in the passage above, we have it when the horses shy at Lensky's corpse and in the passage describing winter. Nabokov always translates it "sensing." Now, it is true that почуять may mean to become aware of something by other ways than by smelling, but it is quite obvious in these passages that smelling is meant, and the three translators quoted by Nabokov for the passage describing winter who deal directly with the word at all make it either *sniff* or *scent*. *Sniff* goes a little further than *scent*, but it does not violate the sense. What we get here, however, from Nabokov is an egregious example of his style at its most perverse-pedantic impossible:

> *Winter! the peasant celebrating*
> *in a flat sledge inaugurates the track;*
> *his naggy, having sensed the snow,*
> *shambles at something like a trot.*

"Inaugurates" is here improperly used, and "naggy" (лошадка) is another of those dictionary words which can only appear grotesque. Borrowing from the versions that Nabokov scorns, I should prefer to translate the passage as follows:

> *Winter! the peasant, rejoicing,*
> *Breaks a new track with his sledge;*
> *His poor horse, sniffing the snow,*
> *Attempting a trot, plods through it.*

I am sorry to say that, though Arndt is no great poet and that his effort to stick to the rhyme scheme sometimes leads him to a certain far-fetchedness, his version is, in general, much closer to *Onegin* than any of the others I have sampled and is likely to give the reader a better idea of what the poem sounds like in Russian than Nabokov's so tortured version. Here is Arndt's translation of the quatrain above:

> *Winter . . . the peasant, feeling festive,*
> *Breaks a fresh fairway with his sleigh,*
> *Snow underfoot, his nag is restive*
> *And, barely trotting, plods his way.*

There is nothing in the Russian about the nag being restive, but I believe that "feeling festive" is the best thing that anyone has hit upon to render "торжествуя." (Another new translation by Eugene M. Kayden, published by the Antioch Press, is by no means so good as Arndt's. He has only a sprinkling of rhymes, and he perpetrates one terrible one: *feet-weep*. Here is his version of the peasant and his horse:

> *Winter! . . . the peasant-man, rejoicing,*
> *Breaks fresh the highway with his sleigh;*
> *His pony, sniffing the new snow,*
> *Trots easily along the way.*

"The peasant-man" is awful, and "trots easily" is definitely wrong: the horse is having trouble.) It must be said that Nabokov's style and rhythm somewhat improve beginning with Tatyana's dream. The translator gets into a kind of stride and does not so often stumble over his self-implanted impediments.

The most curious feature of Nabokov's *Onegin* is the tricks which the commentator plays in dealing with his own native language. He tells us that the word нету is "an old-fashioned and dialect form" of нет. This, I find from the Pushkin dictionary, is true; but why does he not differentiate it from the нету meaning *no more* which is in constant colloquial use, and which one usually gets for an answer when one asks for some book in the Soviet bookstore in New York. He twice asserts that the adjective злой is the only one-syllable adjective in Russian (in the feminine and neuter, it may be noted that it has two syllables). But how about the one-syllable predicative adjectives: рад, горд, пьян, добр, мёртв, etc? In his guide to the Russian alphabet, he tries to explain the character *ë*, called and pronounced *yo*—which has caused so much trouble in transliteration. Except in dictionaries, grammars and schoolbooks, the *ë* is rarely given its dots but is simply written like *e*, because the Russians know where it occurs and do not feel they need go to the trouble of making their language easier for foreigners. Ordinarily, it is never written except when there is a chance of misunderstanding, as when it is necessary to distinguish between все and всё, the former of which, in the singular, is *all* applied to people and the latter *all* applied to things. The name Krushchyov has, so far as I know, never been properly transliterated except in the Moscow *Daily News,* the Soviet paper in English, and, consistently, in the Canadian press, because, in the latter case, the Soviet Embassy, I have been told, complained and set the journalists right. We, however, are stuck with Khrushchev, as we already were with Potemkin and Budenny, which ought to be Potyomkin and Budyonny. Now, Mr. Nabokov arouses one's hopes when we find such correct transliterations as Lyov, Pyotr, Pletnyov and Oryol; but then he discourages these hopes by writing—except in the index, where, for some reason, both spellings are given—what

H

ought to be Kishinyov and Mogilyov as Kishinev and
Mogilev.

On certain points, I volunteer suggestions. May not
some light be thrown on the fact—which Mr. Nabokov
discusses—that the adjective красный meant both
red and *beautiful*, since the peasant women in old Russia,
as described in *Hakluyt's Voyages*, were in the habit of
painting large red spots on their cheeks in order to
beautify themselves? In connection with the "pensive
vampire" of *Onegin*, III, 12, Nabokov takes account of
certain vampires which figure in romantic literature and
with which Pushkin may have been familiar, but he fails
to mention the legends of vampires translated by Pushkin in his *Songs of the Western Slavs* from the faked folk
ballads of Mérimée, which Pushkin took to be genuine. I
would call his attention, also, to the fact that the applica-
tion by the French of the word *goddams* to the English
was not, as he seems to think, invented in the eighteenth
century. The French were referring to the English as "goddams" in their wars with them in the fifteenth century.

The commentary, the appendices and the scholarly
presentation suffer in general from the same faults as
Nabokov's translation—that is, mainly from a lack of
common sense—something that is not detrimental to
the fantastic fiction he writes, of which it is, in fact, an
essential element, but which in an erudite work of this
kind is a serious disadvantage. The first requisite for
such an enterprise as Nabokov has here undertaken
would have been to print the Russian text on the
opposite page from the translation; but, instead of this,
he gives us a facsimile of the edition of 1837, which,
with the index, takes up the whole of Volume Four but
of which the print is too small to be read without a mag-
nifying glass. He has elsewhere invariably transliterated

the Russian—a procedure which is confusing and useless. Transliterated Russian means as little to anyone
who does not read Russian as if it were printed in
Russian characters, and for anyone who does read
Russian it is an unnecessary nuisance to have to trans-
pose it back into the Cyrillic alphabet before one can
recognize it. This alphabet, since five useless characters
were got rid of at the time of the Revolution, is one of the
few features of Russian that are really convenient and
logical—far more practical than the English alphabet.
And there can be no really simple and satisfactory way
of transposing it into English. The one system by which
it has been possible to provide a full set of Roman
equivalents for the characters of the Russian alphabet,
with its varied combinations of vowels, is the laborious
scholarly one which, producing as it must such outlandish effects as a Dostoevsky that ends in *ij,* is impractical
for ordinary use. There is a workable standard system
established by the Oxford publications, and we might as
well stick to this—though the system employed by Nabokov does have the distinct advantage that it transliterates
xa, the Greek *chi,* as *h* instead of *kh* and is thus closer to
the real pronunciation. Hemingway and Khrushchyov in
Russian begin with the same letter. Mr. Nabokov, in explaining his system, has provided a guide to pronunciation which he evidently imagines to be useful to the
reader with no Russian since he prefixes it to each
volume except the last. But this guide is strangely
unreliable. An accented *o* is *not* pronounced like the
first *o* in *cosmos* (though the English way of pronouncing
this sound is a little closer to Russian); the variable
Russian *e,* which is one of the principle problems for a
foreigner, is *not* invariably, if ever, pronounced like the
first two letters of *yellow*; there is nothing about the dif-

ference between the hard and the soft *l*, and the instructions for managing the "soft sign" would be certain to mislead the student.

In a tedious and interminable appendix—or rather, one that terminates only at the end of ninety-two pages —Nabokov expounds a system of prosody, also invented by himself, which he claims may be accommodated to both English and Russian verse. In the vocabulary of this system, a syllable becomes a "semeion." This is a Greek word that is not to be found in the English dictionary. It usually means *sign* or *signal* but one finds in the last definition in the complete Liddell and Scott that it has also been used by one Aristoxenus, a fourth-century B.C. writer on music, to mean a "unit of time, a note." A "scud" is made by Nabokov to refer to "an unaccented stress"—that is, what we call a secondary accent. But this system is ridiculous and will not work. The point is that when Russian versification took over from German versification the technique of accentual stress, this system did not really fit the rhythms of the language, which, in turn, produced in Russian poetry something quite distinct from German or English verse. The English-speaking foreigner is at first surprised, if he takes to scanning Pushkin's blank verse, to find that there are few substitutions of feet—hardly even a trochee for an iamb. Such blank verse is unthinkable in English. We remember the virtuosity of Shakespeare and Milton, who can maintain the basic iambic rhythm while constantly, with the utmost flexibility, manipulating other kinds of feet. Yet the effect of Pushkin's poetry is never monotonous, and this is because the main stresses in the so often long Russian words are more emphasized than they are in English—the other syllables seem likely to go more or less slithering—and Pushkin is always shifting these stresses. This Nabokov understands very well, but a prosody designed to deal with it cannot be used for English poetry, which Nabokov does not quite understand. In order to deal with English verse, you need to talk about only five feet: the iambus, the trochee, the anapaest, the dactyl, and the spondee. The very conception of the spondee seems for some reason to irritate Nabokov. He denies that real spondees exist, for the strange reason that "no poem, not even a couplet, can be wholly made up of them." He cannot see that two lines which he quotes—Tennyson's "On the bald street breaks the blank day" and Marvell's "To a green thought in a green shade"—both contain pairs of spondees. The way that Nabokov has accented these lines shows that he has not heard them correctly. This appendix, however, contains admirable pages on the differences between Russian and English. For example: "The Russian iambic tetrameter [the meter in which *Onegin* is written] is a solid, polished, disciplined thing, with rich concentrated meaning and lofty melody fused in an organic entity: it has said in Russian what the pentameter has said in English, and the hexameter in French. Now on the other hand, the English iambic tetrameter is a hesitating, loose, capricious form, always in danger of having its opening semeion chopped off, or of being diluted by a recurrent trimeter, or of developing a cadential lilt. The English form has been instrumental in producing a quantity of admirable short poems but has never achieved anything approaching, either in sheer length or artistic importance, a stanzaic romance comparable to *Eugene Onegin*."

The commentary, also, to some extent, suffers from being overdone. It is impossible for Nabokov to mention any poem without specifying its stanza form, meter and rhyme scheme—information which is generally quite useless, since it can give us no real idea of the poem; and he supplies us with more information than we need—one sees the lepidopterist here—about the flora and fauna mentioned in *Onegin,* to a degree that we are almost surprised that we should not be given the zoölogical data on the bear in Tatyana's dream. One is grateful to him, however, for identifying, dendrologically, the черёмуха, so much celebrated in Russian literature—it figures very effectively in one of Nabokov's own Russian poems—but impossible to be visualized by the foreigner, who will have found it defined as "bird cherry." It is, it seems, the European *Padus racemosa,* which Mr. Nabokov describes as follows: "The Russian word, with its fluffy and dreamy syllables, admirably suits this beautiful tree, distinguished by its long racemes of flowers, giving the whole of it, when in bloom, a gentle pendulous appearance. A common and popular woodland plant in Russia, it is equally at home among the riverside alders and on the pine barren; its creamy white, musky, Maytime bloom is associated in Russian hearts with the poetical emotions of youth." This is the Nabokov we know. The Nabokov who bores and fatigues by overaccumulation contrasts with the authentic Nabokov and with the poet he is trying to illuminate. It has always seemed to me that Vladimir Nabokov was one of the Russian writers who, in technique, had most in common with Pushkin. (I turn with relief to this aspect of our variously accomplished editor who is perhaps not ideally qualified to be one.) No poet surpasses Pushkin—not even Dante—for the speed, point and neatness of his narrative. How much ground in how short a space *Onegin* covers! How compact and yet easy in every stanza! The fairy tale of the Tsar Saltan—one of the great triumphs of style in literature—tells a story in its first eighty lines, too charming to be called "exposition," and creates the whole situation with which the rest of the poem will be occupied. I first read Pushkin's *Gypsies* on a short railroad journey and then, talking about it with a Russian friend who had not reread it for years, discovered that she was surprised to learn that it was not a poem of considerable length. Pushkin has moved so quickly that you feel, in its few pages, that you have spent as much time with the gypsies as the fugitive hero has and have been witnessing a fully developed drama. Now, Nabokov himself can do this. The best of his short stories and novels are masterpieces of swiftness and wit and beautifully concealed calculation. Every detail is both piquant and relevant, and everything fits together. Why, then, should this not be true of his commentary and his two appendices (for the one on Pushkin's Negro great-grandfather also makes rather heavy weather of Hannibal's African provenance)? Why not simply translate the short document in German which provides us with our principal information? It is as if this sure hand at belles lettres, once resolved to distinguish himself as a scholar, has fallen under an oppressive compulsion which prompts him to prove himself by piling things up. The truth is that in the *Onegin* his brightest moments occur when, as in the passage just quoted, the author of *Conclusive Evidence* slips into a shimmering sentence or performs a sly feat of prestidigitation.

Mr. Nabokov's most serious failure, however— to try to get all my negatives out of the way—is one of interpretation. He has missed a fundamental point in the central situation. He finds himself unable to account for Evgeni Onegin's behavior in first giving offense to Lensky by flirting with Olga at the ball and then, when Lensky challenges him to a duel, instead of managing a reconciliation, not merely accepting the challenge, but

deliberately shooting first and to kill. Nabokov says
that the latter act is "quite out of character." He does
not seem to be aware that Onegin, among his other
qualities, is, in his translator's favorite one-syllable
adjective, decidedly злой—that is, nasty, *méchant*. This
note is sharply struck in the opening stanza, when
Onegin complains about the slowness in dying of the
uncle from whom he is to inherit. This is quite in Evgeni's character, and so is his provoking Lensky by
making advances to his fiancée. You are told, just
before this happens, that Evgeni is "secretly laughing,"
that he is "approaching the moment of revenge."
What revenge? His revenge on Lensky for being capable
of idealism, devoted love, when he himself is so sterile
and empty. He has just rejected Tatyana when she
offered him her own love, which was so much better
worth having than Olga's. He thinks Lensky a fool yet
he envies him. He cannot stand it that Lensky—fed on
German romantic literature—should be fired by ec-
static emotion. So, taking a mean advantage—raising
slowly, we are told, his pistol, in malignant cold blood—
he aims to put out that fire. There are no out-of-charac-
ter actions in *Evgeni Onegin*. Nabokov has simply not
seen the point.

And now for the positive side. The commentary, if
one skips the *longueurs,* does make very pleasant
reading, and it represents an immense amount of
labor—labor which the author, in a letter, once described to me as "аховый," a delightful Russian
adjective which means that something makes you say
"ach." This I can well believe. I imagine that nobody
else has explored Pushkin's sources so thoroughly. Mr.
Nabokov seems really to have done his best to read
everything that Pushkin could possibly have read, and
has shown that he took over from poetry and fiction a

good many current phrases. He underrates Pushkin's knowledge of English and quite disregards the evidence. There is a tradition—I have not been able to trace it to its origin—that Pushkin, in the early twenties, began to read Byron with the young Raevskys, who had an English governess. Mr. Nabokov scoffs at this, but it seems extremely plausible. It was at this time that Pushkin began to write his Byronic tales, *The Prisoner of the Caucasus* and *The Fountain of Bakhchisara,* and he could hardly have given them this form if he had not known something of them in the original. And though Nabokov finds the rhyme pattern of the stanza of *Onegin* occasionally embedded in La Fontaine's *Contes,* it would hardly have been possible for Pushkin to have arrived at this stanza—though it is, of course, not identical with Byron's—if he had not had some first-hand acquaintance with *Don Juan.* He could certainly not have got this, as Mr. Nabokov seems to suppose, entirely from Pichot's French prose translation. Nabokov himself notes that Pushkin had English books in his library, but asserts that he could not read them. Of the most important evidence he says nothing at all. The volumes of Pushkin's notes and miscellaneous papers published by the Soviet government—*Tetradi Pushkina* and *Rukoyu Pushkina* —contain many extracts from English writers which Pushkin has copied out in English: passages or whole poems by Byron, Wordsworth, Coleridge and Barry Cornwall and a quotation from Francis Bacon. Mr. Nabokov does not seem to want to admit that Pushkin's competence in languages was considerable. These volumes contain passages, poems and documents in French, German, Italian, Spanish and Polish, and show that with Hebrew and Arabic he had at least got as far as the alphabets. He was capable of composing Latin epigrams and at the time of his death had been studying

Greek. He had transcribed and translated two odes of Sappho.

Nabokov has also studied exhaustively Pushkin's relations with his Russian predecessors and contemporaries, and there is a good deal of excellent literary criticism. I except from this the literary *obiter dicta* which are partly the result of Nabokov's compulsion to give unnecessary information (he cannot mention a book, however obscure, which has influenced or been mentioned by Pushkin or which contains something similar to something in *Onegin* without inserting his opinion of it); and partly the result of his instinct to take digs at great reputations. In one paragraph, we are told, for example, that a novel by Mme de Staël is "insipid," one by Nodier "lurid but not quite negligible," and both Balzac and Zola are described as inferior novelists. Dostoevsky is identified as "a much overrated, sentimental and Gothic novelist of the time" (what is Gothic about Dostoevsky?); Balzac and Sainte-Beuve as "popular but essentially mediocre writers." *Le Rouge et le Noir*, also, is "much overrated," and Stendhal has a "paltry style" (Stendhal's unadorned style is as much "a part of his act" as Nabokov's Fabergé fanciness). Chaikovsky's *Evgeni Onegin* is first a "silly," then a "slapdash" opera— though Nabokov has always declared that he does not like music and knows nothing about it, and the fact that Chaikovsky's libretto has no more to do with Pushkin's poem than Gounod's *Faust* has with Goethe's is of no importance whatever. He is particularly irritating in his flip comment on the productions of other countries, the local status of which he does not understand. He makes a point of characterizing *Rasselas* first as "insipid," then as "watery"—certainly not appropriate adjectives for the always close texture of Dr. Johnson—as if great claims had ever been made for it in England. *Rasselas* has always been tinged with a certain pathetic interest because Johnson wrote it as a potboiler to raise money for the funeral expenses of his mother, and it does convey some of the sadness which Johnson felt in general in connection with human ordeals: "Human life is everywhere a state in which much is to be endured and little to be enjoyed." But—in spite of the fact that Hilaire Belloc claimed to have read it through every year—it has hardly been popular and is rarely explored. (Nabokov sometimes makes complete blunders—as when, in *Pale Fire*, he seems to think that the heroic couplet was Wordsworth's characteristic verse form.) When Nabokov is not being merely snide and silly but taking his subject seriously, he gives us excellent little essays—on Derzhavin, on Baratynsky, on Zhukovsky, on Karamzin, and a comparison of the character of *Onegin* with Benjamin Constant's *Adolphe*. Before trying to formulate some definition of what is usually meant by classicism and romanticism, he is good on the inadvisability of trying to deal with literature in terms of literary "schools": "As happens in zoölogical nomenclature when a string of obsolete, synonymous or misapplied names keeps following the correct designation of a creature throughout the years, and not only cannot be shaken off, or ignored, or obliterated, within brackets, but actually grows on with time, so in literary history the vague terms 'classicism,' 'sentimentalism,' 'romanticism,' 'realism,' and the like straggle on and on, from textbook to textbook. There are teachers and students with square minds who are by nature meant to undergo the fascination of categories. For them, 'schools' and 'movements' are everything; by painting a group symbol on the brow of mediocrity, they condone their own incomprehension of true genius.

"I cannot think of any masterpiece the appreciation

of which would be enhanced in any degree or manner by the knowledge that it belonged to this or that school; and conversely, I could name any number of third-rate works that are kept artificially alive for centuries through their being assigned by the schoolman to this or that 'movement' in the past.

"These concepts are harmful chiefly because they distract the student from direct contact with, and direct delight in, the quiddity of individual artistic achievement (which, after all, alone matters and alone survives); but, moreover, each of them is subject to such a variety of interpretation as to become meaningless in its own field, that of the classification of knowledge. Since, however, these terms exist and keep banging against every cobble over which their tagged victims keep trying to escape the gross identification, we are forced to reckon with them."

In one special department of criticism, Mr. Nabokov is remarkably competent. With all the recent combing of literature for masked symbols and significant images, with all the exegesis of texts in which the critic diagrams ideas, philosophical, theological and political, which can never have entered the author's head, there has been shown remarkably little sensitivity to the texture and rhythm of writing, to the skill in manipulating language, for the rendering of varied effects. The explanation of such effects, with illustrations from Pope and Milton, used to be part of the apparatus of the "rhetoric" of old-fashioned grammars; but they have lately been so much neglected—really, so little understood, as one can see from the current non-versified "poems" which yet do not have the virtues of well-managed prose—that Edith Sitwell has been foolishly ridiculed for devoting attention to the subject. Mr. Nabokov—although, for the purpose of his "literal" translation of Pushkin, he has condemned himself to wear a hair shirt—has this sensitivity highly developed. He is himself adept at such effects, and is enormously appreciative of his poet's skill in assonance, alliteration, enjambment, changing the tempo by speeding or retarding, and all sorts of other subtle devices for fitting the language to the matter. Nabokov's discussion of such achievements seems to me the department of his commentary which is most valuable to the student of Pushkin or to the student of any kind of poetry.

There is, however, also, a good deal of detailed information on the manners, habits and costumes of the period, and succinct and, I believe, mostly accurate accounts of the main events of Pushkin's life. Particularly satisfactory I found the extensive discussion of Pushkin's relations with the Decembrist conspirators. The poet had planned a Tenth Canto, in which he was to make Onegin try to give his futile life an aim and to banish his chagrin from the past by joining the small band of rebels who wanted the Tsar to grant Russia a constitution. To have such a work around, of course, involved a serious risk, and a note on one of Pushkin's manuscripts shows that at some point he burned it. But fragments of a draft have survived, some of them in cryptogram. Mr. Nabokov—though not telling us, as we should like to know, exactly what this cryptogram was— has minutely examined these fragments, and, in some cases, come to conclusions that differ from those of previous editors. There is also a full discussion of the omitted and unfinished canto on Onegin's travels, and all variants, first sketches and discarded stanzas— though only in translation—are included. One wishes that Nabokov had omitted certain parts of the appendices and commentary and included Pushkin's drawings on the margins of his manuscript, of which only descriptions are given.

This *Onegin,* it is important to mention, has, aside

from its intrinsic merits, a special interest as a part of Nabokov's whole "*oeuvre*." The principal theme of his work—from his early novel in Russian, *Mashen'ka,* to the English *Pnin, Lolita* and *Pale Fire*—is the situation, comic and pathetic, full of embarrassment and misunderstanding, of the exile who cannot return, and one aspect of this is the case of the man who, like Nabokov, is torn between the culture he has left behind and that to which he is trying to adapt himself. Nabokov, the product in Russia of an English-speaking household, the son of an Anglophile father who led the struggle, as one of the leaders of the "Kadet" party, for a constitutional monarchy in Russia, Nabokov, with his Cambridge education and his brilliant command of English, had already, in his first English book, *The Real Life of Sebastian Knight,* which still seems to me one of his best, written a parable of the hide-and-seek of his Russian and English personalities. And there is a drama in his *Evgeni Onegin* which is not Onegin's drama. It is the drama of Nabokov himself attempting to correlate his English and his Russian sides. As in *The Real Life of Sebastian Knight,* they continue to elude one another. When he tries to invent a prosody in which both languages will be at home, English poetry will not submit to it; when he tries to translate *Onegin* "literally," what he writes is not always really English. On the other hand, he sometimes betrays—in his ignorance or misapprehension of certain matters—that he is not quite at home with Russian. Yet Nabokov's work, here as elsewhere, has been serving a useful function of interpretation, cross-fertilization. In spite of his queer prejudices, which few people share—such as his utter contempt for Dostoevsky—his sense of beauty and his literary proficiency, his energy which seems never to tire, have made him a wire of communication which vibrates between us and that Russian past which still provides for the Russian present a vitality that can sometimes inspire it and redeem it from mediocrity.

Finally, it ought to be said that these volumes have been admirably produced. They are not, like so many American books, tastelessly bound and too heavy, with pages of type so wide that the eye finds it an effort to follow the line. The ordinary New York publisher would no doubt have crammed all the material into a single volume which would have been cumbersome to carry around, to travel with, to read in bed. But these volumes, with their narrow measure and their sharp and distinguished type, together with their sky-blue covers and their titles stamped in gold on red, are among the most attractive books that have recently been brought out in this country.

July 15, 1965

The best account I have seen of Nabokov's *Onegin* is a long article in *Modern Philology* of May, 1966, by Mr. Alexander Gershenkron of Harvard: *A Manufactured Monument*. Professor Gershenkron is better qualified than I am to deal with the subject. Though he does justice to Nabokov's "real intuitions, numerous flashes of brilliance and a mass of solid learning," he is familiar with the literature of Pushkin scholarship, and is able to point out Nabokov's unacknowledged borrowings from certain Soviet commentators whose work Nabokov denounces as "worthless compilations."

My article on Nabokov's *Onegin* set off a long and varied controversy, to which the most animated contribution was made by Mr. Nabokov himself. Like all persons who enjoy malicious teasing and embarrassing practical jokes, he is invariably aggrieved and indignant when anyone tries anything of the kind on himself. My own attempts to tease Nabokov were not recognized as such but received in a virulent spirit, and his retaliation was protracted to the extent that he was moved to shift the debate from the *New York Review of Books* to the British monthly *Encounter*, whose readers, if they had not been following the *Review,* would have been at a loss to understand what he and I were talking about. The dialogue was picked up months later in the *New Statesman,* an English weekly, in which, contrary to all the evidence, Mr. Nabokov reiterated his assertion that Pushkin knew no English to speak of—by which time he and I had no doubt come to give the impression of the inextinguishable quarrel between the two Ivans of Gogol's story, one of whom had called the other a goose. (I have revised my original text in eliminating actual errors such as writing as if всё were the plural as well as the singular of the neuter of весь.)

In an attempt to correct any possible injustice that I might have seemed to have done to Mr. Nabokov's work in other departments of literature than the scholarly, I have read most of his early novels, originally published in Russian, which I had not before read; but I have found them rather disappointing. I know that they have been much admired both by Russian and by English-speaking readers, which latter have now had the benefit of translations by the author himself or by translators whose work he has checked. The heroes of these stories were almost always more or less "displaced persons" surrounded by rather absurd inferiors; they, however, possess an inalienable distinction and at moments a kind of communication with a higher world than that of banal contemporary reality. This reality is illustrated by the hero's minute and copious observations in the course of usually solitary excursions through the streets of Berlin and other cities. There

is often a very young girl with whom, as in the case of
Lolita, this character is more or less in love. Mr.
Nabokov has gone on record, in one of his interviews,
as explaining that he regards a novel as a kind of game
with the reader. By deceiving the latter's expectation,
the novelist wins the game. But the device exploited
in these novels is simply not to have anything exciting
take place, to have the action peter out. In Машенька
(*Mary*), the hero does not stay to meet at the station the
girl he has once half-loved in Russia and whom he has
hitherto been looking forward to seeing again. He
decides that, having had the tender passages of the past,
he has had what is most worth having and gives up and
goes away to France. In *King, Queen, Knave,* the lover
and his mistress are discouraged from murdering her
husband. In *Invitation to a Beheading,* Cincinat is not
executed but, dissociating himself from his accusers,
simply gets up and walks away. (It is curious to contrast
this ending with one of Solzhenitsyn's prison camps from
which there can be no escape.) In *The Defense*
(Защита Лужина), the expert and obsessed chess player
decides to commit suicide rather than face the challenge
of the debonair Italian champion. I believe that Nabokov succeeds better in some of his short stories such as
Spring in Fialta, when the illusion does not have to be so
long kept up. Yet I think I may be missing something
from which the virtue of these stories derives. It is
something of which we are made to feel the power in the
passages devoted to Nabokov in the memoirs of Nina
Berberova *(The Italics Are Mine),* the former wife of the
poet Khodasevich, who knew well, having shared in,
the life of the Russian émigrés in Europe. Nabokov
seems to have been the only writer who dealt intimately
with this life instead of echoing the old Russian culture which the émigrés now could never rejoin. "I

stand at the 'dusty crossroads,'" Berberova writes, quoting Blok, "and look at his (Nabokov's) 'royal procession' with thanks and the awareness that my generation (including of course myself) will live in him, that it did not disappear, did not dissolve itself between the Billancourt cemetery, Shanghai, New York and Prague. All of us, with our entire weight, be we successful (if there are such) or unsuccessful (a round dozen), rest on him. *If Nabokov is alive, it means that I am as well.*" But she goes on to say that "Nabokov is the only Russian writer (both within Russia and in emigration) who belongs to the *entire* Western world or the world in general, not Russia alone." And it is true that he gives the impression of being a man of a larger world than that of many of the Russian émigrés; yet it is them that he represents. Berberova compares him to "Joyce, Kafka, Beckett, Ionesco, Jorge Luis Borges," all more or less "displaced persons," and says truly that her "native language . . . has ceased to be what it was in the narrow nationalistic sense of eighty or a hundred years ago." But if there had been no Russian emigration, this fiction of Nabokov's could never have existed, although it could hardly have been anything but an international product, independent, multilingual, self-contained.

Vladimir Nabokov, as a Russian, has a rather peculiar status. The son of Anglophile parents, who spoke English in the household, he was educated at English Cambridge where he seems for the first time to have studied Russian seriously. I have known a good many Russians of various classes and degrees of education, but I cannot remember a "background" into which Nabokov seems to fit. His parents were rich, but his father had been a leader in the Duma of the party which was working for a constitutional monarchy and hence a "liberal" whose interests were contrary to those of the old conservative upper classes. And Vladimir is also liberal in so far as he follows his father's example: anti-monarchist, anti-pogrom. The elder Nabokov was murdered by a fanatical "Black Hundreds" assassin who was aiming to kill Milyukov, and Vladimir has always been suspicious of the representatives of the old regime. I have been very much amused, in reading the White Russian paper Новая Время, to see that these unreconstructed reactionaries seemed to be exhausting their indignation on the advocates of constitutional monarchy to the extent that they had none available for the Bolsheviks themselves. So Nabokov, in the other direction, despises the Communist regime and, it seems to me, does not even understand how it works or how it ever came to be. His knowledge of Russia, in fact, is very special, extremely limited. His account of his boyhood in his memoir *Speak, Memory* betrays his entirely privileged but very isolated position. He tells us that his honored father, who wanted to be true to his democratic principles, sent Vladimir to a kind of school where his companions would not be rich men's sons and aroused a certain amount of the ridicule inspired by class discrimination by having him brought there in a limousine—which seems to show a strange lack of tact. One wonders, why not at least a bicycle? This does not seem to occur to the son, and one wonders how much Nabokov is aware of his double snobbery: on the one hand, to social inferiors; on the other, to the stupid old-liners, whom he has never ceased to dread. With the ordinary vulgar Russian, among whom he includes the makers of the Russian Revolution, he feels no solidarity at all, and somewhere refers to himself as an Englishman. His memories of old Russia are exclusively atmospheric and picturesque—delightful childhood impressions. A meeting of literary intelligentsia he caricatures in *The Gift*. Yet I once in New York heard him recite his Russian poems to an enthusiastic Russian audience: here he dropped all his Cambridge Anglicism and soared away on a flight of eloquence in the tradition of the Russian platform poetics of Mayakovsky and Yevtushenko: in defiance of the censorship of the Soviet Union:

Каким бы полотном батальным ни являлась
Советская сусальнейшая Русь,
Какой бы жалостью душа ни наполнялась,
     не поклонюсь, не примирюсь.
Со всею мерзостью, жестокостью и скукой
немого рабства — нет, о, нет,
еще я духом жив, еще не сыт разлукой,
     увольте, я еще поэт.

The spirited accent of these later Russian poems is quite different from the conventional nostalgia of the patriotic verses in his early book, Горный Путь. I have been glad to have my opinions of such works of his exile as *The Paris Poem,* and *Fame,* in the last of which he speculates on the probable disappearance of his work but affirms his own conviction of inspiration—composed after he came to this country—confirmed by Russian readers. They are much more impressive than his early poems or than his relatively light English verse. He speaks himself of his "sparser output" . . . "in a belatedly discovered robust style."

Indeed his move to the United States seems to have had on him a fortifying effect. Of his novels written here in English, *Bend Sinister* seems to me the weakest. It suffers from the addiction to *Schadenfreude* which pervades all his work. Everybody is always humiliated.

The special torment devised to destroy the hero's son gives the impression not so much of the fiendishness of the Nazis as of the sado-masochism of the author; and in his next novel, *Pnin,* he goes so far as to bring in himself to humiliate in prospect in his own person his humble little Russian professor, who dreads Nabokov's brilliance and insolence. But the professor is somewhat sentimentalized. The sadist, here as often, turns out to have an underside of sentimentality. He compensates for this, however, in *Lolita.* Having had to invent Europe, he says, he had now to invent America; and his panorama of middle-class homes and motels is more vivid and more amusing than his dreary and prosaic German vistas. There is also something here like emotion—the ordeals of a torn personality. And one is brought at this point to wonder whether Nabokov is not better now in English than in Russian. He confesses in a postscript to his Russian translation of *Lolita* that his Russian is now to some extent failing him. His resources in English are amazing—though he does sometimes get something wrong, as Conrad occasionally writes Slavic idioms. Their publishers of course should have corrected these, but both Nabokov and Conrad may have had too much faith in the literacy of people who work in publishers' offices.

As for *Ada,* I could not get through it. The first chapter is watered-down *Finnegans Wake.* The rest, with its scrambled geography, its polyglot conversations, which turn out, when put into English, to be perfectly commonplace, and its highly intellectualized eroticism, bored me as Nabokov rarely does. This is a brilliance which aims to dazzle, but which cannot be anything but dull.

1971

SVETLANA AND HER SISTERS

Two years ago, there appeared in Paris the Russian text of a short novel called Опустелый Дом,* by Lydia Chukovskaya, the daughter of Kornei Chukovsky, the well-known translator and critic and a pioneer in Russia of the English kind of nonsense rhymes for children. The Chukovskys seem today to occupy a unique position in Russia. Chukovsky, now eighty-five, has managed to survive the purges and to maintain his high reputation. He has recently published an amusing book on the deterioration of language in Soviet Russia, Живой как Жизнь —both by way of increasing vulgarities of usage and by way of the official bureaucratic jargon from which the Russians, it seems, have come to suffer as much as we Americans do. His daughter has recently distinguished herself by her courage in addressing to Mikhail Sholokhov an indignant open letter in which she denounced him for his rabid attack on the writers Daniel and Sinyavsky, whose sentences to hard labor and banishment he seemed to think too indulgent. The government has refused publication of her novel, which deals with

* This title is evidently taken from one of the poems in the *Requiem* series of Anna Akhmatova:

Я давно предчувствовала зтот

Светлый день и опустелый дом.

(I have long had a premonition of this: a bright day and an abandoned house.)

the cruelties of the purges, on the ground that, in spite of
the downgrading of Stalin and the "rehabilitation" of
his victims, it does not for the present want the scandal
of those years given any further publicity. The book has,
however, been published in French and has now been
translated into English under the title *The Deserted
House*. It was written just after the events it describes, in
the winter of 1939–40, and is a remarkable exercise in
incisive and disciplined narrative. I should not be
surprised if it became a Russian classic.

The Deserted House is the story of the widow of a
Leningrad doctor, who has been living, as accommoda-
tions in Russia go, in comfortable circumstances,
although since her husband's death, not long after the
Revolution, she has had to share her apartment with
other people. She has been made, however, apartment
head. She has learned to type and has found a job in one
of the publishing houses, where she is now at the head
of the typing department. She takes great satisfaction in
her work and is animated, like so many others, by devotion to the service of the Soviets. She believes what she
reads in the papers, and her son, her only child, is even
more single-mindedly dedicated. Kolya lives with his
mother until he is sent away to the Ural Engineering
Works. She misses him but is made very proud when
someone shows her his photograph on the front page
of *Pravda*. He has invented a new kind of cog-wheel
cutter. But then, after the murder of Kirov, the progress
of Soviet improvement seems to be going wrong. Two
old friends of Olga Petrovna's are inexplicably arrested.
What could they have had to do with this murder?
"Everywhere there is more and more talk of Fascists,
spies, terrorists and arrests. . . . Just think, these
scoundrels wanted to murder our beloved Stalin. It was
they, it turned out, who had murdered Kirov. They have
been causing explosions in mines and the derailing

of trains. And there has been hardly any establishment in which they have not placed their henchmen." The director of the publishing house—whom she had thought such a nice man—suddenly disappears, and the papers in his office have been rifled.

What follows is the gruesome period of terror, suspicion and informing that continued through the late thirties. Olga Petrovna loses touch with her son, and though she waits for hours and days in queues and applies to a succession of officials, she cannot find out anything about him. She is hard put to it to think up explanations, and she is naïve enough to write to Stalin. At last she is told that her son has confessed to being a terrorist and has been exiled for ten years. Her best friend, who has been dismissed from the bureau, poisons herself with veronal. She had been charged by the Party Organizer, who is the watchdog in the office for the secret police, of having blasphemed against the Red Army by writing, through a slip in typing, *Krysinaya* (Rat) instead of *Krasnaya* (Red) *Armiya*. At a meeting of denunciation, Olga Petrovna calls attention to the fact that her friend did not write *Krysinaya,* the adjective from *rat,* but actually only *Krysnaya,* which meant nothing—on account of these two vowels' being close to one another on the typewriter. She had already been under suspicion on account of her father's having been a colonel in the old army, and she had therefore been excluded from the Komsomol. But the lame and sullen Party Organizer, who is now immensely enjoying himself, will not accept this explanation. (Having thus given up his colleagues, he is soon arrested himself.) And now Olga Petrovna is also dismissed from the bureau for having spoken in defense of her friend. She is sunk in despair; by the people in her flat she is treated now as a pariah. She has an hallucination in which she thinks that her son has reappeared. But at last he does succeed in getting a letter out to her. He explains that he had confessed because he had been beaten into it; this has deafened him in one ear. A friend whose husband has been deported and who is now being deported to a different place, with no prospect of making a living there, tells Olga for God's sake not to make an appeal to the authorities: it would get both her and Kolya into worse trouble to report that he has been beaten into a false confession! All she can do is go back to her room and immediately burn the letter. There is no hope of rescuing her son, no way out of her own ostracization.

It is bound to occur to the reader that Olga Petrovna, for an educated woman, has been rather remarkably obtuse, and it is clear that certain of her friends have had a more bitter reaction and a glimmer of comprehension as to what has been going on, but they would hardly dare to talk about it. Yet may there not in the Soviet Union have been many such Olga Petrovnas? Harrison Salisbury, in an article in the New York *Times,* tells of a woman writer, Galina Serebryakova, both of whose husbands were liquidated—one a former Ambassador to London—who spent twenty years in prison camps without ever suspecting that these men had not been guilty of the crimes of which they were accused. How many of our Soviet sympathizers continued for long to believe in the plots that Stalin was supposed to be punishing! Who could imagine, in the West and among Westernized Russians, that so important a ruler as Stalin could not only have gone insane but could have proceeded, with no restraint, to make so wholesale a holocaust of millions of people who opposed or were suspected of opposing him?

And what about the household of the despot who was causing all this torment and terrified chaos? You had here, also, disappearances, suicides and incomprehension as to what was happening. Those revelations of

Stalin's daughter, Svetlana Alliluyeva, which can be used for arresting headlines, are already pretty well known through the excerpts from her memoirs which have been published in the New York *Times*. The two instalments in *Life* did more justice to the family story, but it is a pity that these memoirs should first have appeared in this scattered and fragmentary form. Many people found them disappointing and neglected to read the book, but it is only from the full text, *Twenty Letters to a Friend,* now published in a poor translation, that one can get any real impression of the life and personality of Svetlana. The childhood that she spent at Zubalovo, an estate which had once belonged to a rich oilman, against whose operations her father had at one time led strikes, does not in some ways seem so much different from the life of a well-to-do family under the old regime. The children had governesses and tutors, though they were not supposed to call them so, and they were made to learn foreign languages. There were rides along fir-planted drives and the gathering of mushrooms in a birch grove that seems to be inevitable in Russian memoirs. The relatives of her mother's family and the family of Stalin's first wife were always in and out of the house, and her father's official associates are made to seem extremely genial: Bukharin, who brought them hedgehogs for pets, as the young princess in *The Idiot* did Myshkin; Budyonny, who played the accordion and sang Russian and Ukrainian songs, in which Papa Stalin joined; Ordzhonikidze, whose wife became a great friend of Svetlana's mother. There were picnics with Yenukidze, Mikoyan and Molotov. There was the classic figure of the Russian nurse who remained with the family all her life—a prop of common sense and devoted love, enduring through all vicissitudes. In a passage which has unaccountably been left out of the English translation, Svetlana declares that "In our

century of momentary changes and precipitate metamorphoses it is exceptional and gratifying to find con-
stancy and strong family traditions—when they have
somewhere been preserved." This sentence is significant,
since it emphasizes the difference between the conditions
of Svetlana's childhood and those after her mother's
suicide, when her father abandoned the family and the
government employees descended on them.

But the original difference from the old regime was
that everybody, like the family in Chukovskaya's story,
was working for the Revolution. That some of her
relatives were Chekists would not have disturbed the
young Svetlana, because, from the point of view of the
milieu in which she grew up, they were brave fighters
against the class enemy. And her grandfather, the father
of Svetlana's mother, was an electrical engineer who
built the Shatura power station; her uncle Pavel was a
military attaché to a Soviet trade mission in Germany;
her mother, still a young woman, was a student at the
Industrial Academy at the same time that she kept up her
music and French. They belonged, in fact, like most of
the Communist leaders, to the more or less cosmopolitan
and very well-educated intelligentsia who had mainly
made the Revolution—that group to which Stalin had
never belonged and which he envied, came eventually
to hate and did his best to exterminate. Stalin's first
break with this group as represented by his wife's family
occurred in 1932, when Svetlana's mother committed
suicide. She had been treated by Stalin with coarse rude-
ness at a banquet in celebration of the fifteenth anniversary of the October Revolution. She never drank,
because alcohol was bad for her, and Stalin roughly
ordered her to drink. Nadya left the table and went home
and shot herself, leaving, as Svetlana was eventually
told, a letter of indictment against him—political as well
as personal. She had been married only seven years. Her

Aunt Anna later explained to Svetlana that her mother and father had begun to quarrel as early as 1926 and that her mother had wanted to leave him. But at the time of her mother's death, Svetlana had been told only that her mother had died suddenly of appendicitis, and she did not find out what had actually happened until, very much later in life, she read in some magazine published in the English-speaking world that her mother was a suicide. After this, for the first time, she began to dare to doubt her father. She now believes that he was shocked and bewildered at having thus been betrayed by the defection of his wife, whose loyalty he had taken for granted. He did not go to her funeral and would not visit her grave. He ridiculously blamed her death on that "filthy book," Michael Arlen's once-fashionable *Green Hat*—but it is hard to see what Party worker Nadya could be thought to have had in common with Arlen's heroine of the dissipated twenties, the promiscuous Iris March, though the latter did kill herself. Could Stalin really have read Michael Arlen? He also became suspicious of Nadya's brother and sister, who he thought must have set her against him, and this suspicion of her family grew. He came rarely now to Zubalovo, and the family no longer got on well together. The atmosphere of old Russia faded. The servants were dismissed, and the place was taken over by state employees, who, in an effort to convert the old-fashioned estate into a replica of another place which Stalin had now made his home, pulled up the bird cherry and lilac bushes and covered the sandy roads with gray asphalt. They behaved "as if we did not exist. Most of them were often changed; we never had time to get used to them nor did they get used to us, and feeling that the 'Master' lived apart from the family and did not evidently care much about them, the 'helpers' were not at all amiable."

Having decided that Nadya's family and his first

wife's family were against him, Stalin now had Nadya's brother-in-law shot and the brother of his first wife, who had stubbornly refused to "confess," first exiled—upon hearing which his wife fell dead—and afterwards executed. Yenukidze, Nadya Stalin's godfather, disappeared, denounced as "an enemy of the people;" Ordzhonikidze shot himself; Bukharin was executed. Svetlana, who wants to do her best for her father, has convinced herself that Beria was the demon who led him on into the ever-expanding suspicions that brought on the proscriptions of the purges. No one in the family, she says, had ever liked Beria; her mother had not wanted him in the house. She suggests that it was he and not Stalin who, to settle an old score, had Kirov assassinated; she is unable to bring herself to believe that her father should have had this old friend killed. But, as other reviewers have pointed out, there had already been Yezhov and Yagoda as head hangmen for the secret police before Beria came up from Transcaucasia. Svetlana prints the curious letters that were written to her by her father and accompanied by pineapples and tangerines—in which he whimsically calls himself her secretary, insists that she give him orders, and replies to her, "I submit"—and she tells of her grief at his death, at which she was summoned to be present. But she says that in her father's last years she found it very hard to get to see him and that when she visited him at his dacha she found it extremely painful because it was so difficult to talk to him. She does not see how he could have taken seriously the apotheosis that became official. She thinks that it was all "the system, in which he himself was held prisoner and in which he himself was stifling from lack of companionship, from loneliness, from emptiness."

There is so much more of interest in these memoirs, and they have already been so much written about, that there is no point in trying to summarize the whole story. Alliluyeva is particularly interesting on the attitude of her father toward his Georgian origins. Her mother's family were also mainly Georgian, and they took their Georgian background for granted and were very much attached to their old Caucasian home. But her father, the ruler of Russia, wanted to be known as a Russian. It will be remembered that his conflict with Lenin, just before the latter's death, was provoked by the problem of the treatment of the minority peoples in the Soviet Union, whom Lenin wanted to handle with tolerance but whom Stalin insisted on dragooning. He would be furious when delegations from Georgia arrived and, according to Georgian custom, presented him with magnificent gifts. One of Svetlana's brothers said to her, when they were children, "Did you know that Papa used to be a Georgian?" The novelist Leonid Leonov, according to Harrison Salisbury, thinks that Stalin was actually afraid of Russia because he felt himself an alien there. I happened to be in Moscow in 1935, when Stalin gave his first broadcast. It was awaited with much curiosity and received with dissatisfaction. He may have deferred it so long for the reason that he feared this unfavorable effect. He did not seem to the Russians one of them, because he still had a lisping Georgian accent.

Poor Svetlana has been subjected to an all but overwhelming vulgarization, which is a disgrace to the Western press and television, eager for exploitation of what they regard as the sensational aspects of the case, and to the Soviet public-relations departments, perhaps at this time more anxious about the "image" of themselves to be foisted on their own people than about even that of the Soviet Union to be projected abroad. One of the highest-ranking Soviet agents, Victor Louis, has been sent out to Western Europe peddling a version of Svetlana's text, which she had left behind in Russia and which she has subsequently somewhat cut before allowing her memoirs to be published. The reason for dispatching Louis to try to get the uncut version published is apparently, in accordance with the traditional Russian strategy of deliberately confusing any question which is likely to become embarrassing, to neutralize the imagined hostile efforts on the part of the non-Communist world to throw cold water on the celebration of the fiftieth anniversary of the October Revolution. The Russians have been assuming that the publication of the memoirs was to come as a climax to these efforts, and have attempted to bring pressure on our government to get this publication delayed. Though there is nothing in the memoirs that is critical of the Revolution itself, Svetlana is an outspoken defector, who has declared, since she has been in the United States, her disapproval of what she calls "the system." But the British and American and German papers which had bought her self-edited text have been in a position legally to prevent Louis's customers from printing the other text, and what have appeared in these latter periodicals are unsigned résumés, which in Germany, at any rate, have been presented in such a misleading way as to cast doubts on Svetlana's veracity. Svetlana, in one of her interviews, has declared that these contain statements which she herself has never made. The first instalment in *Stern* is headed "*Mein Vater war ein guter Mensch,*" though Svetlana has amply acknowledged the cold-blooded brutality of which her father was capable. The second, reporting an interview with Khrushchyov, is headed with what purports to be a quotation from him ("*Hier irrt Svetlana Stalin*") and makes him refute an assertion never made by Stalin's daughter—that her father had a great love of nature—by declaring that he had never looked at nature except in the films, where the kolkhozes were prettified for propaganda. What she had really said was no more than that, at Zubalovo, he had shown a peasant's interest in having his orchards and vegetables well cared for. The third of these instalments includes an interview with her children which contains no actual denials but is headed "*Mutter ist ein bisschen durcheinander.*"

All these articles are illustrated by photographs, some of them not very attractive, which have been confiscated by the Soviets from family albums and sold not only to *Stern* but also to *Life* and the New York *Times*. The American television interviews with Svetlana—a strikingly handsome woman in perfect possession of herself and quite able to parry questions in English—seemed tainted by a kind of hostility, by an impulse to degrade their subject. A popular line had been that she was doing it all for money—though the contract with the publishers had apparently been made by her lawyer without her knowing much about such matters—and this cynicism has been shaken only by the announcement that she has now given, as she announced she was going to do, large sums to organizations for the relief of exiled Russians. The low point of this degrading process has been reached by an article in *Esquire,* which is announced on the cover by a huge photograph of Svetlana painted with Stalin's mustache like a disfigured poster in the subway and which, under an acrid pretense of exposing everybody and everything, provides interminable columns of irrelevant elaboration sometimes punctuated by snide exclamations.

Thus America has exploited Svetlana and at the same time accused her of exploiting herself. The Soviets denounce her as a traitor and a tool of the United States, and intimate that she is off her head, while the more fantastic White Russian émigrés, who do not want to believe that the daughter of Stalin can have anything good about her, declare variously that her sojourn in Switzerland was for the purpose of collecting money which her father had stashed away there and that her interest in religion is an impudent pretense, since she is really a Soviet spy. The last idea that any of these critics seems to be able to entertain is that her religious convictions are sincere and that she may have left the Soviet Union with something like a sense of mission— to repudiate her father's "system" and to try to make amends to the world for his crimes. No one seems to ask himself what it would be like to be Stalin's daughter, brought up on the gospel of the class struggle and later a witness to the horrors that this gospel was made to produce, and at the same time to find oneself a serious, affectionate and spiritually minded woman—I cannot find any better phrase for a non-Hindu adherent to Buddhism—in an officially atheist country dominated by Marxist cant, whose government hampered her movements and tried to curb the expression of her thought. Why are the motives imagined for her so often only sordid ones?

And I regret to report that the vulgarization to which she has been subjected has hardly been mitigated in the English translation supplied by Mrs. Priscilla Johnson McMillan. I was in doubt, when I began comparing passages of this with Alliluyeva's Russian text, whether the trouble was that Mrs. McMillan did not know Russian well enough; but I soon came to realize that what threw everything off was that the translator had simply no literary sense—no sense of tone, phrasing, language. Hence low-grade English and off-track inaccuracy where Svetlana is dignified and perfectly clear. "My mother for some reason went to Karlovy Vary [Carlsbad]" appears as "One time my mother went to Karlovy Vary." "I keep on living, as I did ten years ago, outwardly one life, inwardly quite another." The last phrase is rendered by Mrs. McMillan as "something quite else again"—all right for a Broadway columnist but not for a literate woman. One paragraph in the translation is made to begin as follows—"My mother, on the other hand, refused to go to the Academy in a car or even let on to the other students who she was" (Russian: "Mama was embarrassed to drive in a car to the Academy, she was embarrassed to say there who she was")—and to end "She did her best to adhere to these standards because they suited her, her parents and the other members of her family and because that was how she'd been raised" (Russian: ". . . because they were close to her own, to her family, to her relatives, and to her upbringing"). The questionable phrase "picked on" is used first for what would be better translated "persecuted"; then, in speaking of Stalin's treatment of his son, for "and in general *behaved like a pigheaded brute* [самодур]." The important incident of the banquet which resulted in her mother's suicide is made to seem somewhat more violent than it is in Svetlana's account. Translation: "And when the spring uncoiled at last, it did so with ferocious force. What caused the spring to give, the immediate occasion, was trivial in itself, so trivial one would have said it happened for no reason at all. It was a minor falling out at a banquet in honor of the fifteenth anniversary of the October Revolution. My father merely said to her, 'Hey, you. Have a drink!' My mother screamed, 'Don't you dare "Hey" me!' And in front of everyone she got up and ran from the table." There is nothing about screaming or running in the Russian, which would be better translated: "The spring was to fly apart [there is nothing about its being coiled, which would hardly be an appropriate metaphor for the kind of pressure applied] with terrific force [why 'ferocious'? Nadya was not ferocious]. This is how it happened. The occasion was not in itself important, and it did not make upon anyone any special impression—the kind of thing of which one would have said [or, of which it was said] that it happened 'for no reason at all.' It was merely a small enough spat at a banquet in celebration, etc. . . . My father merely said to her, 'Hey, you, drink!' [The occasion for this was undoubtedly one of those tiresome innumerable toasts that one is forced to drink at Soviet banquets. He would hardly have said, 'Have a drink!'] And she merely burst out, 'I'm not "Hey" to you'—and, in the presence of everyone, got up from the table and left." Mrs. McMillan invariably writes such colloquial contractions as "don't" and "that's" and "weren't," which have no equivalents in Russian and let down the sobriety of Svetlana's style. The worst of these contractions is "it'd," which no literate person would write, or even say in conversation. And she deprives the Russian relatives of their nicknames and patronymics in a way that makes the description of a literate Russian family sound rather odd. It may be added that since the book is an historical document and the chronology is somewhat confused, an index should have been provided.

The translation by Aline B. Werth of *The Deserted House,* on the other hand, is neat and clear and accurate —although she, too, writes contractions which are out of place in literary narrative—and fills in for the foreign reader some of those boring abbreviations, such as *Partog* and *Uralmash,* that may otherwise present him with blanks.

December 9, 1967

II

The Russian purges, as news, are now an old story, and an Englishman, Robert Conquest, has compiled a comprehensive account of them: *The Great Terror*. Mr. Conquest has examined all the material available and has produced the only scrupulous, non-partisan and adequate book on the subject. He deals coolly with the character and methods of Stalin and the career and murder of Trotsky, the latter of whom he does not idealize but shows to have learned ruthlessness in the same revolutionary school as Stalin. He points out, in the earlier trials, the preparation for the holocaust of the thirties. I have heard a distinguished Italian writer who was a delegate to one of the Party congresses tell of how he tried to protest, on the ground that the accusations would not be true, a proposed discrediting by trumped-up charges of someone in the opposition, and of how Stalin laughed coarsely at such an objection and his henchmen heartily echoed him. The later trials are described in detail, with quotations from the court proceedings—a record of ridiculous falsehoods extorted by systematic torture that embarrasses one for Russia and the human race. A well-researched and well-assembled book—very interesting if you can stand to read such recent history.

The last may also be said of two autobiographical narratives: *Marie Avinov: Pilgrimage Through Hell,* very effectively put together by Paul Chavchavadze from Mrs. Avinov's notes and papers and from conversations with her; and *Journey Into the Whirlwind,* by Evgenia Semyonovna Ginzburg, translated by Paul Stevenson and Max Hayward. (The Russian original of the latter, under the title Крутой Маршрут, has been published, with innumerable misprints, by Arnoldo Mondadori, in

Milan.) These two women began their lives in circumstances completely different; they had in common the misfortune of both having been confined in the Butyrka prison in Moscow, and in the Pugachyov Tower for those condemned to death, in which Catherine the Great had imprisoned Pugachyov and his rebel Cossacks; and they had both been separated from their husbands—in Mrs. Avinov's case forever—who had up to that time been functioning as able and loyal officials. Mrs. Avinov was the great-granddaughter of a Prince Scherbatov, who had been governor general of Moscow, and the granddaughter of the first elected mayor. She describes herself as having been in youth "a rebel, or at least a young woman of advanced liberal ideas," and she married an idealistic young economist. When the Revolution occurred, Avinov was thought sufficiently useful to be kept on to serve the Soviets, and he was eventually put at the head of an economic-planning department in the Far Eastern Altai Mountains. But he was suspect as a former noble and was arrested again and again. He was arrested and sent to jail for having accepted two pairs of felt boots from a friend, a former cotton-mill owner who had learned to make shoes as a hobby before the Revolution, and who now earned a living by doing so. He was accused "of having taken part in a plot to sabotage and wreck the textile industry of the U.S.S.R." After nine months in the Butyrka prison, under peculiarly humiliating circumstances, among a hundred in a cell designed for thirty, his wife was sent out for over two years to a small town beyond Turkestan in Central Asia, where, as a "political deportee," she was not allowed to find employment. When what was called her "free deportation" came to an end, she was allowed to return but obliged to live at least three hundred miles from Moscow, and chose a small provincial town close to the western border. This was very soon invaded by the Germans, and at first, since she spoke German and greatly admired German literature, she got on with them very well. Like many other Russians, she hoped that the Germans would rescue them from the perils of the Soviet regime. She made special friends with a chaplain of the occupying regiment, for she had never submitted to the government in abandoning her religion. But the Nazis proved as bad as the Russians: "It was painful to see how mistaken had been my image of a noble German 'Crusade of Liberation.' " One day, an officer arrived from Germany and announced that Hitler had ordered the abolition of Christianity and a return to the pagan northern gods. All the churches were now to be closed, as most of them had been in Russia, and swastikas instead of crosses were to be stuck on the soldiers' graves. In the mess, the officers were drunkenly shouting, "*Wotan über alles!*" Discussion of religion was forbidden. The Germans were as brutal as the Russians, and freely shot natives who offended them. After the unsuccessful siege of Stalingrad, when it was evident that the Russians were about to counter-attack, an aristocratic German general, who recognized a class equal in Mrs. Avinov, had her sent away to Berlin, from which she made her way to France and thence to the United States. She arrived here in 1947 and is at present living on Long Island. She succeeded in finding out that her husband was still alive, but a brother-in-law persuaded her not to make any effort to get him out, because if she did so they would certainly conclude that he had actually been a traitor and shoot him. Later, she was visited by a man with "thin white hair, bags under tired watery eyes . . . and cheeks grown puffy from many years of semi-starvation,"

whom she had known years ago as a "round-cheeked
and rather naïve" young student of economics, a protégé of her husband's. He told her that Nika had been
shot but had enjoined him to try to find his wife and
to tell her that he still loved her, that his thoughts were
still with her, and that death would come "as a release
and a blessing."

Mrs. Ginzburg's experience was a good deal worse.
You wonder she survived at all. She spent eighteen years
in jail and exile. She had been suddenly separated from
her children, and never saw one of her sons again. The
only positive idea that occurs to us as we read these harrowing books is that Russians are indomitably tough
and can endure almost anything—that is, until one
remembers that millions did not survive. Evgenia
Ginzburg and her husband had been active Party
members; he had been "a leading member of the Tatar
Province Committee." She was accused, on no evidence
at all, of having criminally failed to denounce a professor of her acquaintance for his imputed Trotskyism.
This kind of thing very much puzzled her, as it did so
many of the other accused—though some of them
believed that there had really been treachery and
"wrecking," or that the persecutions were really due
to the wickedness of Yagoda or Yezhov, the successive
heads of the secret police; that Stalin did not know about
them; and that everybody would be released when the
"Leader" found out what was going on. In prison,
some refused to fraternize with the traditional political
opponents of the Party, the Social Revolutionaries and
the Mensheviks: "One mustn't let one's mind be swayed
by pity . . . above all, we mustn't play into the hands
of enemy propagandists." Mrs. Ginzburg gives instances
of meeting women with whom she had formerly been

on friendly terms but who had been turned into virulent repudiators of everyone accused of heresy. One who had been persuaded to spy on and denounce other prisoners by the promise that she would afterwards be liberated was told, when she had done her work, "And now, my dear, you are going to be shot." Nobody could at first imagine that punishment for imaginary offenses had been adopted as a deliberate government policy. "Every region and every national republic was obliged by some lunatic logic to have its own crop of enemies so as not to lag behind the others, for all the world as though it were a campaign for deliveries of grain or milk." One is appalled by the hatefulness and unnecessary sadism that were brought into play by this campaign, to realize that it is possible for a large number of human beings to devote all their time and energy to making life miserable for their fellows. What satisfaction, one asks, could have been derived by the wardens and interrogators—once the victims had been locked away—from continuing month after month to torment them on petty false charges, sometimes gratuitously invented, such as writing on the walls of the washrooms, leaving nail marks on the books they had borrowed from the library, and talking or singing in their cells? Even fear of being charged themselves with showing too little zeal can hardly account for this. The interrogators, we are told, were trained to practice in their mirrors the looks of contempt and loathing with which they tried to paralyze their victims. No brief summary can give any idea of the suffering and degradation to which these women were subjected: constant abuse, plank beds, scant and silent exercise, food so revolting that they starved themselves rather than try to eat it; nights made horrid by the shrieks and groans of prisoners who had not yet been sentenced because they had not yet been made to confess. Evgenia spent two years in what was meant to be solitary confinement, though the press of the condemned became so great that another woman was put into the cell with her. Special national holidays, such as May Day and the Anniversary of the Revolution, were celebrated by transferring the prisoners to even worse underground cells, where they lay or stood upright in darkness. As one of these special punishments, at the time of the first big series of bogus trials (how could added torments in the prisons act as warnings to the people outside?), the window of Evgenia's cell was kept shut in the stifling summer weather except for ten minutes a day. When Evgenia became unconscious, a relatively humane doctor, who had said he had no authority to interfere with prison regulations, did succeed in having the window opened for twenty minutes instead of ten.

When at last these women were dismissed from the prison, all their photographs of their families were taken from them and flung on the ground and walked on for fear they would write messages on them and slip them outside on their way. They were now forced to travel on foot and in overcrowded boats and trains which remind one of the days of the slave trade. Though there was plenty of water available, they were nearly forced to die of thirst, and there was a special car reserved for the punishment of such offenses as aggressively demanding water. It is evidence of the life-giving power of literature that Evgenia was able to lighten the ordeal of this hardly bearable journey by reciting pages of Pushkin and other poets, as Marie Avinov had distracted her companions by repeating to them the stories of *Ivanhoe, The Three Musketeers* and *Around the World in Eighty Days*. This journey ended near the Pacific in Elgen, not far from the Arctic Ocean, where the cold was, of course, extreme.

Evgenia was to spend, in all, eighteen years of her life in jail and in arctic exile. The latter years were, however, made more tolerable when she came into contact with a doctor who knew a relative of hers, a surgeon in Leningrad, and who had her made a medical attendant in a children's home. (The translation by Max Hayward and Paul Stevenson reads well in idiomatic English. The character called Brotteaux in Anatole France's *Les Dieux Ont Soif* is confused, as he is not in the original, with Balzac's César Birotteau.)

It is nagging and annoying, it goes against the grain, to be obliged to take account of these books, so unrelievedly negative. The only fascination such memoirs can have for the Western reader derives from the accumulation of horrors, from the suspense of watching how far systematic malignancy can be made to go and how much, in the rare cases of survival, a strong and proud spirit can bear.

There has, however, emerged just now another Soviet story, which startlingly and dynamically offsets these depressing records. Stalin's daughter, Svetlana Alliluyeva, has now produced a second book, of a quite different order of importance from the first. Her *Twenty Letters to a Friend* was written six years ago in Russia and had to be smuggled out for fear of having it confiscated. It was mild enough, consisting chiefly of early memoirs of her life in the country with her mother's family, and an account of her late discovery of her mother's suicide and of the scene of her father's death. This was given such exaggerated publicity and first published in such an unsatisfactory way—simultaneously in two sets of fragments in *Life* and the New York *Times*—that unless one later read the whole book it made hardly any impression, and some readers found the book itself puzzling. Svetlana's new book, however

—*Only One Year* (in an excellent translation by Paul Chavchavadze; Harper has also published a Russian edition)—is, on the contrary, a story of her life which is outspoken to an astonishing degree, and a unique historical document, which will take its place, I believe, among the great Russian autobiographical works: Herzen, Kropotkin, Tolstoy's *Confession*. The "year" which gives its title to the book is 1967, when Svetlana was allowed to go to India for the purpose of scattering in the Ganges, according to the Hindu rite, the ashes of her late Indian husband and when, suddenly making the decision not to return to the Soviet Union, she took refuge in the American Embassy and was flown out that night to Switzerland. There she stayed in a convent under an assumed name, and, on the intervention of Mr. George Kennan, was thence admitted to the United States. This narrative is, however, interrupted by frequent flashbacks which cover her whole previous life, with the exception of those phases and incidents which have already been dealt with in the *Twenty Letters*. The book is close-packed with incident, with ideas and with information. I do not know how far consciously its scheme was planned, but the result is immensely effective: the Russian instinct for storytelling and dramatic presentation makes it a narrative so moving, even harrowing, that at one point it sent me to bed with a headache. It was at that point where Svetlana seems to say to you, after telling of her life in India and creating tense expectation as to whether or not she will succeed in escaping, "Very well, if you were not satisfied with my other book and believe, as some said, that I was whitewashing my father, I am going to tell you now exactly what it was like to be Stalin's daughter, growing up in the Soviet Union, living through the period of the purges and attempting to arrange for myself a tolerable life under the conditions of the postwar period." This comes

with a kind of explosive force. Svetlana, as had already
been plain, is a strongly religious woman; she was saved
from a neurotic girlhood, when she was strictly confined
in the Kremlin and lost half the school year through
illness, by something in the nature of a religious revelation, and she had herself baptized in the Orthodox
Church, an action still rather dangerous, after her
father's death. She has something like a sense of divine
mission in connection with both her decision to break
with the Soviet Union and her writing of this second
book. Of the first of these actions she says, "I myself
took the decisive step, in Delhi. No one helped me or
advised me or knew what I was doing. But I believe that
all our thoughts and acts are in the hands of God,
and I knew that, lacking this support, for which I had
previously been prepared and which came to me
as an inspiration and a decision impossible to set
aside, I should otherwise never have had the strength
to take such a step by myself." And the book is a moral
declaration that has the boldness and the passion
of *Doctor Zhivago*—which was discovered by Svetlana in Switzerland and made by her the subject of
an eloquent article. One feels that, whatever the consequences may be, she has resolved to leave *One Year*
as a testament with which the spiritual mediocrities
of the Soviet Union will eventually have to come to
terms.

During her years of living in the Kremlin, almost her
only opportunity of escaping from it was provided by
the public school which, like all Soviet children, she had
to attend, and, later, by the university; but she was
ashamed to ask her school friends to the Kremlin
because she had to get passes for this. It was only through
these school friends that she learned what was happening at the time of the purges. First, the relatives of her

mother with whom she had grown up were executed or
sent into prison or exile. They had been zealous workers
for the Soviets, and she found it quite impossible to
imagine them as "wreckers." She knew that it could only
have been by the order of her father that his in-laws had
been "liquidated," but she did not understand at that
time that it was because they knew too much about her
mother's death—her suicide, caused by the brutality
both public and private of her father. Then a man with
whom she thought herself in love was suddenly accused
of spying and sent for five years to the Arctic, followed
by another five years in a concentration camp. It
seems evident to the reader, though I do not believe
Svetlana is conscious of this, that since her early affectionate relations with her father had been broken and
obliterated, she has been searching for a father substitute. This first love, banished by her father, was twenty
years older than she, and her third husband seventeen
years older. The priest who baptized her and on whom
she much depended was an old man who died not long
after, and there appear older men in her memoirs with
whom her relations also seem filial. (She explains at one
point, in fact, that she has always liked older people.)
The culminating occurrence in her relations with her
father seems to have come when, on one occasion, while
she was visiting him at his dacha, she overheard a telephone conversation which had ended by Stalin's
saying, "A car accident," in a positive tone which indicated that he was not asking a question but giving some
kind of order. She could tell that the man "had been
murdered—there had been no accident." She knew now
that her father was a merciless despot, and her alienation
from him became complete. This is the terrible story she
has to tell, at once one of the most astonishing and most
distressing of history. She went to her father and said

to him that she no longer wanted to be called Stalina (since Stalin was, after all, only a *nom de guerre,* and she found it too forbidding and metallic); that she wanted to take her mother's name instead, which is legal in the Soviet Union. He said nothing, but she felt this had stung him.

Svetlana has described in her previous book his unresponsiveness and moroseness in these years. He had repudiated his unfortunate son, Jacob, who had been taken prisoner by the Germans, declaring, when asked about him by a foreign correspondent, that there were no Russian prisoners in Hitler's camps—"only Russian traitors"—and that he had no son called Jacob. Svetlana became convinced that the methods by which he annihilated millions of Soviet citizens were kept as indirect as possible, and denies a story once circulated that, on seeing at his country place some unexplained footprints in the snow, he had himself shot a guard who had failed to report them. She says that it was quite unlike him to shoot any offender himself, and that the moment he had been informed that his opponents had been disposed of, he dismissed them completely from his mind and was untroubled by pangs of conscience. She makes an attempt to explain her father which, since she knew his Georgian mother and had family information about his early life, makes some genuine contribution to the subject. Josef Dzhugashvili was the only child of a shoemaker, for whom, after his father's death, his mother made every sacrifice to enable him to study for the priesthood. This mother was the only human being for whom he seemed ever to have shown any affection. But he had been a rather bad and destructive boy, and at the seminary—although, apparently, he acquired there a little more education than his detractors have liked to assume—he learned to despise the priesthood, which undoubtedly in Georgia, Svetlana says, was extremely corrupt and crude. Having never been exposed in youth to any teacher who had any real sense of religion, it was possible for him to develop, she says, into "a moral and spiritual monster." He was not, she insists, a typical Georgian. The Georgians are gay and gregarious: they love banquets at which they sing and have formalized discussions that recall the ancient Greek symposia. But Stalin had no hesitation in destroying his old Georgian friends and never showed any regional benevolence toward Georgia. When he revisited his native place and was met on the road by enthusiastic ovations, he said only "Fools! The Georgians are fools!" and had the car turned off along another road. Svetlana makes no attempt to explain in any psychiatric way her father's mental condition. She says that she is no Dostoevsky. She admits that he occasionally lost his temper, as when once, trying to telephone and finding the line always busy, he hurled the apparatus against the wall; but she believes that he was much "too cold a man" for such "fits of passion as Othello's." He always, Svetlana says, knew exactly what he was doing, and she does not consider him to have been insane. The word "paranoia" is never mentioned, and I get the impression that her notions of insanity may perhaps be rather antiquated.

Svetlana had, of course, been brought up on Communism almost, as she says, "from diapers." "At the university, I went through a course in the historical and social sciences. We seriously studied Marxism, we analyzed Marx, Engels, Lenin, and of course Stalin. From these studies I only came to the conclusion that all this theoretical Marxism and Communism had nothing whatever to do with the actual life of the Soviet Union. In the economic sense, our socialism was more like state capitalism. Its social aspect was a kind of strange hybrid: a bureaucratic barrackslike system, in which the secret police resembled the German Gestapo, and the backward rural economy the villages of the nineteenth century. Marx had never dreamed of anything of the sort. Progress was forgotten. Soviet Russia had broken with everything in her history that was revolutionary, and had got onto the usual rails of great-power imperialism, having replaced the liberal freedoms of the beginning of the twentieth century with the horrors of Ivan the Terrible." The October Revolution she regards as "a fatal mistake—it is impossible after fifty years not to recognize this"—for she believes that "the proletarian revolution of Lenin" was made to take place prematurely in Russia. "The Social Revolutionaries understood better than the Bolsheviks the historical problems and the destiny of the huge disorganized peasant country." It was only in the fifties and sixties that she began to learn about pre-revolutionary Russian history, the history of the Revolution itself and the political role played by her father, from such works as Isaac Deutscher's *Political Biography* of Stalin, Djilas's *Conversations with Stalin* and John Reed's *Ten Days That Shook the World*. It is remarkable that her natural intelligence, overcoming such cramping limitations, should have enabled her to learn from these books when she was supposed to shut her mind against them. For her, what she calls the romanticism of the early days of the Revolution is now something completely old-fashioned, which really died out after the Spanish Civil War and of which one now hears only "echoes." She has an amusing account of a dinner at the Molotovs' at which Mrs. Molotov is telling Svetlana what a great man her father was and throwing around the cant clichés of the early years, while the young Molotovs are silent and drop their eyes and do not know where to look. Svetlana is amusing in a grim way in describing the annual celebrations of the anniversary of October which she had to attend from childhood. She always knew what the speeches were going to be before they began, and she says that the loudspeakers have been becoming louder and louder; she suggests that the reason for this may be a fear on the part of the authorities that the officially rallied crowd, instead of responding with the usual cheers, might break out with "*Doloy!*" ("Away with it!")

But she declares she has not much interest in politics. From the moment when you experience the power of religion, she says, you can no longer take Communism seriously. What difference, from the point of view of moral character, does it make whether an individual is a capitalist or a Communist, a peasant or a Western bourgeois? It is worthwhile to quote her declaration of faith made in connection with her baptism into the Orthodox Church. (It should be noted here that she tells us that she does not have any preference for any of the religions above the others. Judaism, Roman or Greek Catholicism, Mohammedanism, Buddhism and the Protestant churches all aim at the same ideals.) "Baptism," she explains, "was for me a great symbolic event. Neither the dogmas of Christianity nor its rituals were important for me, but eternal Life, eternal Good. The rite of baptism consists in rejecting evil, in freeing oneself from evil, from the lie. I believed in 'Thou shalt not kill,' I believed in truth without violence and bloodshed. I believed that the spirit of truth is stronger than material values. And when all this entered into my heart, the remnants of the Marxism-Leninism that had been taught me from childhood vanished like smoke. I knew now that no matter how much sinful and cruel man might declare his power on earth, truth would triumph sooner or later, and former glory would turn to dust."

She does, nevertheless, touch on politics to the extent of insisting that the seeds of the system which her father carried to such exterminatory lengths had already been planted by Lenin and inherited from old Russia. She scoffs at the idea that in her father's case it was a "cult of personality" which perverted the progress of the Soviet Union. Yet her horror at her father's role is something from which it is difficult for her entirely to free herself. She had thought that by writing her previous book she had more or less dismissed the past, but she realized after it was published that she had not fully portrayed Stalin or explained her own situation. "When I was writing *Twenty Letters,*" she says, "there were ringing always in my ears the words of the priest who baptized me: 'Do not judge your father. The Highest Court has now dealt with him: in his life he raised himself too high, but now there is nothing left of his glory. God straightens out and corrects what is wrong. But you cannot—you are his daughter.' "

Her account of her sojourn in India is interesting in a special way. She had never lived before in a foreign country; and she observed people, customs and landscapes with her usual close attention. Her husband's family belonged to a very high caste, and—in spite of the existence in Russia of what were called the "ten first families"—she had had no experience of a caste-bound society. She thought nothing of mixing with the "untouchables" and engaging, if convenient, in their menial work. She could not understand at first that every servant had a special duty which he was limited to performing. When the daughter of a rajah, her relative by marriage, got married for love to a man of lower caste, she could not be given the family jewels which would otherwise have come to her, and when she visited her parents with her husband, a new atmosphere of formality prevailed. In India, although Svetlana was living in the country there, she was constantly pursued by her Embassy, and it was attempted to abbreviate her permit of absence and get her back to the Soviet Union. A woman companion was posted to watch her, whom with difficulty she at last shook off. She has a disdainful account of a lunch at the Ambassador's house just before she was supposed to leave, when she was told that in the country she had been starved to death, and that she must now drink up and eat plenty in the good old Russian fashion. They were extremely nervous about her. Her attitude toward the Soviet "élite," in general, is one of cool and slightly contemptuous superiority. After a chapter describing a number of her friends, scientists and cultural specialists who, by disassociating themselves from politics, found means to pursue their interests and to survive both the purges and the war, she takes up, one by one, in a later chapter, a number of the Soviet leaders—their personalities, their households, their habits. Svetlana, in the post-revolutionary society, occupied a unique position. She grew up as a sort of princess, enjoying more comforts than most girls yet closely guarded and not allowed much freedom. Till at last she acquired a small apartment, where she lived with her two children, a boy who is now a physician and a girl who is studying geophysics, she had never had a home of her own. The results of this are paradoxical. One feels at first some astonishment that, schooled under Soviet pressures and subjected to the Soviet restrictions—though there are still in her education inevitable historical gaps—she should have been able to learn so much, that her innate good sense and good taste, brought to bear on the extensions of an acquired perspective, should have guided her to arrive at what seem to us in the West more or less normal views.

It is strange for anyone who has been in Russia to find her reacting as a foreigner does to its ineptitude, sloppiness and dirt. The daughter of the leader of the Soviet Union, coarse though he himself may have been—his carouses with his colleagues, at which she was forced to be present, disgusted her and made her sometimes withdraw—she cannot accept his vulgar successors. There is a curious and interesting scene in which she goes to apply to Kosygin for permission to regularize legally her union with her Hindu mate. It is years since she has been in the Kremlin, and she recognizes with distaste the stale old official carpets and green cloth covers on the empty tables among which, in her girlhood, she had languished so long. One feels that she is made uncomfortable by being forced to appeal to Kosygin in the office which her father had occupied. He asks her whether there aren't plenty of nice Russian boys with whom she would be better off than with her elderly asthmatic Hindu, and he tells her to go back to the collective, where it will be seen to that they will not discriminate against her on account of the downgrading of her father. She has difficulty controlling her temper. Her petition is never granted.

Svetlana says she is happy in the United States. She has bought a house in Princeton and a Dodge car, in connection with the latter of which she has defiantly said, in a letter that has been published in the *Novoye Russkoye Slovo,* that she does not feel the slightest compunction for having yielded to a "bourgeois" ambition. She has discovered, as many have done before, that Americans are in some ways very much like Russians—that is, they are informal and friendly. A difference, however, which she noted between the Soviet officials and ours, when she took refuge in our Embassy at Delhi, was that the young Americans there always smiled at her, whereas the officials of the Soviets were usually tense and morose. Her accounts of the American households she visited when she first arrived make rather amusing reading: from what she tells us about them one can fill in a more complete picture. Her relative freedom here has given her a new self-confidence, which enables her to express opinions that, as in the case of her frank doubts about the wisdom of the October Revolution, may seem to us rather startling. Our complaints of our own country seem to her like those of spoiled children— spoiled, that is, by our freedom and affluence—who are scolding their provident parents. This seems strange to depressed Americans, who may feel that she is overrating us. It is rather odd to find her concluding her so often fantastic story at a table in the Princeton Inn, not long before celebrating Christmas, with Louis Fischer and Mrs. George Kennan, where they drink to the "only one year" that has included her visit to India, her narrow escape to Switzerland and her publicized advent to the United States. A tame enough conclusion, this seems, to a book which I believe will reverberate through the whole contemporary world.

September 27, 1969

SOLZHENITSYN

We have known about the Russian purges, but we have not really been able to imagine them. The Nazi concentration camps have confronted us more immediately, since they were opened up by the Americans, and we have seen the photographs of piles of emaciated corpses. We were not aware that the Russians, with their undiscourageable literary gifts, had been assiduously writing up what had happened to them under Stalin's insane tyranny: Anna Akhmatova's harrowing *Requiem,* which seems almost too intimate to be published; Miss Chukovskaya's *The Deserted House,* which deals with a similar situation, of a woman whose son has been snatched away with no explanation and no possibility of communication; the memoirs of Mrs. Avinov, Mrs. Ginzburg and Mrs. Mandelshtam (which last, in its protracted misery, becomes at last almost unbearable), together with other first-hand accounts of hardship and humiliation. But the most thoroughgoing exposé has of course been that of Alexander Solzhenitsyn.

Solzhenitsyn had graduated with honors in physics and mathematics from the University of Rostov and had taught physics in a school at Rostov. (I mainly follow the short biographical sketch in the collected works, published in Germany.) His career was interrupted in 1942 by the war, and he became commander of an artillery battery. He distinguished himself in the field, received a commission as captain, and was decorated with the Order of the Red Star. In February of 1945, he was arrested for criticizing Stalin in his diary and in letters to a friend, and for alleged "anti-Soviet agitation." He was charged with having participated in "the creation of an anti-Soviet organization," and sentenced to eight years in labor camps and afterwards to "perpetual exile." It was only as a result of the "unmasking of the 'personality cult'" of Stalin at the Twentieth Party Congress that he was at last "rehabilitated." He now went back to teaching physics in Ryazan. Friends tried to persuade him to come to Moscow, but he refused, "because he feared that he would be deprived of the quiet and repose so necessary to him in the literary work to which he had decided to devote himself." When, later, he did want to go to Moscow, the authorities refused him permission. His imprisonment had, however, been somewhat alleviated by permission to teach physics. Solzhenitsyn's long short story *One Day of Ivan Denisovich* (the title is so in Russian), a description of life in a labor camp, was published in *Novy Mir* under the somewhat looser regime of Khrushchyov, in 1962. But his more elaborate novels, so damaging in their criticism of Soviet society— *The Cancer Ward* and *The First Circle*—have never been published in Russia. What happened to Solzhenitsyn as a result of these books is well known. He was expelled from the Writers' Union; he was awarded the Nobel Prize but he would not go to Sweden to get it, because he was afraid of not being allowed to return to the Soviet Union. He was determined to remain in Russia and to work for a more enlightened government.

One can well understand how embarrassing Solzhenitsyn must seem to the Writers' Union, who are committed to representing the regime in the most favorable possible light. Solzhenitsyn, who had fought against the Germans, whose activities as a scholar had been abruptly cut off by the war, who had been condemned for a long term of years to the waste of his time and energies on rudimentary forms of labor, resolved to spare nothing and nobody, to make known what had been going on in those years of meaningless repression, and to continue to protest against the Stalinist practices that were still being imposed in Russia. One cannot beyond a certain point sweep the crimes of the past under the carpet. If Stalin's reign, while it lasted, constituted one of the blackest periods of human history, if its followers are functioning today, we must face it, we cannot blot it out. Let the repulsive story be told. There is a man of great talent to tell it. And the Russians have too long been masters of making of the most sordid, the most painful, the most degrading aspects of their lives absorbingly dramatic stories.

In Solzhenitsyn's case, *The Cancer Ward* presented, surely, from the literary point of view, a very peculiar challenge. How would it be possible, one might wonder, to provide an interesting narrative out of the materials furnished by a lot of patients suffering from, many dying of, cancer, with their staff of doctors and nurses? The subject is unpleasant, depressing—in its medical aspects, highly technical. The scene is a provincial hospital, far from Moscow and attached to Tashkent, with all the deficiencies and ineptitudes characteristic of such an institution. The present writer has had first-hand experience of a similar hospital in Odessa, where he was quarantined for nearly six weeks, and he can vouch for the veracity of Solzhenitsyn's picture, which is also

based on first-hand experience. True, the central Solzhenitsyn-figure is finally cured and dismissed.
The story has been somewhat enlivened by two incipient
love affairs, with a nurse and a woman doctor, both of
whom have practically invited him to live with them.
But although the excitement of emergence from the
hospital, the renewal of the colors and movements of
life—he is fascinated in watching a zoo and made to feel
the personalities of the animals—intoxicates the ex-
patient, he fails to visit either of his women, and,
his senses and ambitions blurred, ends by simply
writing to one of them a friendly note, and at last,
stretching out on the baggage rack, with his duffelbag
under his head, takes a train to the little Eastern town
to which, like the author, he has been exiled "in per-
petuity" and in which he has made for himself a quiet,
fairly comfortable life. Yet an interest on the part
of the reader in the life of the cancer ward is aroused.
We want to know how the people will behave, how each
of them will meet his fate. An official who is a patient,
accustomed to certain privileges, is disposed at first
to resent what he regards as unwarranted indignities;
he calls the Solzhenitsyn-figure a "class enemy," and in
the end drives off in his car. The Uzbeks and Kazaks can
hardly speak Russian, and keep up their spirits by
playing cards. The old men are almost past caring
about anything but their treatments; a young man who
lost a leg and who has been "thinking pleasant
thoughts—how he'd learn, briskly and smartly, to walk
on crutches"—has a crippled erotic passage with a
girl who is about to lose her breast. Solzhenitsyn's constant resourcefulness at sustaining our interest in all
this, shifting our attention and varying the mood from
one of these wretched groups to another, is an impressive exhibition of skill.

This novel, in spite of its gruesome subject, seems to me the better, perhaps because it was the first written, of Solzhenitsyn's two large-scale works. The characters are more vivid, the emotions are conveyed more tellingly. It is a long book—it seems to me a little too long. *The First Circle* is even longer; in the Russian German-published edition, it runs to two volumes. Though the action covers only three days in 1949, it involves so many characters and so many "confrontations" that it seems to go on for years. We are again confined to an institution—a special prison for technicians and scientists who are still supposed to be useful—and the relations and personalities of the inmates, here on a much higher level, are traced with the same particularity as those of *The Cancer Ward*. A suspense ought to be kept up by the doom that, without his knowing it, hangs over the State Counsellor Innokenty Volodin, but by the time we have got to the end we are likely to have forgotten the opening incident, in which Volodin incurs official displeasure by warning a colleague, a professor, that he is himself in danger for having promised to "give something"— actually, only "some kind of medicine"—to his fellow-professors in Paris, any traffic with any kind of foreigners being at that time, of course, suspect. Volodin, however, has every reason to believe that he has been assigned to the ambassadorship in Paris, but he finds that instead of this he has been condemned to the dreaded Lubyanka Prison. His realization of this, his confinement in a narrow cell, in which he is watched constantly through a peephole, his being stripped, searched and otherwise humiliated provide one of the most horrible scenes in literature. The Solzhenitsyn-character, a mathematician who is thought to be unfaithful to the official line, is transferred to an even worse prison, and Solzhenitsyn is said—*Time*, March 21, 1969—to have written a sequel, *Arkhipelag Gulag* (Gulag is the labor-camp administration), which deals with his experiences there. This has not yet been translated, though it is reported to have been circulated in an underground way in Russia. One wonders how many non-Russians will be able to face something even more oppressive than *The First Circle*.

In all these chronicles of frustration and injustice, however, a few positive elements appear. Ivan Denisovich, enduring, sticks stoutly to his métier and persists in doing sound rather than slipshod work (though it seems to me just as boring to read about his conscientious bricklaying as about any other kind of bricklaying). Nerzhin, the Solzhenitsyn-character in *The First Circle,* maintains his intellectual dignity and makes friends with the gatekeeper at the prison, who— recurring theme in Russian fiction since Tolstoy's worthy peasant Karataev—in spite of having been subjected to endless ordeals of disaster and deprivation which would crush a less humble, less resilient soul still also endures and is not discouraged. Nerzhin, when he is sent away to another prison, gives this man what he has come to regard as his only precious possession, a volume of Essenin's poems. But the sole trace to be found in these books of the original Soviet ideology is Solzhenitsyn's conviction, or the conviction of one of his characters, that capitalism is doomed.

And it is evident, though not allowed to become too insistent, that Solzhenitsyn is sincerely religious, and that, as in the case of other Russian writers, it is his faith, something quite alien to the cant of the Soviet doctrine, that has helped him to survive and reject the official propaganda. A prayer of his, not included among his collected works, has been circulated, and it sounds authentic: "Thou wilt give me what I need," he ends his appeal to God, "to reflect them [the radiance of thy rays of light to humanity]. And so far as I may fall short, Thou wilt assign the task to others." In such sketches as *Travelling Along the Oka* and *Easter Procession* (the latter of these was lopped of its bitter ending in the translation published by *Time*), it is clear that he resents the profanation of the churches and the rites of the Orthodox Church. The best treatment I have seen of Solzhenitsyn, which brings out the pattern of his work and emphasizes these positive elements, is the study in Miss Helen Muchnic's *Russian Writers: Notes and Essays*.

But Miss Muchnic, too, is a Russian, and it is true of most of the Russians I know that they perfectly understand Solzhenitsyn and are in sympathy with what seems to me his somewhat masochistic point of view. In an Anglo-Saxon reader, there is something that ultimately rebels against this.

It is not that the incidents of his picture are false. The horrors that he tells of are fully confirmed by the testimony of other writers, who, like him, have known them at first hand. But such a reader, who is outraged at first by these chronicles of senseless suffering, of protracted degradation and torment, who is stirred to indignation against the oppressors, may end by becoming impatient with the beings who are thus oppressed. Such a state of things, feels the Anglo-Saxon reader, should not be allowed to exist. Such relations between human beings are certainly quite abnormal. The existence of a Stalin, after all, implies the existence of a nation that will stand for the horrors he inflicts. That many of these people have been led to believe that they were paving the way to a glorious future, to a

regeneration of humanity, and that this will demand the
survival through periods of formidable hardship, the
resolute extirpation of the class enemy, and that one
cannot doubt the wisdom of the leader who has been
appointed by the Communist Party to enforce its discipline and accomplish its tasks—one has to allow for
all this. And yet would not Anglo-Saxons have put up
somewhat more resistance? The religion of Protestants
is more pugnacious. In characterizing the poet Nekras-
sov, the Vicomte Melchior de Vogüé, who probably
in his time knew Russia better than any other foreigner,
writes that "you will not find in him the common fund
of mysticism of other Russian writers , of resignation,
of love for the suffering which they denounce." The
Russian religion itself, all obedience and resignation to
inevitable misfortune, involves a humiliation. And the
unvaried frustration in Solzhenitsyn becomes in the
long run monotonous; one feels that it is systematic,
that, except for his recognition of the virtue of sheer
endurance, it is Solzhenitsyn's only theme. We always
expect what is going to happen: someone is going to be
cheated, to be disappointed, squelched. Ford Madox
Ford calls attention, in his book on Henry James, to
the apparently abnormal unhelpfulness of the narrator-
observer of James's *Four Meetings,* to whom it never
occurs to offer to lend five or six pounds to the little
New England schoolteacher who has been stranded at
Le Havre and cheated of her dream of a visit to Paris, or
to tip her off to the fraudulence of the supposed French
countess who is swindling her. So in Solzhenitsyn's
Matryonin Dvor (translated as *Matryona's Home,* or
House) we wonder why *his* narrator-observer—even
when Matryona complains that she has not "a man to
stick up for me"—should never lift a finger to intervene
when his long-suffering peasant woman is clearly being
exploited and robbed. Though he is lodging all through

this in her house, he simply looks on at the outrages, to which she makes no resistance. This lodger, like Solzhenitsyn's other heroes, has emerged from a long term in prison and is consequently under a cloud, so that for him to try to protest would be futile and only make for her more trouble; and we have been told that when Matryona in the past has attempted to appeal for a pension that has been due her she has invariably been given the runaround by the Soviet bureaucrats. But we recognize that we are here inescapably in Solzhenitsyn country as soon as we learn that Matryona's cat is lame in one paw and unable to catch the mice that hide behind the layers of wallpaper, that when she does succeed in catching the cockroaches she eats them and they make her sick. Of course, she eventually escapes, and gets killed, and Matryona is deeply grieved. But these are the least of Matryona's trials. She is willing to work in the fields without pay. The representatives of the government—an unhelpful woman doctor, who comes when she is very ill; the wife of the chairman of the local collective, who forces her to help shift manure— are, naturally, very snippy and unpleasant. (It is true that officials in the Soviet Union habitually treat with the greatest contempt those peasants in whose name the Communist Revolution is supposed to have been made. Each item in Solzhenitsyn's picture is derived from a real condition.) Matryona allows her rapacious relatives to take down an annex to her *izba,* which leaves one side of her house very flimsy, and when they are dragging the boards away on sleds she goes with them in order to help them, and, as a result of this, is horribly mangled and killed, at an unguarded crossing, by locomotives driven backward with no lights. Yet for Solzhenitsyn, when he reflects on her, Matryona becomes a heroine. "We all lived by her side," he concludes, "and failed to understand that she was that most righteous person without whom, according to the proverb, the village cannot stand. Nor the city. Nor all our earth." But to the kind of Anglo-Saxon I have mentioned, Matryona seems a simpleminded and too devoted victim who allows herself to be exploited and crushed. It is not that this exhibition of peasant brutality and meanness is any darker than Chekhov's *Muzhiki* or than Leskov's *Lady Macbeth of the Mtsensky District,* and it is impossible to overrate the prodigies of incompetence and bureaucratic indolence of which the Russians are capable. But, reading Solzhenitsyn in bulk, we are given the impression that nothing can ever come out right, and that the disappointments have been somewhat contrived. In the story called *The Right Hand,* a veteran of the Revolution, incapacitated by dropsy but equipped with the correct certificates, is refused admission to a hospital by one of Solzhenitsyn's supercilious officials, a young woman who is reading a comic about an exploit by a Soviet soldier. In the play of which the title has been translated *The Love-Girl and the Innocent,* we are again in a labor camp, where an incipient amorous relation between two of the finer-grained inmates is frustrated when it turns out that the girl, by a camp convention, is supposed to be at anyone's disposal and is claimed by the camp doctor, so that she can only go to meet her lover surreptitiously in off-hours. In another story, *For the Good of the Cause,* a new technical-school building built with enthusiasm by the students for their own use is suddenly assigned without a qualm on the part of the bureaucrats to an institution for research. Here the story is merely a mechanical instance of official callous indifference. It makes its point but is rather abstract. It helps to pile up the indictment, to show how all human values are being sacrificed to inhuman planning, but it is itself rather lacking in human interest, as, for example, *The Cancer Ward* is not. One does not know how to criticize the dryness of some of these pieces of Solzhenitsyn's. In this dryness they are different from Pasternak's *Doctor Zhivago,* with its central theme of rebirth, but Pasternak was never in prison, and his book was the product of a more hopeful moment. One is curious to see Solzhenitsyn's next novel, which has been announced as abandoning the present and dealing with the wars of the Revolution.

In the meantime, one must congratulate the Nobel Prize judges on honoring this very courageous man and very gifted writer, who, even with all the forces of Soviet stupidity and conservatism against him, is finally in a position to defy the ridiculous Writers' Union and the publishers who will not print his writings, because he has been penalized already with all possible appalling punishments and can hardly be frightened by further threats.

August 14, 1971